Meteorite Hunter

Other Books by Roy A. Gallant

Meteorite Hunter

The Search for Siberian Meteorite Craters

Roy A. Gallant

McGraw-Hill

New York   Chicago   San Francisco
Lisbon   London   Madrid   Mexico City   Milan
New Delhi   San Juan   Seoul   Singapore
Sydney   Toronto

Library of Congress Cataloging-in-Publication Data

Gallant, Roy A.
 Meteorite hunter : the search for Siberian meteorite craters / Roy A. Gallant.
  p. cm.
 Includes bibliographical references.
 ISBN 0-07-137224-5 (acid-free paper)
 1. Meteorites—Russia (Federation)—Siberia. 2. Gallant, Roy A.—
Journeys—Russia (Federation)—Siberia. I. Title.

QB755.5.R8 G35 2002
523.5′1′0957—dc21

                 2001052165

McGraw-Hill

A Division of The McGraw·Hill Companies

Portions of this book appeared in somewhat different form in Sky & Telescope, and appear here with the permission of Sky Publishing Corporation. Other portions of this book appeared in somewhat different form in *Meteorite* magazine and together with photographs are used by permission of that magazine's editor Dr. Joel Schiff.

1 2 3 4 5 6 7 8 9 0 DOC/DOC 0 8 7 6 5 4 3 2

ISBN: 0-07-137224-5

Printed and bound by R. R. Donnelley & Sons Company.

This book is printed on recycled, acid-free paper containing a minimum of 50% recycled de-inked fiber.

To my Russian friends and colleagues
who have helped make all my research expeditions
to Siberian meteorite impact sites
the highlight of my professional life.
Thank you, one and all—
and I'll be back at the drop of a meteorite!

And there fell a great star from heaven, burning as it were a lamp.
(Rev. viii, 10)

Contents

Foreword

During the past decade or more, there has been a growing interest on the part of scientists and the public alike in that branch of astronomy that studies past and potential future collisions of Earth with those rogue and life-threatening objects of the Solar System called Near Earth Objects (NEOs). They are errant chunks of matter left over from the time the Solar System was formed nearly 5 billion years ago, the orbits of which have the nasty habit of crossing Earth's orbit from time to time. The Solar System is not the neat and tidy place imagined by classical scholars up through the seventeenth century. It is a chaotic nook of the Universe where conditions are never quite the same from one day to the next as gravitational perturbations of its myriad denizens continuously interact and so keep them in a state of flux.

Before the turn of the last century the cosmic debris that assaults us periodically tended to be perceived more as harmless curiosities than as serious threats to our planet's ecological stability. However, in July 1994 world attention was riveted on the mind-boggling fireworks display resulting from a train of twenty-one comet fragments of Shoemaker-Levy-9 tearing into Jupiter's atmosphere with a force that would have devastated our small planet. It was a terrifying cosmic event in our own planetary backyard, one never before witnessed by humans and a reminder of the awful forces that have shaken our home planet countless times in its geological past. The drama will surely be repeated many more times before Earth dies.

That Earth has long been bombarded by smaller celestial bodies of the Solar System is attested to by multiple astroblemes, or "star wounds," that are well known to astronomers and geologists. They are the scars left by those cosmic mountains of stone and metal called asteroids and by comets that have intercepted Earth during its Keplerian dance around the Sun. Those events, however, took place in the very distant past and not during our period of recorded history. Because they happened so very long ago, we tend to look on them as abstractions having little or nothing to do with our mundane affairs. Shoemaker-Levy-9, however, observed on television by hundreds of millions of Earth's inhabitants, in the minds of many became a Sword of Damocles held high above our heads, a terrifying warning that disaster has struck before and can strike again. The ultimate questions, of course, are what, if anything, can we do in the face of such a threat? And can we afford to wait until we are targeted before starting to develop an efficient system to protect our planet against a major threat from space—as rare as such a strike may appear in our lifetime?

There are other questions as well: Is there a regularity in occurrence of such catastrophic events? What is the probability of one occurring tomorrow, next year, or next century? Are we presently in possession of adequate technical means to prevent such catastrophes? There are answers to these and several other germane questions, but I will not discuss them here since they are addressed in Chapter 8.

No matter what your brand of mathematics may be, the threat of a collision with a large asteroid or a comet nucleus is real and of a magnitude that dwarfs threats of other natural cataclysms such as earthquakes, volcanic eruptions, hurricanes, or tsunamis. However destructive those common natural catastrophes may seem, their forces pale with the realization that a collision with an NEO would have the potential of ending our present level of civilization perhaps in an hour or less.

Each week or month, observational astronomers continue to find previously undiscovered objects sharing Earth's space, reminding us, contrary to the ancients' belief, that outer space is not empty but teeming with potential intruders. Both near and remote space within the Solar System is inhabited by large asteroids, smaller meteoroids, and comets by the hundreds of millions. Among them are some quite troublesome objects that not only can cross Earth's orbit, but that approach our space home at dangerously close distances from time to time. Over the past several decades, there have been instances of rather large asteroids nearing Earth to within distances of only hundreds of thousands of kilometers, which on an astronomical scale means virtually hitting the bull's eye. Every year the probability of destruction by such dangerous episodes grows.

But you might ask, "How can that be? Does it mean that the arsenal of cosmic bombs is actually increasing with the passage of every year?" No. The matter is not related to a cosmic factor but to human society. As our global society develops and becomes increasingly complex, it also becomes more frangible. In the first place, its fragility is related to our fast-growing human population, which is on the log phase of a sigmoid growth curve. In nonmathematical language, that means that the growth-rate curve is pointing nearly straight up. Such rapid growth must lead to an unavoidable escalation in areas of increasing population density as individuals migrate to urban areas and as populations compete for preferred habitats. Therefore, the probability of a cosmic "shell" striking a high-density area of human population tends to increase. The 1908 explosion of a cosmic missile over the Tunguska, Siberia, forest wilderness was one of immense power, exceeding a minimum 500 times the equivalent of the atomic bomb exploded over Hiroshima during World War II. Yet that event went practically unnoticed due to its remoteness from sizable areas of human habitation. In the 1930s a similar event occurred in the upper flows of the Amazon River. Again, due to its remoteness, the event is known only to a small circle of specialists.

Population specialists tell us that in some fifty years the global population will be double that of today if it continues to grow at its present rate. In Russia we have a song that says, "Sorry, there are no more vacant seats in our horse drawn coach." It is not only a matter of our planetary "coach" becoming overcrowded, but also that it carries a pretty dangerous cargo. It doesn't take much imagination to picture what could happen if an asteroid a kilometer or so in diameter impacted a densely populated industrial region containing hazardous technological facilities including nuclear power plants, radiation graveyards, or germ warfare laboratories. Such an impact would reduce the Chernobyl tragedy to the pop of a child's balloon. The catastrophe would most likely be of a magnitude that would require human intervention for untold thousands of years.

With the above as background, readers of Roy Gallant's fascinating book *Meteorite Hunter* should be better able to appreciate his graphic descriptions of Siberian meteorite impact sites and their importance to our understanding of the role asteroidal and cometary impacts have played in our planet's geological history. Readers also will come away with more than just a superficial knowledge of what meteorites are and how the science of meteoritics has evolved. There are numerous impact scars on Earth's land surface and seafloor, and Siberia has its share, not because our land is a magnet with a penchant for attracting cosmic missiles but simply because Siberia is so large.

Readers of *Meteorite Hunter* will also be introduced to our beautiful Siberia and its peoples. Siberia makes up a significant region of Eurasia and is known hardly at all by outsiders. Roy Gallant has come to know Siberia not by hearsay, but from spending a decade of summers organizing his expeditions; hiking miles and miles through our forests that we call the "taiga"; and traveling by horseback, boat, and on foot through bogs and streams often blocked by felled trees and occupied by bears, wolves, and vipers to reach remote meteorite impact sites. He has learned firsthand what endless swarms of merciless Siberian blood-sucking insects are. He has managed to visit practically all major known meteorite sites of the Asian part of Russia, among them Sikhote-Alin, Chinge, and the fall site of the famous Pallas Iron. He has explored the giant impact crater of Popigai in the far north of Yakutiya and participated in expeditions to the Tunguska meteorite epicenter. Each of those events has its own unique destiny: the Pallas Iron played a significant role in the history of the science of meteoritics; the Sikhote-Alin and Chinge sites present classic studies in meteoritics; the Popigai crater, with a diameter of about 100 kilometers represents an impact site on a giant scale; and the Tunguska Event continues to tantalize its investigators by veiling its actual cause, despite investigations by the world's leading meteorite scientists. The first expedition of the Tunguska site was in 1927 and was organized by the Russian scientist Leonid Alexeyvich Kulik, founder of the science of meteoritics in Russia, but that catastrophic explosion—the largest known explosion in the history of civilization—to this day remains a major mystery and one of the most scientifically intriguing plots of planet Earth.

Strictly speaking, we can hardly apply the notion of a "meteorite" to the Tunguska phenomenon of 1908. The term *meteorite* implies a natural cosmic object that intrudes into Earth's atmosphere, burns its way through it, survives, and ends up on Earth's surface where it can be discovered and, once discovered, can be investigated. There is nothing like that in the case of the Tunguska "meteorite." The object—whatever it was—never reached Earth's surface, having exploded at a height of no less than 5 kilometers and not leaving any common meteoric matter in the region directly beneath the blast.

A number of investigators have suggested that after releasing its explosive energy, the object might well have skipped back out of the atmosphere, like a flat stone skipping on impact with the water, and continued its movement along a trajectory that took it back into space again. The Tunguska object couldn't have been an iron asteroid, as believed by Kulik. It lacked a number of telltale signs; for instance, there was no smoke tail typical for big iron meteorites similar to what occurred during the Sikhote-Alin meteorite shower of 1947 in the Russian Far East. Some have proposed that the Tunguska object was a stony asteroid, and others, that it was the nucleus of a comet. Although both options have their pros and cons, there is not yet enough hard evidence to allow a sound choice between the two. But I am now treading on material that is presented in more detail in Chapter 1.

The new millennium inherits the problem of the Tunguska meteorite as one of the most fascinating scientific mysteries of the previous century, a unique enigma that has continued to gain momentum over more than seventy years. Of all the cosmic collision events of several past centuries, the priority, no doubt, belongs to our Tunguska meteorite. This can be explained not only by the inherent scientific interest in the event, but also by the obvious circumstance of repetitions of similar events, the probability of which is estimated by some as one occurrence every 200 to 300 years. If I seem to have spent too much time talking about Tunguska, it is only because of the importance of the event to science and to the lives of every reader of this book, as a forecast of what will surely occur many more times in the life of our planet, if not in our lifetime. My bias may also be accounted for by my being the principal scientific investigator of some thirty-five expeditions since the 1950s.

Not a small part of Roy Gallant's book is dedicated to his journey to the Popigai astrobleme, the ancient meteorite crater located in Siberia's far north near the polar zone. Earth's collision with an asteroid that caused the formation occurred some 35 million years ago and belongs to one of the most grandiose collision events in Earth's geologic history, exceeding the Tunguska Event by a factor of a million. Such impacts have recently caught the attention of geologists as major events that have helped determine the geological evolution of Earth as a planet—including climatic change, a shift in Earth's poles, and mass extinctions of untold millions of biological species. The origin of the Popigai astrobleme had long been disputed, the presumption of a volcanic origin long holding the spotlight. Proof that the cosmic invader was a giant asteroid, thanks to the brilliant work of Professor Victor Masaitis, has come only relatively recently.

The millions of years that have passed since that calamitous event have not completely erased the scars that our planet sustained from those wounds, and that is why the geology of that impact area is of exceptional interest for an understanding of how our battered planet has long sustained and recovered from encounters with rogue cosmic visitors ever since its formation.

All of this, and much more, is discussed in *Meteorite Hunter* captivatingly and with a scientific knowledge that has earned Gallant the respect and admiration of his many Russian colleagues since his first expedition to Siberia in 1992. Gallant has become an important historian of Siberian meteorite impact sites, and in several of his accounts he has brought to the English-speaking world information previously available only in Russian, and in some instances he has brought to light events never before published. He presents complex issues of modern meteoritics and astronomy at a high scientific level. His book is bound to leave its mark among modern popularizations of science.

Academician Nickolai V. Vasiliev
Committee on Meteorites
Russian Academy of Sciences and
Scientific Director of the
Federal Nature Reserve "Tungusskiy"

Introduction

Roy Gallant is not only a widely published popularizer of science, but an active scientific explorer who has brought to the English-speaking world accounts of Russian meteorite impact sites, a result of his academic skills and his yen for adventure. Gallant is professor emeritus at the University of Southern Maine where he has taught astronomy and for twenty years was planetarium director. His accounts in this book of his expeditions to Russian meteorite impact sites are sometimes hair-raising and always captivating. Until this telling, some accounts were largely unavailable to the English-speaking world.

In the process of preparing this book, despite frequent difficulties of travel conditions, Gallant studied each of the meteorite fall sites he describes. The book's title, *Meteorite Hunter*, very appropriately reflects its contents. The narration leads the reader on three levels through wild Siberia to meteorite impact sites. First, there is an introduction to the broad scene of action—Siberia. Siberia is a huge part of Russia, historically a place of exile for political dissidents and criminals and the place for Stalin's notorious gulags during the Soviet era. In contrast, present-day Siberia is a region of major scientific research institutes that include Tomsk, Novosibirsk, and Irkutsk. Additionally, there are enormous power-generating plants and mining enterprises. Among the natural resources mined are vast quantities of gold and diamonds, nickel and aluminum, and the subsurface products of oil and natural gas. An enormous territory of Siberia is occupied by our famous taiga: beautiful forests so dense that they discourage penetration. And there is the forbidding tundra inhabited by hunters who supply sable, fox, and other furs. The hunters are mostly the native peoples of Siberia: the Evenks and Yakuts, the Chukchas and Oirots, and the Nenets and Dolgans. Our beloved Anton Chekhov wrote of them respectfully, admiringly, and lovingly.

With the broad scene set, a second direction Gallant's narrative takes is a finer focus on the nature of meteorites and a glimpse into the history of meteoritics as a science that evolved over the formative years of the eighteenth and nineteenth centuries. Presenting the history of his Russian meteorite events, including four that were observed by eyewitnesses, Gallant has assembled and cleverly woven a wealth of eyewitness details with facts from the history of meteoritics as a science in a way that makes for fascinating reading for specialists and nonspecialists alike. Two such accounts are the cataclysmic Tunguska explosion of a cosmic body in 1908 and the story of the famous Pallas Iron, which began to unfold in the backyard of a retired Cossack soldier and blacksmith in the late eighteenth century. And for interested readers, Gallant explains how meteorites are classified based on chemical composition and structure—iron meteorites, stony meteorites, and the stony-irons—and their relationships with asteroids and comets.

The author was fortunate in having the opportunity to deal with a wide variety of impact occurrences, including both recent and ancient events. For example, the giant meteorite crater Popigai was formed about 35 million years ago, resulting from Earth's collision with an asteroid about 10 kilometers in size. More recently, the Tunguska cosmic intruder most probably was the nucleus of a small comet some 100 meters in diameter that penetrated Earth's atmosphere to a height of about 5 kilometers above the surface and exploded before impacting the ground. The still more recent Sikhote-Alin meteorite shower of 1947 was the result of the entry into Earth's atmosphere, and explosive fragmentation, of an iron body with a mass of some 300 metric tons. And there was the 1922 stony meteorite shower of Tsarev, most likely from an object of considerably less mass than the Sikhote-Alin object. The famous Pallas Iron long baffled investigators; it was an individual stony-iron meteorite that came to be representative of a comparatively rare class of meteorites called *pallasites*.

The third layer of Gallant's book—his fascinating accounts of ordeals his Russian companions and he experienced in the field—is bound to involve readers the most. Further, the levels and richness of detail with which he describes Siberian nature and the everyday life of Siberian people turn his narration into a vivid and live account that will capture the imaginations and spirit of adventure of western readers, many of whom would be eager to join the author on one of his expeditions, as did seven on his Popigai expedition.

The many travails Gallant and his companions often had to overcome included crossing barely passable terrain: traveling through the taiga, across tundra, through bogs, and across swift streams and small rivers sometimes by foot and other times by one of our rugged Gorkey trucks. Often they were plagued by difficulties of a different sort—swarms of blood-sucking insects (mosquitoes, black flies, and disease-carrying ticks). Luckily they were never threatened by direct encounters with the master of the taiga—the great Siberian bear, a potential encounter with whom they would prefer to avoid even though they were armed against possible attack. Bears may be frequent visitors during expeditions into the taiga, and Gallant's groups more than once found paw prints within their campsite left during nocturnal visits or while the group was temporarily away from camp. During one low-altitude helicopter flight over the forest in Kamchatka, Gallant sighted twenty-six bears.

Of the seven expeditions described by the author, five took place in "real" Siberia. The Tsarev meteorite shower occurred in that area of the middle flow of the Volga River known as the European part of Russia, and the Sikhote-Alin shower rained down in the Russian Far East. The other sites are all located within a narrow longitudinal band between 84° E (Teleutsky) and 111° E (Popigai); and within a wider latitudinal band from 72° N above the Arctic Circle (Popigai) southward to 51° N not far from Mongolia (Chinge).

It was back in 1921 and 1922 when the renowned Russian investigator Leonid Kulik first showed interest in meteorites and arranged a special expedition in search of them. Despite those difficult and unstable times for Russia following the revolution, Kulik nevertheless was intent on building an impressive collection. His expedition turned out to be very successful, and he prepared a detailed report for the Russian Academy of Sciences published by the Academy's *Izvestiya* (Transactions).

In 1971 the Geological and Geophysical Research Institute of the Siberian Branch of the then USSR Academy of Sciences published a brochure entitled "Meteorites of Siberia." It described the results of research into some of the Siberian meteorites and their possible fall sites, although some of the fall sites had been only tentatively established. The introductory sentences in that brochure are still true today: "Siberia from the point of view of meteoritics is a virgin land never ploughed. The number of finds beyond the Ural Mountains is disproportionally small relative to the vast territory. This is especially so if you compare the number of Siberian finds with the number of finds in more densely populated areas, such as Ukraine, for example." Even though more than thirty years have passed since that brochure was published, those introductory remarks retain their significance to the present time. So Siberia remains the land of opportunity for the meteorite hunter.

I feel compelled to draw the attention of the reader to the age of our meteorite hunter. When Roy Gallant set out on his first expedition to Tunguska in 1992 he was age 68, about three years beyond the current life expectancy of Russian males. Yet today our doughty scientific explorer of Russian impact sites is still at it, seemingly with renewed vigor each year. Last year found him climbing among the glaciers of the Altai Mountains. Where he will be next year one can only guess. I am confident that the readers of *Meteorite Hunter* will share my admiration for the heroic deeds of our scientific explorer.

Vitaliy A. Bronshten
Committee on Meteorites
Russian Academy of Sciences
Moscow
March 2001

Preface

The Sleeping Land

Where Eagles Soar

It seems an eternity now, although it has been only a little more than eight years since my first passage through that vast land called Siberia. My memories of that first summer are a kaleidoscope of images, odors, sounds, and periods of profound stillness—not so much a quality of the environment as a response to it. Lying on my back in a hot field with my head cradled in my hands, I watched the flight of seven eagles soaring lightly as they rode first one thermal and then, losing it, plunged briefly to another and again rose carelessly skyward, all as effortlessly as the flow of a river. The rhythm of the rise and fall of each bird brought to mind the cadence of the lines from Arnold's "Dover Beach":

> *Come to the window, sweet is the night air!*
> *Only, from the long line of spray*
> *Where the sea meets the moon-blanch'd land,*
> *Listen! You hear the grating roar*
> *Of pebbles which the waves draw back, and fling,*
> *At their return, up the high strand,*
> *Begin, and cease, and then again begin,*

With tremulous cadence slow, and bring
The eternal note of sadness in. . . .

That summer was one without care. Soon after the last day of classes at my university I flew to that faraway land. The very sound of the word—*Siberia*—evoked mystery, adventure, and a history shrouded in intrigue. According to the Russian author Valentin Rasputin, "The word *Siberia*— and not so much the word as the concept itself—has long sounded as a warning bell announcing something vaguely powerful and imminent."

For more than 400 years, since Russia began to occupy the untamable Siberian wilderness, the gigantic region has remained remote, but it is less so now than it was in the days when it took months to cross its broad expanse by horse and boat. The Russians' conquering hero of Siberia was Yermak Timofeevich, leader of a band of warriors called Cossacks. The name comes from a Tartar word meaning "daredevil," one who has shunned all ties with his social class and becomes a free spirit as ready to fight as gulp down a measure of vodka. The Cossacks came into their own in the 1500s when they avoided the Tartar yoke of feudalism and serfdom by fleeing to the "Wild Field" where, according to Rasputin, "They founded their own settlements, elected chieftains called atamans, established laws, and began a free, new life that was not subordinate to any khanate or czardom." Nevertheless, to survive they eventually came to serve the czar and tirelessly vented their patriotic fervor by defending Russia against her perceived enemies, be they Turks or Tartars. Their stronghold was the land forming the lower reaches of the Don and Volga rivers. It was the Cossacks, under the leadership of Yermak, who played an almost supernatural role in opening up Siberia. They were a proud and ruthless lot of adventurers who let nothing stand in the way of their pursuit of wealth. But there were others before them.

Who were the first Siberians, the mystery people who inhabited the forests and plains east of the great Rock, or Ural Mountains? Foreigners in ancient and medieval times reading Herodotus's *History* were told that "at the foot of some high mountains dwell people who are bald from birth and have flat noses and oblong chins [and who] have goats' feet; and others living beyond them sleep six months out of the year." As late as the 1500s, one Russian written source related old tales describing the Siberians as a people who ostensibly die to pass the harsh winter months and do not reawaken until spring.

Siberia, from a Tartar word meaning "sleeping land," is a giant only slightly smaller than the United States. It extends eastward across northern Asia from the Ural Mountains to the Pacific Ocean. From west to east in the north it borders first the Barents, then the Kara, then the Laptev, and finally the East Siberian seas across the Arctic. It sprawls southward, first across the tundra, then through the great north coniferous forest biome called the taiga, and finally over the steppes of Central Asia to its southern borders with Kazakhstan, Mongolia, and China.

In my opinion, there is no better way to savor that capacious estate than to cross its breadth by the Trans-Siberian Railroad, and to plumb its depth from north to south by river. The Trans-Siberian Railroad was completed in 1905, the year the Russians suffered humiliating defeat in the Russo-Japanese War and three years before a cosmic visitor ripped apart the sky and exploded over Tunguska. To this day, transportation in the region remains poor, however. Most villages are accessible only by dirt roads either alternately choked in swirling clouds of dust or churned to mud by heavy rain, which means that at times they are not accessible at all. In Russia, according to one saying, there are no roads, only directions, which was literally true for some of my expeditions. For instance, you get to Vanavara, the stepping-off point of my expedition to the Tunguska site, by foot, river, or air. North-south traffic in Russia is served by the Lena, Ob, and Yenisei rivers and their thousands of tributaries of central Siberia, and by the Amur River, which flows along Russia's border with Manchuria in the Russian Far East. The Amur eventually empties into the Pacific Ocean near the island, and former penal colony, of Sakhalin.

Dissidents, political prisoners, rapists, murderers, and thieves of every description traditionally have been carted off to Siberian penal colonies—most recently Stalin's notorious gulags—or exiled to remote villages. In 1897 Lenin was exiled for three years to the small and remote Siberian village of Shushenskoe. His exile, however, was something of a lark since he had a comfortable little house, was well fed, and had an ample supply of books and periodicals. In fact, his banishment to Shushenskoe marked one of his most productive periods in churning out Bolshevik literature. He was even married there, to his long-time fellow revolutionary Nadezhda Krupskaya.

Trotsky also ended up as a Siberian exile, and so did Stalin, and most likely at the very time of the catastrophic Tunguska explosion. Most of the political prisoners, dissidents, and their descendants were simply dumped in that vast empty land. Since there were no easy or reliable means of escape, they had no choice but to stay and follow the wish of the government to settle and help tame the inhospitable wilderness and exploit its seemingly inexhaustible natural wealth.

Three-quarters of Siberia is a land of eternal frost, or permafrost, a crust of ice, bog, and soil frozen to a depth of some

300 meters on the average. In places, the frost penetrates to a depth of 1500 meters! Despite the heat welling up from Earth's interior and bearing down from the summer Sun, the permafrost temperature remains a constant $-4°C$. Only during a few weeks of summer does the permafrost melt to a depth of a few meters.

I saw a graphic example of the delicacy of the permafrost layer and what happens as a result of human intervention when I explored the ruins of one of Stalin's notorious gulag prisons a few days downriver from Krasnoyarsk on the Yenisei River. The camp marked one location along an ill-fated railway line, constructed by forced labor, across the tundra from Salekhard, on the Arctic Circle, eastward to Igarka. The railroad, destined never to be completed and never intended to be, was a pet project of Stalin's to help settle Siberia and to condemn untold thousands of "enemies of the state." When Stalin died in 1953, the project instantly came to a halt, testifying to its utter folly. Today, survivors of that grim time and that fateful project describe the railroad undertaking as the Soviet equivalent of Auschwitz and Dachau.

When I picked my way among the ruins of the gulag, the fragility of the tundra was driven home to me. The centerpiece was a derelict railroad engine rusted nearly to dust. Tilted and resting on equally rusted rails, the engine had sunk several feet into the permafrost. This particular section of the rail line was built in 1947. There are numerous other reminders of the fragility of the tundra. Bulldozers and other tracked vehicles used by oil exploration crews break through the thin insulating layer of mosses and lichens and leave vast, heaving ditches that will remain for centuries. Like the railroad engine, structures such as heavy buildings create just enough heat by their weight pressing into the ground to melt the frozen ground below and create swamps, into which the buildings eventually sink, totter, and collapse. Roads are destined to meet the same fate.

My decision to brave the Trans-Siberian Railroad for the 4000 kilometers from Moscow eastward to Krasnoyarsk on the first leg of my journey to the Tunguska site was the right one, although I don't know if I would do it again. In part, it was the realization of a longing I had had since my teens inspired by my reading the works of Tolstoy and Chekhov. Anton Chekhov's moving and graphic descriptions of his three-month crossing of Siberia in 1890, first by horse and carriage and then by steamer, had made me long to see Siberia from the ground rather than from the indifferent perspective at an altitude of 10,000 meters. I wanted to experience the texture of the land from within its fabric, not above it, to sense its aromas, and to mix unobtrusively among its peoples to hear them speak and hawk their wares. Oh, how I came to yearn to speak their language and be one with them.

What is this seemingly endless land like? It is like no place else. Comparisons, which we habitually make when describing a visit to foreign lands, are useless. Siberia is a world unto itself, another planet marvelously varied and self-sufficient in every way. Its environmental, cultural, and spiritual diversity makes Siberia singular, unique, extraordinary, incomparable. The experience of it is unforgettable and unduplicatable.

Cloud Merchants and Wet Fences

On April 29, 1890, while sailing on the river Kama, Chekhov wrote to his family that, "The banks are bare, the trees bare, the earth a mat-brown, patches of snow stretch ahead and the wind is such that even the devil himself couldn't blow as sharply or unpleasantly. When the cold wind blows and ripples the water, which after the spring's flooding has taken on the color of coffee slops, everything turns cold and lonely and wretched; the accordion sounds on the shore seem mournful and the figures in torn sheepskin coats standing motionless on the barges we encounter appear permanently stiff with sorrow. The cities of the Kama are gray; it looks as though their inhabitants occupied themselves exclusively in the manufacture of lowering clouds, boredom, wet fences and street filth."

To this day, on making your way along the dirt, dung-strewn main streets of remote Siberian villages—remote in time as well as place—you can encounter the same types of people described by Chekhov. From the town of Ekaterinburg he wrote: "The people here inspire the newcomer with something like horror; they are high-cheekboned, with jutting foreheads, broad-shouldered, have little eyes and enormously big fists."

On arriving at Krasnoyarsk, Chekhov referred to the world's most voluminous river, the Yenisei, as "that fierce and mighty warrior." During the weeks ahead after my adventure by train, I was to spend eleven days on that fierce and mighty warrior aboard the ship *Anton Chekhov* as it carried me north into the Kara Sea of the southern Arctic Ocean and the outpost of Dickson at 73°N. That is north of Norway, north of Alaska, halfway up Greenland. Even in August you can expect to encounter ice floes when the wind is right. We were lucky. The wind wasn't right, but even at the height of summer we could feel the bite of the cold and heavy glaciated air. What a contrast from the oppressively dry and hot air of the steppe land where eagles soar. Actually, I welcomed the brief chill of Dickson. It meant no mosquitoes.

The train continued to speed me on that three-day hot July journey across some of the most beautiful country I have even seen—across the Ural Mountains; through forests of pine, cedar, birch, spruce, and larch; across expanses of broad and flat fields of wild grasses adorned with little islands of silver birches that glowed pink in the early morning sun, gleamed titanium white by day, and then dissolved to a ghostly gray by moonlight. On and on the train groaned and creaked, sometimes with a rapid clacking of the wheels as they raced along, striking the expansion joints of the rails; other times slowing to a staccato click-clack, click-clack; and sometimes stopping altogether as we were shunted onto a siding to wait for one or more trains to pass from the opposite direction. We traveled at an average speed of 58 kilometers an hour. The hypnotizing effect of this unending Sonata for Iron Wheels often kept me in a state of half asleep, half awake, being neither fully conscious nor deeply asleep.

On crossing the steppes of central Asia and trying to still the shimmering of the ground caused by thermals rising off the hot fields, I almost expected to see a herd of giraffes or a pride of lions in the distance, so similar is this land in summer to the African savanna. It seemed interminable. As we approached villages, the wild grassland abruptly gave way to continuous patches of incredibly lush vegetable gardens, some towering with swaying sunflower plants that would serve as cattle fodder or whose seeds would be lightly fried, salted, and sold at bus and trolley stops everywhere. Husky, hooded female peasants, shawled and heavily clothed, worked plots of potatoes. Seldom did these *bábushkas* look up from their chopping hoes. "Get yourself a nice *bábushka* who will bring you tea and vodka and mend your socks," I was once jokingly advised. On and on, click-clack, click-clack.

The gardens stopped as suddenly as they had appeared and were interrupted by squalid wooden buildings unpainted except for pale blue pealing shutters. At one time, who knows when, the late communist government must have decided to make an ocean of paint—all blue. Throughout Russia, house shutters are to this day almost always that same hue. I doubt Russians will ever run out of blue paint.

No matter what time of day or night the train stopped at a town to take on or discharge passengers, the railroad tracks were instantly lined with dozens of shawled and jacketed *bábushkas*. They stood by makeshift tables or tended baby carriages brimming with cabbage pies and boiled potatoes, collectively wrapped in blankets to keep them warm, and with radishes, raspberries, wild strawberries, blueberries, endless jars of succulent preserves and honey, little cakes, and homemade vodka. At Mareensk we were met by regiments of more peasant food merchants, kerchiefs knotted tightly under their creased and wrinkled chins, their faces browned by the sun and lined by age. Their hands, extended with their offerings, were also brown and calloused and often deformed by arthritis or years of hard use. Children were vendors as well. "My God! How rich Russia is in good people!" Chekhov wrote his family. "If it were not for the cold [and] the officials who corrupt the peasants and exiles, Siberia would be the very richest and happiest of territories." These were Chekhov's "good people," unchanged over a century, survivors of the wretchedness and brutality of Stalin's reign of terror, enduring as tenaciously as the hardy weeds and flowers of Darwin's "tangled bank."

From time to time the train, for no apparent reason, slowed to a crawl—click . . . clack . . . click . . . clack—as we passed a tiny wooden hut with a man or woman standing just outside its cuckoo-clock entrance and holding up a pole with either a plain yellow or red disk attached to the end. These were signals to the engineer announcing whether the tracks ahead were clear (yellow) or not (red). An electronically operated signal system for the railroad had yet to come to Siberia, and still has yet to come eight years later.

I had reserved and held tickets for all four bunks in the first-class sleeping car compartment that I shared with my attractive traveling companion Ekaterina Rossovskaya. It was Katya who was responsible for my embarking on this odyssey, which was to extend unexpectedly into several adventurous years. Since she played, and continues to play, such an important role in my Siberian travels, I should explain the circumstances of our meeting.

It was during the summer of 1991. I was enjoying the seasonal break from my university and writing a book deep in the Maine woods on the mountain lake where I live. I was carefree, single, and in a frame of mind to consider just about any opportunity that suggested adventure. At the time, I was a member of the advisory board of the Center for the Study of the First Americans, located at Oregon State University, from which I had recently returned from a meeting. My involvement in astronomy prompted the director's wife, a recent Russian transplant, to bring up the subject of the Tunguska Event of 1908. Yes, of course, I knew about it, and, in fact, had long had more than a passing interest in the cause of the event.

A week or so after my return home I received a call from Oregon. It was Mila, the director's wife, saying that a Russian friend of hers, who was an authority on the Tunguska Event and who had visited the explosion site, was temporarily on assignment by the Russian government and doing work as an interpreter in San Francisco. Would I like to talk with her? Her name is Ekaterina Rossovskaya, but just call her Katya.

Over the next week or more Katya and I talked for several hours, mostly about Tunguska, but gradually we became acquainted. She struck me as being very bright with a strong and winning personality. She was single and in her mid-thirties. Mila had told her about the astronomy books I had written, which prompted Katya to ask me why I didn't write a book about the great Tunguska explosion. She could even arrange for me to go to the site since she knew, among several other investigators, the principal scientific investigator.

I said I'd jump at the chance if she really thought she could arrange things. She assured me that she could and that she was free for the next two months to begin making arrangements. I suggested that she come to Maine and work from there since she would need a number of documents from me. "Send me a ticket and meet me at the airport. You'll recognize me because I'm Russian and have long red hair." So began our relationship and the years of adventure to follow.

Katya had advised my buying out the sleeping car compartment, saying that it would be unwise to risk unnecessarily displaying my two Nikon cameras, camcorder, and tape recorder, not to mention our bottles of Russian champagne (which is excellent and cheap, by the way) and tins of caviar. Our choice for "climate control" was to suffer the heat inside the compartment or pull down our top window, which provided a flow of hot air filled with soot from the engine. The windows were so crusted with grime that we had to lean out and clean them with tiny pieces of paper napkin soaked with tea. To get as much mileage as possible out of a paper napkin, the Russians to this day unfold the napkin and then cut it into four patches along the folds. It is called a *salfetka* and, as a napkin, is about as useful as a postage stamp.

Each first-class carriage had ten compartments accommodating four passengers each, a narrow corridor running the length of the car, and a toilet at each end. Passengers were supposed to have use of both toilets, but the two *prahvadneetsahs*, or attendants who collect the tickets, sell you bedding, serve you tea, and also act as guards, almost always kept one toilet locked for their private use and for use by important officials. Bureaucrats in Russia are everywhere. The other toilet was nearly always filthy and barely usable. You never sit on the seat of a Russian train's toilet. You adjust yourself above it, brace yourself as well as you can, and take your chances with the swaying and abrupt jolts of the train. Both toilets were kept locked when the train passed through a village or town, and sometimes remained locked out of neglect or forgetfulness of the *prahvadneetsah*s

Each car also had a hot water urn for tea. Previously, tea was 3 kopecks a glass without sugar, or 6 kopecks with sugar (a penny or two). Prices had gone up to 6 rubles (about 25 cents at the time of my trip). Bedding, which consisted of a mattress cover, two sheets, one blanket, and one towel, came to 25 rubles per person (just under a dollar). Previously, the price was 1 ruble. I asked Katya if I might offer our *prahvadneetsah* a couple of my Earl Grey tea bags. She frowned and said no, "because she would think that you were trying to tell her how awful her Russian tea is." A tip would also have offended her and would have been refused because, as Katya explained, "people are expected to take pride in their work and without extra compensation."

"What about bribes?" I asked. "Oh, that's different," she smiled. "How do you think those people standing up night and day in the corridor outside our compartment got permission to do that? They didn't have tickets." One time our *prahvadneetsah* tried to persuade us to let two young men share our compartment. After several determined *"niets"* (noes) from Katya, the matter was settled in our favor. I wondered how much the *prahvadneetsah* was planning to get for selling a place in our compartment.

I once told Katya that I wanted to do some video record-ing in the second- and third-class cars. "Absolutely not," she admonished. "When they see your camcorder, someone is likely to follow you out of the car and mug you, or worse." In 1992 a camcorder was regarded as an extremely expensive item, approaching the price of a car.

In the third-class cars a ticket does not ensure you a seat. There are no bunks, and seats are on a first-come, first-served basis. These carriages usually are so crowded that there is no room to lie down. Bodies occupy the floor wherever there is space; standing room also is at a premium. Even the upper-most luggage compartments have someone lying curled up in them. A car designed for 100 people commonly is occupied by half again that many. People are everywhere, sitting on their luggage, standing in the vestibules between cars and inhaling soot, and in the toilets inhaling odors better avoided. Most Russian males smoke, so the air throughout the train is about as bad as air can get, even without the summer enrich-ment of strong body odors.

The importance of the Trans-Siberian Railroad as the principal means of east-west travel and the distribution of goods was driven home to me by the frequency with which trains passed us going in the opposite direction. Before arriv-ing at Novosibirsk, from which you would drop straight into Mongolia if you slid due south down the map, we were delayed for an hour by the wave of a cuckoo-clock attendant holding her red disk pole. You learn not to ask why there is a delay; no one seems ever to know or care. If you are in a sta-tion and ask a question at the information counter, you have to pay 2 rubles for a simple question and 4 rubles for a com-plex question. Rarely do you get a reliable answer and never a return of your rubles.

During our hour of delay I counted eighteen trains passing us westbound. They carried people, logs, hogs, milled boards, tanks of natural gas, tanks with guns, tractors, trucks, more tractors, marble chips, tires, drilling equipment, military vehicles of all sizes and sorts, dark containers tightly closed, banded, and locked, and endless cars of coal, coal, and more coal. The variety of the Siberian landscape matches the richness of its natural resources—vast quantities of oil, natural gas, coal, iron ore, gold, platinum, nickel, timber, and gemstones galore, some so rare that they are known to occur only at a single site in Siberia.

We were five hours late when we arrived at the Novosibirsk station at 4:00 A.M., but the station clock showed only 11:00 P.M. That was because railroad stations, air terminals, and certain other public buildings throughout Russia display Moscow time, a reminder of who is in charge. I wished I had been traveling with Chekhov, without need of a temporal Big Brother.

Our last stop was Krasnoyarsk, although the train was to continue on for several more days to its final destination, China's capital of Beijing. The engineer had neither gained nor lost a minute over the 880 kilometers from Novosibirsk. At Krasnoyarsk we were still exactly five hours late.

Welcome to Siberia

Northward for some 600 or more kilometers from the Trans-Siberian rail line is the densest region of the taiga and tundra biomes, with swamps and bogs in every direction. Even as late as mid-June the tundra remains frozen at 2 or so meters beneath the downy surface. One Russian writer, Yuri Semyonov, has described the region as a "sinister" land where "the weak and imprudent often perish ... where everything below is decayed and rotten, and everything above withered, where only the corpses of the huge trunks slowly molder away in the brackish water." Mosquitoes here are reputed to be the fiercest, largest, and most numerous of any place in the world. The only protection against them is heavy clothing, gloves, and a "helmet" of netting to protect your face and head. Chemical repellents are nearly useless. The mosquitoes just laugh. One Japanese expedition member to Tunguska called Siberian mosquitoes "flying alligators."

So this was the Siberia I had traveled so far to see, and it was to be my summer home for several years to come as I visited remote meteorite impact sites across the breadth and depth of the land—from the Arctic to Mongolia and from the Ural Mountains eastward to the active volcanoes of Kamchatka in the Russian Far East.

Roy A. Gallant
Rangeley, Maine
2001

Acknowledgments

Many people have played key roles in making this book possible, most of them Russians. The prime mover is Ekaterina (Katya) Rossovskaya, colleague, friend, polyglot, and organizer extraordinaire from Siberia, who in 1992 arranged for the Russian Academy of Sciences to invite me to join its 1992 expedition to the Tunguska explosion site. That expedition somehow led to others and the others to still others, most of them brought together to make up this book. In all cases, there were arrangements for travel across Russia; lodging; interviews with scientists, journalists, politicians, and academicians; and searches for recent and decades-old documents about the impact sites we visited. Katya served as interpreter and translator of dozens of taped interviews and a four-foot-high stack of documents, nearly all in Russian. My deepest thanks go to Katya the Remarkable.

It is hard to know whom to thank next, there are so many, so I will express my deep, emotion-laden appreciation more or less as they came into my life over the years. There is the late Academician Nickolai V. Vasiliev, who had coordinated the scientific research of some thirty-five expeditions to Tunguska. Beginning with our first meeting in Siberia, he spent many hours recounting for my benefit details of the history of the Tunguska investigations over the past several decades. He also expressed his views of the numerous hypotheses that have been put forward over the years to explain what it was that exploded on that June morning in 1908 in what has come to be called "the cosmic mystery of the century." I am indebted to Nickolai for reading relevant sections of my manuscript and for the generous praise in his Foreword for this book, which he completed just one month before his death.

Special thanks go to Dr. Vitaliy Alexandrovich Bronshten, member of the prestigious Committee on Meteorites of the Russian Academy of Sciences, for reading the entire manuscript of this book for accuracy, and for so kindly writing the Introduction. Bronshten is a distinguished scholar and researcher of meteors and meteorites and the author of numerous books and articles, both technical and popular, some of which are noted in the References section of this book.

My thanks also to Dr. Gennadi Andreev, director of the Astronomical Observatory of Tomsk State University (Siberia) and codirector (with the late Academician Vasiliev) of the ongoing Tunguska expeditions, for issuing the formal invitation that made it possible for me to visit Russia and take part in the 1992 expedition.

These acknowledgments would be glaringly incomplete without including special thanks to three remarkable men. One is Yurii Kandiba who, like Katya, has trod hundreds of kilometers of the "enchanted" taiga during many Tunguska expeditions over the years. Kandiba's knowledge of that wilderness area is remarkable, and it served us well as he led Katya and me to regions of the Tunguska epicenter rarely visited. I owe Kandiba thanks also for relating many details of the early history of the Tunguska expeditions, for allowing me to copy a number of archival photographs, and for permitting me to use his map showing the location of various eyewitness accounts of the 1908 blast. Access to other accounts of the blast involved many hours of searches through old Krasnoyarsk newspapers and other Russian publications by Katya's mother, Dr. Tatyana Lvovna Rossovskaya.

The second remarkable person is Vitaliy Voronov, whose knowledge of the Evenki (Tungus people) is extensive and whose reputation as a skillful hunter extends to many and distant parts of Siberia. The third remarkable person is Dr. Yevgeniy Kolesnikov, the well-known cosmic isotopic cosmic chemist of Moscow University and head of its potassium-argon radiometric dating laboratory. Kolesnikov has been involved in the Tunguska investigations for some twenty-five years, and is the leading proponent of the theory that the Tunguska Event was a comet. I thank Yevgeniy for reading sections of my manuscript for accuracy. Another chief investigator is Dr. Alyona Boyarkina, veteran expedition member for some forty years and author of more than 100 academic papers on the Tunguska Event. Her work has taken her over hundreds of square kilometers of the Tunguska epicenter region in search of meteoric matter embedded in peat and, more recently, in the study of geomagnetic anomalies of the soils. My thanks also to Karin Junghans, a specialist in remote sensing from München, Germany for providing a copy of her report, "The Analyses of Remote Sensing of the Tunguska Event."

Among the most deserving of my thanks is Dr. Valentin Tsvetkov, Russia's foremost field investigator of Siberian meteorite impact sites. He led three of my expeditions, one to the Sikhote-Alin site, another to the Chinge site, and a third to Tsarev. It was Tsvetkov who developed a method of estimating the source of impacting objects by analyzing the strewn field distribution of shower meteorites. During our Sikhote-Alin expedition, Tsvetkov kindly arranged for me to interview Korney Shvets, of the village of Meteority, for his eyewitness account of the Sikhote-Alin meteorite shower. He also arranged for us to stay in the home of Alexander Vetrik, chief forester, in the village of Ismailikha. My thanks to Alexander and his wife for their hospitality and generous provisions for our field trip. I should add that Tsvetkov's warm personality, refreshing sense of humor, and tolerance of my occasional frustrations have made him a jovial, ideal companion.

Over the years of my expeditions a number of individuals have served as expedition specialists who assisted in many ways, from setting up camp to cooking, carrying heavy backpacks, driving our expedition vehicles, and always providing companionship with song and storytelling by many campfires. They did it not for the small fees they were paid, but because of their genuine interest in the expeditions coupled with a hankering for adventure. They include mineralogist Dr. Alexander Andreev, Major Alexey Kovalyov, Sergei Parshikov, Dimitri Yurkovsky, Sergei Kovlov, and Sergei Sapelkin, director of the Tandinski Forest District.

Special thanks to Russian historian of astronomy Dr. Alina Eremeyeva of the University of Moscow for background information and a description of her 1970 expeditions to rediscover the fall site of the famous Pallas Meteorite. Thanks also to Dimitri Belakovsky, curator of the Fersman Mineralogical Museum, University of Moscow for providing access to the museum during renovation so that I could photograph the Pallas Meteorite sections and specimens from the Sikhote-Alin shower.

Thanks also to Victor Ivanovich Evmenov, geography teacher at the town school in Kulcheck, for letting our group bunk down in the school gym and for his assistance. And thanks to our driver Nickolai, who courageously got us to our swamp campsite on the Pallas expedition. Although I can nowhere find his last name in my archives, his first name, skill, and daring in driving us through more rivers than I care to recall will live in my memory.

Lida Nikiforova deserves a big hug for providing quarters for Tsvetkov, Katya, and me during our Tsarev expedition. Lida merits warm praise for organizing her village choral group of women to perform for me during a grand evening of entertainment and feasting in her small but hospitable home.

For our Popigai expedition, special thanks go to Dr. Victor L. Masaitis, Distinguished Scientist of the Russian Federation, for traveling from St. Petersburg to Moscow to brief us on our expedition. I also heap thanks onto geologist Dr. Valery Kirichenko, our expedition's chief scientist. And without the extremely valuable assistance of Dr. Michael Martyshkin, head of the Polar Expedition Group in Khatanga and chief manager for organizing all Russian geological expeditions to the Popigai region, our expedition might not have been possible. Thanks also to Drs. John Warme, Keenan Lee, and Jared Morrow, American geologists who joined our expedition and provided valuable insights into the geology of Popigai's northwest crater wall. Also included in my thanks are my son, Jonathan R. Gallant, who assisted as an interpreter, Boris Bidyukov, authority on the Tunguska Event and camp worker, and biophysicist Lena, our camp cook, whose last name also has mysteriously disappeared, most likely in smoke.

For our Teleutskoye expedition, I wish to thank John Anfinogenov, meteorite specialist from Tomsk, for leading our expedition and providing journal and popular accounts of the Teleutskoye shower, and I also thank his wife Larissa I. Budayeva from Tomsk State University for her valuable assistance. Thanks also to Andranik Mgdesyan of Troitsckoye

Acknowledgments

for supplying provisions for our expedition and for arranging an interview with Valentina Markitan, who was kind enough to relate her grandmother's account of the 1922 meteorite shower.

Three scholars who, during the 1996 Bologna, Italy, Tunguska Conference, shared with me their views about the Tunguska Event and comets deserve thanks. They are the late U.S. Geological Survey geologist Dr. Eugene Shoemaker, Dr. Brian Marsden of the Harvard-Smithsonian Astrophysical Observatory, Cambridge, and Academician Victor Korobeinikov of the Russian Academy of Sciences.

My thanks also to astrophysicist Dr. Jerry LaSala, of the University of Southern Maine, for reading and commenting on Chapter 8, and to U.S. Geological Survey senior research scientist Dr. C. Wylie Poag, of Woods Hole, Massachusetts, for permission to use, in Chapter 6, a brief quotation from his book *Chesapeake Invader*, published by Princeton University Press. His book is must reading for anyone interested in large impact structures.

I would be remiss in not thanking Dr. Joel Schiff, editor-in-chief of *Meteorite* magazine for his support and permission to use sections of my expedition articles that first appeared in various issues of *Meteorite*. Small portions of this book also appeared in somewhat different form in *Sky & Telescope* magazine and are published here with the permission of Sky Publishing Corporation. Additional thanks go to Jeannine L. Dickey, who spent endless hours transcribing dozens of taped interviews and organizing them for integration into various chapters. Her brave guesses about the spelling of the many Russian personal and place names were a continuous source of amusement for both of us.

And I wish to thank the Southworth Planetarium of the University of Southern Maine for providing partial funding for my research expedition travel expenses to Russia during the years I was director/lecturer of the planetarium. Last, but not least by any means, my warm thanks to Jean Dickey of Sykesville, Maryland for her generous financial aid that made my Popigai expedition of 1999 possible and so rewarding.

Although I have made all efforts to ensure the accuracy of information in this book, errors have a way of sneaking into a work of this length and complexity. If such errors have occurred, they are mine and mine alone and are in no way attributable to any of those who were kind enough to read parts or all of the manuscript.

Meteorite Hunter

★ Expedition sites
Map locations are only approximate.

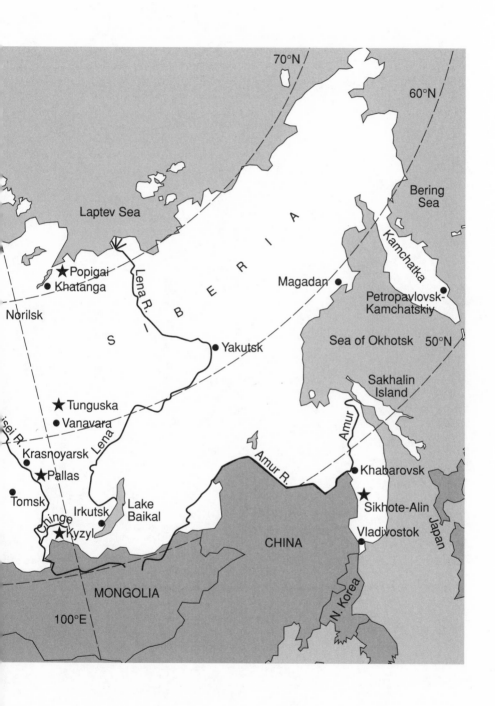

CHAPTER 1

Tunguska:
The Day the Sky
Split Apart

The explosions were heard in the early morning hours of
June 30, 1908, when most farmers were already at work
in their fields. It was a drama that has occurred countless
times in Earth's geological history and one that surely will
play again. But to those unsuspecting peasants it seemed that
the end of the world had come.

The Tungus tribespeople and Russian fur traders who
happened to glance into the Siberian sky that fateful morning
were puzzled on seeing a distant bright spot, a "second Sun,"
approach out of the cloudless southeastern sky, and rapidly
grow larger. Their puzzlement then turned to horror as the
spot billowed into a monstrous fireball brighter than the Sun,
streaking down through the atmosphere and dragging a long
trail of light. It appeared to be heading directly toward their
trading post of Vanavara on the Stony Tunguska River.

With arms raised to shield their faces from the heat and
fierce light, their gaze continued to follow the blinding fire-

Surviving the Tunguska Blast

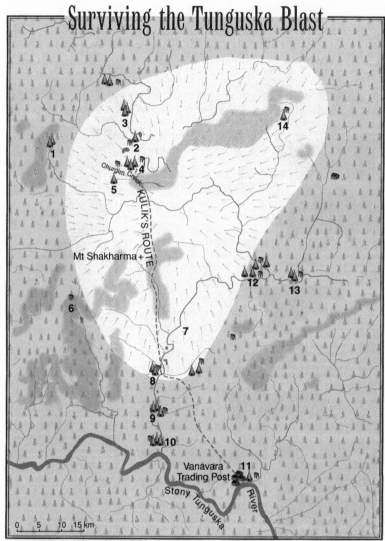

Diagram: STEVEN SIMPSON / YURIY KANDYBA

The often repeated myth in numerous accounts of there being no human deaths caused by the Tunguska explosion are just that—an often repeated myth perpetuated by writers who simply have not done their homework by looking into the eyewitness accounts meticulously screened and cross-checked by both investigator Leonid A. Kulik and ethnographer Innokenty Suslov before 1930. There are hundreds of such eyewitness accounts. Of those few quoted here, at least two people reportedly died as a result of the explosion. And quite possibly there were others, judging from the large number of reindeer and tepees incinerated or otherwise destroyed.

2

Eyewitness Reports

1 Near the Chuvar Range by the upper flow of the Khushmo River: "In the nomad camp of P. Tarkichonok the reindeer herd was burned to ashes. For three days the dumbfounded people lay inert beneath blankets, as if dead."

2 On the Kimchu River close to Lake Cheko: "In the nomad camp of Stepan Dzhenkoul many deer lay motionless in a stupor. All the tepees were carried away by the whirlwind."

3 On the Kimchu River closer to Lake Cheko: "All the tepees were blown into the air; people fell unconscious."

4 From a nomad camp on the Churgim Creek: "In Vasiliy Dzhenkoul's nomad camp between 600 and 700 reindeer were burned, as were the reindeer dogs, all stores, and all the tepees. Luckily, Vasiliy at the time happened to be away tending another of his herds on the Ilimpo River."

5 On the upper flow of the Churgim Creek: "Everything was incinerated. Only ashes remained. The storage hut of Stepan Dzhenkoul was burned, and his birch bark tepee was blown away."

6 From the Upper Lakura River: "All the storage shelters of S. Ankov and his three brothers were incinerated. They lost eighty sacks of flour, all their winter clothing, and stores."

7 On the Chamba River north of the Khavarkita River: In the words of Ivan Aksenov: "While hunting, I was knocked to the ground unconscious and lay motionless, as if dead, then later I awoke."

8 From the Chamba River near the Khavarkikta tributary: "In the nomadic camp of the aged hunter Lyuburman, from the family group of Shanyagir, all the tepees were felled and the old man died of shock."

9 On the Chamba River near the lower Yakuta tributary: "The Tungus hunters Petr Doonov and his son Vasiliy were slightly contused."

10 At the mouth of the Chamba River: "In the nomadic camp of Pavel Aksenov, Pavel, his wives, daughter, and sons Gelencha and Pampunya were stricken with horror."

11 From the Vanavara trading post: "The sky has split apart. When the fire appeared it became so hot that one couldn't stand it. S. Semenov's shirt was as if set on fire. When the loud explosion was heard he was hurled to the ground across a distance of three sazhens [the old Russian measure of length, one sazhen is equal to 2.13 meters]. M. Kosolapov said that he felt 'as if someone had burned my ears.' A hot wind blew past us. The ground and all the huts trembled, causing the sod packing to fall from the ceilings. The glass was blasted out of the window frames. The families of P. Yakochen, M. Kosolapov, A. Kosolapov, and Marfa Bryukhanova all hid inside their huts in horror."

12 On the Chamba River: "God in his displeasure with us tore the sky apart. In the nomad camp of Ivan Dzhenkoul all 200 reindeer in a single instant were incinerated. All of his stores of furs, food, and other goods were likewise destroyed."

13 On the Chamba River: "Akulina was thrown up into the air as if flying. The old man Vasilly, son of Okhchen, was thrown into the air as he slept. He flew for 12 meters until he was hurled into a tree, which broke his arm so that the bone was sticking out. He soon died. In a state of shock Ivan Yerineev lost his tongue. The hunting dogs disappeared."

14 On the upper flow of the Ukagitkon River: "The herdsman S. Dronov lay unconscious for two days. His entire herd of reindeer was killed and all his household burned."

ball as it moved along a northwestward trajectory and disappeared over the horizon. Then it exploded. The sky appeared to split apart in a series of rapid bursts. The deafening roar terrified children and adults going about their early morning chores. Later, some said the explosions sounded like a "cannonade" that thundered across the countryside and resounded for several minutes. Others likened the clamor to "a dozen trains all rattling the rails simultaneously." Those closer to ground zero of the explosion were temporarily deafened by the blast. Those still nearer were struck dumb and speechless and fell to the ground in a state of shock. Some were hurled through the air, and two, according to eyewitness reports, died a few days after the event as a result of the injuries they suffered. One survivor from the Chamba River near the mouth of the Lower Dulyushma River later described what happened: "Akulina was thrown up into the air as if flying. The old man Vasiliy, son of Okhchen, was thrown into the air as he slept. He flew twelve meters and was hurled into a tree, which broke his arm so that the bone was sticking out. He soon died. In a state of shock Ivan Yerineev lost his tongue. His store of two moose skins, a sack of flour, and nets was destroyed. A sack of furs became charred, and a rabbit blanket, sleeping bags, and tepee were all destroyed. The hunting dogs disappeared."

The blast felled trees outward in a radial pattern. At the epicenter of the explosion the forest flashed into a soaring column of flame that was visible several hundred kilometers away. One eyewitness at the Vanavara trading post reported: "When the fire appeared it became so hot that one couldn't stand it. S. Semenov's shirt was as if set on fire. When the loud explosion was heard he was hurled to the ground across a distance of three *sazhens* [the old Russian measure of length, 1 *sazhen* is equal to 2.13 meters]. A hot wind blew past us."

The fires incinerated many Tungus tepees and hundreds of their reindeer and continued to burn for weeks. Ash and powdered tundra fragments sucked by the fiery vortex were caught up in the global air circulation and carried around the world. As the debris mixed with the air over Tunguska, condensation triggered a "black rain" of mud and ash.

A series of shock waves pulsing through the bedrock radiated out from the epicenter, causing the frame buildings in faraway Vanavara to shudder. Sod packing was loosened and jolted from log roofs and rained down on the startled occupants. Windows were rattled and glass shattered. Fishermen repairing their boats along the banks of the Stony Tunguska River were flung into the water. Horses stumbled over the trembling ground and lost their footing. Dogs were flipped off balance. A thousand kilometers away to the southwest, near Kansk, a speeding Trans-Siberian passenger train began to rattle even more than usual, shaking dozing passengers fearfully awake. Unbelievingly, the engineer watched the tracks ahead shiver as if they were being shaken by an earthquake that just wouldn't stop. When at last the rails ended their eerie dance, he brought the train slowly along to the next station and got out to examine each car. He couldn't tell the frightened passengers what had happened. He was as mystified as they were.

Arrival in Krasnoyarsk

That was what I knew about the Tunguska explosion when, in July 1992, I set out for Siberia to find out more about the mysterious event. My mission was to familiarize myself with the region where the explosion occurred, get video footage and still photographs of significant locations within the epicenter, and gain knowledge about the work of several Russian investigators who had been doing research in the area for many years—all as research for a book I intended to write. During the next two weeks in Krasnoyarsk, my activities once at the epicenter were to be more fully orchestrated by some of those veteran investigators. During the days of preparation just ahead, I was to learn just how knowledgeable and valuable a traveling companion Katya was to be.

━━┅ ≋◆≋ ┅━━

When Katya and I scramble off the train at the Krasnoyarsk station, we are met by her mother, Tanya, a stout woman in her sixties, who was a practicing M.D. and is now a pensioner. Although officially retired, she keeps up a small private practice that enables her to get by far better than most. When not traveling, Katya, a single parent, lives with her mother, sister, and four-year-old son in a small three-room apartment lavishly furnished with oriental carpets adorning the walls and magnificent rock and mineral specimens collected by Katya's geologist father. She has not seen him for several years since her parents' divorce. Marcia, Katya's sister, a tall morose young woman, has just begun medical school. By living with Katya, she has picked up enough English so that we have little difficulty communicating. Tanya, always referred to by Katya as "The Mother," speaks hardly a word of English.

Katya and I must be a sight, continually scratching the soot out of our hair and ears. I can even feel it like fine sand whenever I grit my teeth. Both of us are exhausted and want a hot bath, a vigorous shampoo, and a night's sleep without the endless click-clack, click-clack sounds and in beds that stay put instead of rocking back and forth.

We are greeted at the apartment by a smiling barefooted man introduced to me as Yuri Kandiba, a geologist. Not speaking a word of English, he smiles broadly and nods his greetings enthusiastically. Yuri is of medium build and muscular, and wears dark trousers a bit frayed at the cuffs and a T-shirt with horizontal black stripes, the kind worn by Russian sailors. He is a veteran of a dozen expeditions to the Tunguska epicenter and an authority on the history of Kulik's expeditions. Yuri has been hired to serve as our guide for a fee of a $100, which in 1992 Russia is a generous sum for which he seems immensely grateful. He is very eager to get right down to business.

The Mother has prepared a rich red borscht with a large dollop of sour cream, cabbage pie, and vegetables for dinner. Marsha provides a background of lovely Russian choral music and piano sonatas played by the legendary Stanislaw Richter. Then comes a treat of a small glass of *kedrovka*, a clear vodka in which knots of Siberian cedar trees have been allowed to soak for several weeks. It has a very pleasant taste, almost sweet, and is just what I need for a night of motionless sleep. The Mother's next-door neighbor, an airline stewardess, has agreed to rent her apartment to us for the next several days. It isn't much, but we are grateful for it. The sink is plugged up, the bathroom is about the size of a telephone booth, and the unattached plastic toilet seat keeps falling off. But at least you can sit on it, sort of. Our greatest stroke of luck is that the Krasnoyarsk authorities have not turned off either the hot or cold water to apartments in our part of the city. This major inconvenience occurs often during summer, and usually without warning. You wake up one morning, and no hot water, or no water at all. Call the city's water department and you usually get a busy signal, or a rude voice that scolds, "Why are you complaining? Why do you need hot water? It's summer." Click! As much as one-half of the city's population of nearly a million may be without hot water for from two weeks to a month. Before Katya left for Moscow to meet me, a fifth of the city went five days without gas for cooking because of inspection and maintenance operations. These summer shutdowns occur all over Russia, sometimes announced over the radio or television, usually not.

The Expedition

Our 1992 expedition was one in an ongoing series led by Russian scientists who continue to examine the area of the Tunguska explosion for its cause. Since about 1960 expeditions have been organized each summer, and since about 1990 have included foreign investigators. One to two dozen researchers from a wide range of academic disciplines—botanists, geneticists, physicists, astronomers, soil geologists, chemists, remote sensing experts, and others—work together on these trips like detectives at the scene of a crime. They are trying to piece together a full explanation of the mysterious blast from the many clues it left behind.

As the first American to be invited by the Russian Academy of Sciences to take part in a Tunguska expedition, my role was that of a science writer and teacher of astronomy doing research into the history of the Tunguska cataclysm and other Siberian impact sites. On my arrival in Moscow in the summer of 1992, I began my research by spending several days conducting interviews. One veteran of more than a dozen Tunguska expeditions was Yevgeniy Kolesnikov, a specialist in isotopic cosmic chemistry at Moscow State University. For fifteen years he had been collecting peat samples (*Sphagnum fuscus*) from the epicenter region and analyzing them for contamination by cosmic residues. Another interview was with Russia's leading field investigator of meteorite impact sites, Valentin Tsvetkov, who was at the time scientific director of the Moscow Planetarium. We were to develop a close friendship over the years, and he was to play a major role in three of my future expeditions to Siberia. Tsvetkov's principal interest lay nearly 5000 kilometers east of Tunguska where more than 100 craters and pits were formed by fragments of the Sikhote-Alin meteorite shower of 1947. According to Tsvetkov, the Tunguska investigators could benefit by applying methods he had used to study the Sikhote-Alin site.

The 1992 expedition seems poorly organized, at least at the beginning. A German couple find their way to our apartment through telephone calls to The Mother. No one met them at the airport or arranged for a hotel; Katya does the latter immediately. The two expedition leaders are off in Italy. Initially the Germans are told the fee will be $150 each. Then it jumps to $350, and then to $500, which they can't afford. Three Japanese are also supposed to join the group, though they speak not a word of Russian or English.

No one seems to know when the group is supposed to assemble at the airport for the flight to Vanavara. Katya and I decide to fly to Vanavara on our own and wait for Yuri and the group there. We will carry two large backpacks with food, some clothing, and sleeping gear. Yuri will follow along with our other luggage—containing our tent, more food, a small cook stove and gasoline bottles, water bottles, and the rest of our clothing—as soon as the group gets organized. If the others fail to show up, we will gather more supplies in Vanavara, hire a local guide, and walk the 78 kilometers into Kulik's base camp, our initial destination.

On August 2, Katya and I board an aging Yak-40 jet with rickety seats and paint peeling off the interior. We have to carry our luggage aboard and stow the larger pieces in a walk-through baggage section in the rear of the plane. Smaller pieces are stuffed into narrow open overhead bins, under our seats, or just left in the aisle. The two seats behind us against the rear bulkhead are piled high with duffel bags, sacks of potatoes, and dried fish. None of the luggage is secured, and the overhead bins don't have doors or tie-downs. A barefooted man with a large dog climbs over the luggage in the aisle and claims the last seat. One passenger stands all the way, leaning against the haphazardly stacked cargo in the rear luggage compartment. He has apparently bribed either the stewardess, or more likely the pilot, into giving him a place on the plane. Any Federal Aviation Administration (FAA) inspector who might enter on our scene would flee in horror. Being a commercial pilot myself, I am more than a little apprehensive. Our bored and sleepy-eyed stewardess lolls across the two rear seats opposite us in utter disregard for any activity inside the plane. She remains that way throughout the flight.

The 850-kilometer flight of an hour and forty minutes is, fortunately, humdrum, with the stewardess sleeping soundly all the way, curled up in her double seat. There is not even a seat belt check. Since the buckle on my seat belt is broken, I have to knot the two ends together. Everyone sleeps, including the dog. On landing in Vanavara, we taxi to the parking area by a log shack that serves as a combination ticket office, waiting room, and control tower. Two dogs come bounding out onto the taxi strip, tails wagging, to cheerfully welcome us. "Maybe they're here to meet our doggie passenger," Katya observes.

"Now what?" I ask once we are inside the waiting room. "It's a waiting room, so wait here," Katya commands straight-faced and disappears through a heavy, creaky wooden door and into a small office. From time to time, she boastfully reminds me that she was once a sergeant in the military reserves. There are two wooden benches and a set of scales for weighing luggage in the waiting area. I lean against a wall, let my backpack slip to the floor, and sit on it. Through one of the windows I watch two militia types in camouflage coveralls help a handcuffed prisoner out of their jeep. One holds a rifle in one hand as the three make their way toward us. Katya returns with the news that the telephones aren't working. A strong wind the day before blew down the lines, so there is no way to call the one hotel in town. "Wait here," she orders again, indicating her imaginary sergeant stripes, and disappears through another door, this one to a tiny room that seems to have something to do with airport administration. Meanwhile the two militiamen, who have deposited their prisoner somewhere, saunter into the waiting room and eye me with suspicion as they chat softly.

A few minutes later Katya, looking grim, reappears. "I just asked if a helicopter had been reserved for a flight to Tunguska. They say they don't know anything about such a reservation, and they can't find out about the other expedition members because the telephone lines are down." The two militiamen take renewed interest in me when Katya appears. Slowly they approach us, and as I am about to reach for my passport they smile and begin talking with Katya. "*Karashaw, karashaw . . . ocheen karashaw*," Katya keeps saying, and she too is all smiles. Understanding *karashaw* to mean "good," and *ocheen karashaw* to mean "very good," I decide that some smiling of my own is in order. The two men grab our backpacks and lead us to their jeep, chatting away as if we are old friends reunited after a long absence. I never do learn what happened to the prisoner.

The jeep rocks and bounces its way along the unpaved streets littered with the soccer-ball-size rocks that are continually pushed up out of the roadbed by frost. There are more potholes than smooth surface of roadway. We stop by the roadside across from the entrance to what I presume is the hotel. Our militia escorts again grab our backpacks and beckon to us to follow them down over the steep slope of the roadway, then across the boarded sidewalk that provides footing during the brief summer season when the permafrost melts and there is mud everywhere. Running parallel to the town's system of boardwalks is a continuous wooden tunnel enclosure on stilts. Inside is a pipeline that carries hot water to the main buildings in the town. The roadways all are some 1.5 meters higher than the boardwalks to facilitate drainage during the muddy season in April and May.

Before leaving us, the senior militia officer tells Katya that they will return the next morning to drive us to the airport so that we may inquire about the rest of our expedition. The hotel is a barracks-style building with about twenty small rooms. It is state operated, which means that the service is predictably bad and is there to serve the many visiting government oil exploration and minerals engineers. In a tiny area that serves as a lobby, a young man sits in front of a black-and-white television set. Katya clears her throat a couple of times to get his attention, but he ignores us. Now, Katya doesn't like to be ignored and is about to unplug the television when, without looking up, he says that the woman who is the manager isn't here, and he doesn't know when she'll be back. Just then, two little girls appear, and in Russian Katya tells them to "Go find mama." Moments later the manager appears and eyes us in a manner that is not inviting. She then notices the two militiamen sitting in their jeep, smiling, nodding, and pointing to us. She asks for our passports, writes something in a large red book, stamps the entry with a resentful thump, gives us a key, and points down the hall.

"The room is expensive," Katya says, putting me on. It is $3 a day. The toilets and wash area are several doors farther along the corridor. The room is narrow, no more than 5 or so meters long and a little more than 3 meters wide. The floor is bare boards, and the long wall is adorned with a lovely oriental carpet, most likely made in Afghanistan. (Russians usually decorate their walls rather than cover the floors with carpets.) Two flimsy iron frame beds, probably surplus from some military barracks, are arranged end to end along one wall. An uncurtained window at one end of the room looks out onto a wooded area. A naked light bulb with a pull chain dangles from an electrical cord sticking out of a hole in the ceiling that looks as if it had been smashed in with a hammer. Katya slides out of her backpack and collapses onto her bed, giggling "What a lovely little room. Aren't you happy they found this hotel for us?" I stretch out on my bed and gently bounce up and down to test the springs. On my second bounce the bed collapses amid a clattering of metal, and I find myself flat on my back on the floor with metal slats and springs in disarray around me. Once she sees that I am not hurt, Katya begins laughing uncontrollably.

The Demise of a Culture

In the years (late 1920s and early 1930s) following the early expeditions to the Tunguska site, Vanavara was a trading post where a few hundred migrant Evenk reindeer herders and hunters of bear, wolves, and highly prized sable did business with Russian fur traders whose principal medium of exchange was cheap vodka.

Over the decades the vodka, and then the Soviet government's attempt to "civilize" the Evenks, led to the demise of the Evenks' culture. First, the government tried to keep them in one large permanent settlement, a state collective called the *kolkhoz*, instead of permitting them to continue their ancient migrant ways. They were no longer allowed to have their own reindeer herds, but were forced to manage a large single herd owned by the state. No longer could they trade freely, but were instructed to sell their furs only to the state at a fixed price. At the same time, the Communist government placed all the Evenk children in state-run boarding schools far from home and taught them to speak Russian in preference to their native language. Deprived of their pride in being able to support their families by trading competitively and owning their own herds of reindeer, many Evenk men turned increasingly to alcohol. They watched in despair as their culture suffocated under the stifling mantle of Soviet socialism. Even their names were taken away from them. Earlier the Tungus clans had named their children after objects and living things in their environment—Axe, Knife, Fox, River, and so on. But then the government encouraged parents to give their newborn infants traditional Russian names—Avel, Naum, Afanasiy, Andrey for boys and Mariya, Darya, Anna, Polina for girls. So in a short time the Tungus lost their names, and the state forbade them to practice their pagan religion. Even their god of fire, Ogdy, was dead.

Today there is only a handful of full-blooded Evenks in the region. On finishing school far away, the Tungus children chose life in the cities over returning to the taiga and a culture they no longer knew. When I was on a later expedition to the Popigai impact crater above the Arctic Circle east of Vanavara, I witnessed the same situation with the Dolgans, the native people of that region.

Vanavara now supports a population of about 10,000, which includes local inhabitants and the oil exploration crews that visit the settlement for weeks or months at a time.

The government workers live mostly in long wooden barracks situated here and there around the town. The high officials stay in our hotel. In 1992 Vanavara was decidedly a one-star town and not a pleasant place. During the first three months of that year there were twenty-seven robberies and six murders. Our militia friends told us to be careful and to talk to no one who might attempt to stop us on the streets.

A little after 6 o'clock the evening we arrive, we decide to explore the town and soon find a restaurant complete with dance floor, bar, and about a dozen tables. We sit down near a window overlooking the parking lot and are served up a reasonably good three-course dinner of salad, fish, then beef with rice, and tea, all for 123 rubles, which comes to 95 cents. Only three other tables are occupied. A group at one seems a bit heavy with vodka and keeps looking over at us throughout our dinner. They probably have overheard us speaking English. Just before we are about to leave, three men weave their way over to our table. Two of them start to speak Russian to Katya while the third decides to practice his few words of English on me. Katya looks nervous, which makes me nervous. How are we going to get out of this one without appearing rude and creating an unwanted and possibly nasty scene? At that moment I happen to glance out into the parking lot and see a military jeep. Our friends have been observing us through the window, probably even following us around town earlier, and they begin walking rapidly toward the restaurant when they see our visitors huddled over our table. A minute later they have the three in firm grips and march them back to their own table. I pay the bill, and we are escorted under armed guard to the safety of our two back seats in the jeep. For the next hour, our escorts take us on a sightseeing tour of Vanavara and the banks of the Stony Tunguska River.

I drift off to sleep that night with complete confidence that our newly found friends from the militia are our guardian angels, but with less confidence that my bed will retain its integrity. All other militia types I have encountered since my arrival in Russia have been rude, stern, and threatening with their authority. Ours have nice genes. They say they will pick us up in the morning and take us to the airport to meet the flight from Krasnoyarsk. But will the rest of the expedition be on the flight? Will a helicopter costing about $2000 an hour be chomping the air ready to whisk us off to the epicenter site of the greatest known explosion in recent geological history?

What Caused the Mysterious Explosion?

Russian investigators studying the Tunguska site since about 1930 had been able to piece together what ensued: On the morning of June 30, a fireball cascaded down from the Siberian sky, trailing a blaze of light some 800 kilometers long—the distance from central Maine to New York City. It approached Earth from an azimuth of 115° and rapidly descended at an angle of 30° to 35° above the horizon. Then at about 7:15 A.M. local time, it exploded at an estimated 5 kilometers above the sprawling forest and some 70 kilometers northwest of Vanavara. [The point of the explosion, as determined by my global positioning system (GPS) navigation aid during my 1992 expedition to the site, was 60° 55′ 04″ N, 101° 56′ 55″ E.] The flash of the explosion was reported from as far away as 710 kilometers in the village of Znamenskoye in Irkutsk Province. The sky appeared to split apart in a series of rapid bursts crossing a distance of 15 to 20 kilometers. Its force was 2000 times that of the atomic blast that devastated Hiroshima, Japan in 1945. That's 40 megatons of TNT producing energy of 10^{23} ergs. The object, whatever it was, had an estimated mass of between 1 and 5 million metric tons and a diameter of around 156 meters.[*] It is difficult to comprehend the magnitude of the explosion that felled trees over an area of some 2150 square kilometers (more than half the size of Rhode Island), shook an enormous region of desolate Siberian taiga to its bedrock, rattled vodka bottles more than 800 kilometers away, and sent pressure waves through Earth's crustal rock twice around the planet. The accompanying fiery vortex devastated an area of some 1000 square kilometers and sucked ash and powdered tundra skyward to a height of some 20 kilometers.

Following the explosion, unusually colorful sunsets and sunrises caught the attention of observers in western Europe, Scandinavia, Russia, and western Siberia. The climax of visual displays occurred on the night of June 30, though they continued over several weeks, weakening exponentially. *The New York Times* of July 3, 1908, reported "remarkable lights . . . observed in the northern heavens," and scientists mistakenly attributed the dazzling skies to electrical disturbances in the atmosphere caused by solar outbursts. Similar light displays had been reported in 1883 at the time of the Krakatoa volcanic explosion in the Sunda Strait, said the *Times*.

These optical fireworks, or "light nights," were most prominent over eastern Siberia and central Asia. They included a night sky bright enough to cast shadows and allow a newspaper to be read. Ice-coated dust grains at heights of 75 to 90 kilometers created noctilucent, or night-

---

[*] The figures cited in this chapter are the most recent estimates, at the time of this writing, of Russian investigators

shining, clouds that illuminated much of the sky, and by day there were halos around the Sun. A marked decrease in the air's transparency was recorded in the United States by the Smithsonian Astrophysical Observatory in Cambridge and the Mount Wilson Observatory in California.

Disturbances in Earth's magnetic field were reported 900 kilometers southeast of the epicenter by the Irkutsk Observatory. These were magnetic "storms" similar to ones produced by nuclear explosions in the atmosphere. A seismograph station 4000 kilometers away in St. Petersburg recorded tremors produced by the blast, as did more distant stations around the world. While all this had been determined with reasonable certainty by the time of our 1992 expedition, one great mystery remained: What was it that exploded over the Siberian countryside that fateful morning and became the most devastating known assault on our planet in the history of civilization? I was to find that there was still no consensus on the identity of the cosmic visitor to Tunguska, though there were many hypotheses. However, the various teams of Russian and foreign investigators do agree on one thing, that the event transcends scientific curiosity and raises a host of social, medical, and economic concerns of global importance.

Expedition Ho!

In the morning, our militia friends come to our hotel with news that the rest of the expedition will be arriving within the hour, that an MI 17 helicopter is being preflighted, and we should hurry. It takes us less than ten minutes to stuff our belongings into our backpacks, which are then whisked away with urges of "*Davai, davai, davai!*" meaning "hurry, hurry, hurry." On the way to the airport, the driver presents me with a souvenir of a scabbard for my hunting knife. It is traditional Tungus, consisting of a 25-centimeter length of a deer's forefoot complete with hoof. The upper part is a flap with slits for a belt to fit through. My knife slides smoothly into my new prize, the blade point safely tucked into the small black hoof. Even Katya is impressed, and simply says, "Wowww!" as she strokes the scabbard with her finger.

The same two dogs that met our flight the day before are busy greeting each of the seventeen other expedition members as they form a human conveyor belt to hand down duffel bags and bulging backpacks and stack them into a huge pile. Our German friends smile and wave. We immediately spot Yuri, who shuffles our two heavy duffel bags into position for loading aboard the helicopter. Vasiliev and Kolesnikov greet us warmly, and eventually we are introduced to our other companions, among whom are three Japanese and one Englishman. The rest are Russian, among them a female interpreter-cook. Since Katya, Yuri, and I will be off on our own for most of our week at the epicenter, Vasiliev has arranged for a second English-speaking expedition member to be available when Katya is not. One of the senior investigators is Alyona Boyarkina, a researcher at Tomsk State University and a veteran of more than thirty expeditions to Tunguska. Among her work over the years has been mapping of the area of trees felled by the explosion; collecting thousands of soil, peat, and snow samples for analysis for cosmic dust; and more recently the study of the magnetic properties of the soils in and around the epicenter region.

When I ask Alyona if she thinks her line of research may one day explain what caused the 1908 explosion, she answers, "Not straight away, perhaps. But there are numerous hypotheses. For instance, let's take the plasma hypothesis, one suggesting that a fragment of the Sun's hot gases was hurled toward

Earth. According to the hypothesis, if a piece of that plasma collided with the atmosphere, there should be strong magnetic disturbances imprinted in the soil. So my research, by itself, cannot answer the question. But it can help support or perhaps contradict certain hypotheses." The plasma hypothesis, by the way, was suggested in 1984 by A. N. Dmitriev and V. K. Zhuravlev. It has a 100,000-ton mass of matter ejected from the Sun hurtling to Earth and then somehow exploding over Siberia. Theoretician V. A. Bronshten dismisses the idea, citing "pseudo-scientific terminology and general philosophical reasoning" as substitutes for valid science.

Within an hour the huge helicopter comes screaming toward us from the opposite end of the airport and sandblasts us unmercifully as it chops the air briefly before touching down a few meters away from us. We all scramble aboard, tossing, hauling, and shoving the small mountain of duffel bags and backpacks up into the bowels of the giant bird. Then we are off, skimming low over the beautiful endless taiga on our way to the epicenter and Kulik's base camp. Sure beats walking, I think to myself. Katya squeezes my hand and grins, happy to be off on another adventure. But ten minutes later she has gone silent and white. "You'd better give me a plastic bag," she says. "I'm going to be sick." And she is for the remainder of the flight.

In the Footsteps of Leonid Kulik

Despite the many eyewitnesses unlucky enough to have been within 80 kilometers of the blast's epicenter, the Tunguska fireball event went virtually unnoticed by scientists when it occurred. It was all but ignored for two decades. When investigations were finally launched, they met a bizarre set of circumstances.

Following the explosion, the local Tungus inhabitants regarded the region of devastation as bewitched or enchanted. They believed their disobedience had so enraged Ogdy, their god of fire, that he had punished them. Travel through or hunting in the region was therefore forbidden, a taboo honored by all but the courageous or foolish.

"Now, Roy, respected friend," Yuri said to me one day as we were hiking through the forest, "I am about to tell you something, a bit of history, that is not generally known." And his account follows: The first "expedition" into the area was carried out in 1910 by a wealthy Russian merchant named Susdalev, who cunningly manipulated the presumed bewitchment of the region to his own ends. He wanted the Tungus people's assurance that other Russian merchants would be kept out of the territory so that he might reap a disproportionate profit in the local fur trade.

Susdalev's guide was one Ivan Aksenov, an eyewitness who had been knocked unconscious by the explosion. Aksenov led Susdalev and a group of hunters, shamans, and chiefs to a lake they suspected had been formed by the impact of Ogdy's fireball. There Susdalev sank a large spruce pole into the tundra to claim the territory as the Tungus people's sacred ground. He formalized the occasion by having the costumed shamans sing ritual songs, all on cue. Susdalev was probably the first outsider to view at least the edge of that vast area of trees felled by the terrible blast.

Seventeen years after Susdalev's incursion into the site, Leonid Kulik began his legendary expeditions. A geologist, Kulik was the first scientist to explore the Tunguska site, and he was determined to find the cause of the explosion. As Academician Nickolai Vasiliev has written, "The destiny of a scientist is inseparable from the problem that scientist is investigating. Perhaps there is no better example of this in the history of science than the way the destiny of the father of Russian meteoric science, Leonid Alexievich Kulik, was shaped by his obsession to unravel the mystery of the Tunguska 'meteorite.' It has never been proved that the 1908 event was a meteorite, although to the end Kulik believed that his tireless search would one day uncover a telltale nugget of cosmic iron."

Kulik met resistance when he tried to employ a local Tungus to guide him into the enchanted area. Only with the assistance of an influential member of the Presidium of the Soviet Executive Committee was Kulik put in touch with a Tungus named Ilya Potapovich Petrov, who reputedly knew the location of the area of felled trees. Better known as Lyuchetkan (meaning "a friend of Russians"), Petrov was reluctant to visit the site. Kulik persuaded him with two sacks of flour, building materials for the roof and floor of his house, and several rolls of cloth. After two false starts, they were forced back by snow so deep that it came up to the breastbones of their horses. An entry in Kulik's diary reads: "The loads of supplies and equipment were pushed this way and that and torn by the branches and rough tree bark of the taiga that crowded in from all sides. Our caravan continuously got stuck in dense thickets since the horses could not go through the forest as easily as the deer slips through lightly. After endless reloadings of sacks of fodder, and with the horses strained to the breaking point in the deep snow, we returned to the trading post to work out a different way to travel."

By mid-April 1927, with pack reindeer instead of horses, Kulik, Lyuchetkan, and another Tungus had managed to hack their way through nearly 100 kilometers of taiga, across rivers and streams, and through bogs and swamps. Kulik's second guide, Pavel Aksenov, at first refused to go beyond the edge of the region of flattened forest, but Kulik persuaded him to carry on for a few more days. On April 15, the little group reached the base of the twin-peaked Mount Shakharma.

On climbing the mountain, Kulik was astonished. He could hardly believe his eyes. From horizon to horizon, across 25 kilometers, there was utter devastation. Thousands of trees had been torn from the ground by the pressure wave. Their uprooted ends pointed universally to the north while their tops pointed southward. Birch, cedar, larch, and pine limbs were strewn everywhere. Not even the wildest descriptions of the Tungus could have prepared Kulik for what lay before him, a chaos of twisted, broken, and scorched debris that left him dumbfounded. He simply stared. Lyuchetkan slowly raised his arm, pointed over the macabre scene toward the northern horizon, and said solemnly, "That is where the thunder and lightning fell down." Kulik had become the first scientific investigator to gaze on this bizarre scene.

Sixty-five years later I stand atop that same ridge of hills and gaze over a tranquil taiga of lush green that stretches away forever.

The Dock and Vitaliy's Mammoth

"Roy, respected friend," Yuri begins again one day as the three of us stop to rest during a 10-kilometer trek through the forest to another of Kulik's camps, this one on the Khushma River and named The Dock. Yuri has become an authority on Kulik and obviously has also become very attached to the man, as many biographers become attached to their subjects. "You must understand that in Russia Kulik is still a scientific legend and much honored, even though he died needlessly in the Great Patriotic War [which the Russians call World War II]. So much has been written about him exaggerates to make the legendary Kulik even bigger than life; and some of it has even been fictionalized, to the disappointment of our scientific community.

"But what I am about to tell you now, respected friend, about his collecting birds, is not known, and as a researcher into Kulik's life I believe it to be true, not just part of the Kulik legend. Kulik's laboratory and study were in the large cabin behind where we were eating by the fire last night. It is where he slept also. As you saw this morning, bottles of some of his chemicals still rest on the shelves where he left them, as well as equipment from his photographic laboratory. And there were the many birds that Kulik had collected, examined, and skinned, some of which he mounted in lifelike poses. Kulik did not intend these bird specimens to be exhibited in a museum. So why did he collect them? He cut open the crop of each bird—that little sac where the bird stores stones to grind its food before digesting it. He was interested in those stones. Since the birds peck stones out of the peat, Kulik thought that their crops might contain tiny meteorite fragments. I tell, you, respected friend, Kulik overlooked *nothing*."

When we arrive at The Dock and have slipped out of our backpacks, a slight but muscular bearded man of about fifty is grinning at us over a fire. He is Vitaliy Vornonv, dressed in baggy khaki trousers, sneakers, a tan shirt with sleeves rolled up, and a red bandana. Hanging from a rawhide thong looped around his neck and secured by a second thong tied around his waist is a heavy bark sheath containing one of the largest hunting knives I have ever seen. A high-powered army rifle, loaded, leans against the log shelter wall. Hanging from a tripod of poles is an old ammunition canister of boiling water. After introductions and greetings, a young man of about sixteen, who is Vitaliy's apprentice, produces a spit of five huge trout which he caught an hour earlier in the river only a few yards away. One by one the fish are slipped into the boiling water headfirst and allowed to cook for about three minutes. The rest is very memorable gastronomic history.

As a child, Vitaliy had spent many seasons traveling with the Tungus and living in the taiga. He says that as a boy he was accepted in all tepees. Being a child, he was not permitted to speak, except on certain occasions; but he listened, observed, and learned. He came to know the Tungus language and ways intimately, having traveled with them on their nomad treks for hundreds of kilometers through the taiga. Later, he wandered alone in the taiga for three years, living off the land. When he returned to Vanavara, it took him several months to adjust to having other people around. Today his reputation as a skilled hunter and guide is well known over a large region. When shooting sable, he nearly always manages to send his shot through one of the animal's eyes in order not to puncture the fur.

Later that night, full of trout, we sit around the fire and listen to Vitaliy recount episodes from his life with the Tungus.

"The most horrible thing that could happen during a hunt was the loss of the dogs," Vitaliy begins. "If you lose the dogs, the hunt is over. During one hunt I was on with my Tungus family, the dogs ran ahead through the snow to chase an elk. When they did not come back, we returned to our tepee and waited. We waited one day, then another, then the third day. Our nomad camp was in mourning. When the dogs are absent for one day, there is always hope that they will return. If they are not back in two days, we become alarmed. And when they do not return after three days, they usually are dead.

"By the end of the third day we had lost all hope. No one spoke in the tepee except the old man. We, the young hunters, had no right to talk. I remember the night vividly. It was late. The wind was so strong that the whole taiga was moaning. No one went to sleep. Then the old woman, whose name was Nadyora, meaning 'hope,' began to cook food for the dogs. She took a piece of birch bark and with a knife like the one I wear cut out of the bark the shapes of three running dogs. She then bound them with a thin string of rawhide and poised them above the dish of hot food, their heads pointed down as if eating hungrily. Next she took the bowl outside and walked a short way into the taiga. I heard the wind howling and the woman singing. She hit a stick against the bowl, Bang! Bang! Bang! and continued to sing, but I could not hear the words clearly, only that she sang about the dogs. Then she returned to the tepee and placed the bowl just outside the entrance. After that she took her sleeping position with her head pointed at the entrance, as is the custom of the hostess, who must always be alert. Everyone went to sleep.

"In the morning I was the first to awake and quietly went outside. All the dogs were lying near the entrance of the tepee and the bowl was empty. Twice I was the witness of such a shaman method of making the dogs return safely."

In the flicker of the firelight with the dense dark just beyond, Vitaliy's sonorous voice and the soft caressing of his words casts a spell over me. I feel magic in this place, and I do not want the spell broken. Luchetkan, Stepan Dzhenoul, Ivan Aksenov, the hunter Lyuburman, all are there materializing and dissolving and materializing again in wisps of smoke just beyond the fire, waiting for their turn to tell me their tales about the wrath of Ogdy and the awful fireball he hurled down onto them. I feel one with them. All that night I have uneasy dreams.

The next morning I am awakened by the crackling of a fire outside my Tungus tepee of heavy slabs of bark supported by thick poles both inside and out. Vitaliy built it the previous year. Katya is feeding small sticks to the flames and boiling water for tea. Meanwhile, Vitaliy has stoked up a fire in the small log cabin banya which was built by Kulik when he established The Dock as his first camp.*

After a breakfast of dark Russian bread and hot instant cereal, we walk over to the edge of a steep gravel embankment that leads down to the Khushma River. I look down on a nearby bend in that river. Years earlier Kulik had looked up from his raft to the place where I now stand, his bespectacled eyes searching for a suitable place to build his first camp.

My image of Kulik on his raft is suddenly replaced by a grinning Vitaliy poling his way around the bend toward us in a small flat-bottomed boat shaped something like a canoe. He has been fishing. Made of planking and a little more than 4 meters long, the boat has one seat spanning the midsection. Its sheet-metal bottom reveals telltale patches of tar used to seal leaks. Vitaliy maneuvers his small unstable craft against the shore and motions for me to climb in. For the next two hours the two of us glide smoothly and silently along part of the route traveled by Kulik. Because the summer season is dry and late, the river is low and calm. I can recall few times in my life when I have felt more at ease and more a part of the land than during those tranquil and unhurried hours on the river with *boyo* ("friend") Vitaliy. Kulik, also a lover of the land, must have felt the tranquility of this

---

* A banya, which is a near relative of a sauna, is revisited in Chapter 4.

river. From time to time Vitaliy has to get out and tow the boat through shallow water with the bow painter slung over his shoulder. He insists that I just sit and enjoy the voyage. We hardly speak, Vitaliy not knowing a word of English and my Russian then virtually nonexistent, but we somehow communicate our mutual respect and love for this wilderness. Bird song fills the air, beaver swim unconcerned in front of us, a startled young duck beats its wings clumsily and propels itself along the water surface as it takes flight, and trout seemingly the size of dolphins jump for low-flying insects. Twice we stop by deep, shaded pools where Vitaliy expertly works his fishing pole whittled the night before by our campfire. The first strike comes after thirty seconds, the second in another forty seconds. Both are fat trout more than a foot long. Deftly he smacks the head of each fish on a rock and tosses it into the boat. Within the next five minutes he catches two more.

This section of the Khushma is rarely visited. Its high banks of soft and crumbling sediments are a paleontologist's paradise. On one trip Vitaliy spotted the lower jaw of a saber-tooth tiger, which he carefully pried out of the sediments. On another he recovered a 40-pound mammoth tusk as smooth and polished as if it still belonged to its owner. There are Tungus accounts of the late spring thawing and slumping of the soft riverbanks revealing entire carcasses of mammoths that roamed these forests 10,000 years ago. The cold and deeply frozen ground—in winter as hard as a concrete tennis court—that preserved Vitaliy's mammoth tusk and saber-tooth jawbone also has been responsible for preserving the peat and trees felled by the 1908 blast. The scars of catastrophe do not heal quickly in the land of eternal frost.

Occasionally a large cedar hanging like a frontier gate across a narrow part of the river forces us to bend low as a strong thrust of Vitaliy's pole glides us beneath it. On his raft, Kulik had encountered many such fallen trees blocking his way and had to chop his way through them. But when Kulik was here, the river was swollen, swift, and treacherous with blocks of ice the size of a mastodon's head from the spring melt. Our boat brushes its way through small forests of glistening lily pads which serve as landing platforms for dragonflies. Every now and then I scoop up a handful of cold water and let it trickle down my throat. Even in the deeper parts of the river the water is so clear that it seems not to be there at all. Fish in deep pools appear as if suspended motion-less in the air. It is an enchanted moment in an enchanted land. I feel that if God had ever created a perfect Universe, surely it would have been here.

Later in the day, Yuri, Katya, and I climb into our back-packs and, after saying our farewells to Vitaliy and the boy, set out northward through the taiga back to Kulik's base camp. Every now and then Yuri lets out a short series of yelps to alert bears and the region's large wolves to our presence. I wonder if the beasts will be frightened away or attracted. At one stage Yuri recalls one of Kulik's diary entries in which he described hiking through this part of the forest of toppled trees. He said that on mornings when the wind rose he had to be constantly on guard against the twenty-year-old giants toppling around him. "I kept my eyes on the treetops so that, if they fell, I should have time to jump aside. This method of advance had its unpleasant side, for with my eyes turned upward I did not see what was under foot, and I continually stumbled against adders (a venomous European viper) that abound everywhere in this region."

When I ask Yuri if there are still adders in the area, he vaguely shakes his head, but I can't tell if he is shaking it yes or no. In any event, with my eyes often turned upward to the precarious trees, I fail to see a single snake.

After about an hour away from The Dock, we climb a steep cliff face with a waterfall, the Churgim Creek. The cool spray feels good against my hot face. Although there are plenty of places for good foot purchases, the sharply angled rocks are slippery, and our backpacks make the climb tricky. Not far beyond the top Yuri indicates that we should rest by the base of a tree that has a long vertical burn scar, a remnant of the fire that followed the blast. It was most likely here, Yuri says, that the Tungus herdsman Vasiliy Dzhenkoul had been camping on that fateful morning of June 30, 1908. According to the account he left, the fire came roaring through the canyon where we were resting and incinerated between 600 and 700 of Dzhenkoul's reindeer, his dogs, and all his stores and tepees.

Lighting a cigarette and hunkering down, Yuri then relates the following account of how Kulik was first led to this spot. "The Tungus and Russian traders in the Vanavara region all came to know Kulik as a famous man, a scientist, and called him Professor. He also had a reputation for his ability to treat people with illness. His father was a highly respected doctor and most likely taught his son a number of useful nostrums. Once, when Kulik was at the Chamba River, a Tungus shaman approached and asked Kulik to cure his daughter who was seriously ill. It turned out that her condition was too advanced, and the girl died. She was buried near their nomadic camp and, according to Tungus tradition, the shaman's clan left that camp and set up a new one some distance away.

"In appreciation for Kulik's attention, the shaman offered to show him the most direct route to the 'enchanted' region, or epicenter of the explosion. He arrived in his best shaman garments and led Kulik here, to this very location on the Churgim Creek. He then pointed up this canyon and said, '*Boyo*, you must go along this fire rivulet.' The shaman then left. And that is how Kulik successfully reached his destination and set up his base camp. But there is more to the story. Later, Kulik learned that the shaman was killed by his own people, probably because he violated the taboo and revealed the location of the enchanted land."

So, What *Was* the Cosmic Visitor?

After Kulik's expeditions, the Tunguska Event was largely forgotten. Then in 1946, world attention was refocused on the mysterious explosion by a curious and controversial idea. A backdrop for the idea had been provided in 1945 when the United States exploded the first atomic bomb over Japan.

The man to ignite the controversy was Aleksander Kazantsev, a forty-year-old engineer who had graduated from the Tomsk Technological Institute in 1930, the same time that Kulik was probing the Southern Swamp adjacent to his base camp in search of the meteorite he was convinced to his dying day lay buried somewhere nearby. Kazantsev was a talented spinner of tales of science fiction and fantasy. In 1936 he had won first prize in a national science fiction film scenarios competition. As an engineer, Kazantsev was thoroughly familiar with Kulik's expeditions and had read detailed descriptions of the flattened and scorched taiga, of the oval structures that Kulik had presumed were small "craters" caused by the impact of meteorite fragments, and of so-called telegraph pole forests in the central region of the explosion.

The "telegraph poles" were trees that had been left standing but which had had all of their branches, except for stubs, snapped off by the force of the explosion. As part of a Soviet team, Kazantsev had visited Hiroshima after the atomic bomb explosion to examine the devastation, and what he saw there excited his imagination. Just as the Tunguska forest had been scorched and felled, virtually all the buildings and other structures outward from ground zero in Hiroshima had been scorched and flattened—except for one curious scene. A few hundred meters from the ground-zero point there stood a miniature "telegraph pole" forest, a small cluster of trees stripped of their branches.

Additional similarities between Hiroshima and Tunguska led Kazantsev to write a science fiction story in which Kulik's meteorite was transformed into a Martian spaceship with a nuclear reactor engine that blows up over the desolate Siberian taiga. Later Kazantsev was to embellish this scenario. The Martians, he said, had come in search of water for their dried-up world and had been examining nearby Lake Baikal, Earth's deepest and largest body of fresh water, containing 20 percent of the planet's fresh water.

When Kazantsev's story was published in the Russian science fiction magazine *Around the World (Vokrug Sveta)* in 1946, it caught the attention not only of the public, but of scientists as well. Had Kazantsev not been highly respected among the scientific community, his fairy-tale account probably would have been dismissed with a coffee-shop giggle. But he did not end his tale there. He wrote further accounts in which he applied his considerable scientific knowledge to graphically describe the effects of a nuclear explosion over the Tunguska forest. In the eyes of some, his fictionalized accounts had merited the dignity of an alternative "hypothesis."

While many members of the public responded to this new nuclear hypothesis with enthusiasm, the scientific community reacted with indignant condemnation. Virtually every important astronomer in what was then the Soviet Union pounced hard on the provocative hypothesis in articles criticizing Kazantsev's preposterous views, which he had spent ten years refining and promoting. In 1958, his most elaborate publication of all appeared, an article entitled "A Guest from the Cosmos." His 1963 book by the same title had as its theme the visitation of a Martian spaceship powered by a nuclear engine that blew up.

Twenty-six years later, in 1989, a group of Japanese members of the UFO organization *Sakura*, "a special UFO research corps," was invited to join the first International Tunguska Expedition at the invitation of then President Mikhail Gorbachev. Katya, who was a member of that expedition, scoffed, "The Japanese tried to convince all the scientists that the 1908 explosion had been caused when the nuclear engine of a Japanese spaceship blew up. They said that the spaceship had left Japan 2000 years earlier and was returning home." Then laughing, she added, "but somehow I guess it overshot the Narita Airport runway in Tokyo by 6500 kilometers."

In ordinary times most scientists simply would have shrugged off Kazantsev's fantasy as not even being nutworthy. But the postwar years were not ordinary times for Soviet science. A new breed of scientist, whose skills had been honed with the technology that grew out of World War II, wanted to reexamine Kulik's "meteorite" hypothesis and began to search for alternative causes of the Tunguska Event. Oddly enough, the seed of one such proposed cause was provided by a most unlikely source—Kazantsev himself. According to Vasiliev, "Kazantsev had the explosion occurring not on the surface but at a certain height above the ground," a notion now universally accepted by modern research into the event. His spaceship fantasy also raised the question: "Could the explosion have been some form of a naturally occurring nuclear phenomenon?" In other words, could it have been some unknown state of matter entering Earth's atmosphere?

The controversy stirred up by Kazantsev seems to have played at least some part in persuading the Academy of Sciences to resume the Tunguska expeditions. But the strongest argument to do so came from A. A. Yavnel, who in 1957 examined soil specimens that Kulik had brought back from his 1929-1930 expedition. Yavnel reported that the samples contained small globules of magnetite and meteoric dust remarkably similar to meteoric materials from the famous Sikhote-Alin iron meteorite shower of 1947, second in size only to the Tunguska Event in recorded history. Yavnel concluded not only that the Tunguska object was a meteorite, but that it belonged to the class of irons.

The Academy quickly organized a new expedition for the summer of 1958. It was to be led by the Russian geochemist Kirill Florensky. Kirill achieved scientific prominence in the USSR, as had his famous father Professor P. Florensky, who died in one of Stalin's notorious gulag death camps. The 1958 expedition included an impressive group of experts. In addition to Florensky, there was an astronomer, a mineralogist, a soils expert, a physicist, two chemists, several laboratory assistants, and workmen. By that time twenty years had passed since the previous expedition and fifty years since the explosion.

The expedition had two goals. One was to collect and analyze numerous peat samples from different locations within the epicenter region for possible telltale meteoric particles. The soil sampling program was carried out in an area of more than 1000 square kilometers where the forest had been destroyed. Samples were taken at 5-kilometer intervals but were more closely spaced in the central region. The other goal was to begin work on mapping the area of felled trees. Florensky, like the famous Krinov, was a firm believer in Kulik's meteorite theory. Meanwhile the controversy flourished. Others held an opposing view, favoring a nuclear, or, more likely, some other aboveground explosion hypothesis. But what kind of explosion?

On his return to Moscow, Florensky had a new map drawn up on the basis of the expedition's new topographical survey. He was puzzled to find that, according to the map, the epicenter of the explosion did not appear to be in the Southern Swamp, as Kulik had believed, but on its western border. And imagine his astonishment, and further disappointment, when examination of the new expedition's eighty soil samples failed to agree with Yavnel's claim that Kulik's 1929-1930 samples contained fragments of nickel and other metallic particles implicating an iron meteorite. As it turned out, the Kulik samples examined by Yavnel had been mixed accidentally with samples from the Sikhote-Alin site when they were stored by the Committee on Meteorites. With that discovery, the mystery of the remarkable similarity between the Kulik and Sikhote-Alin samples was solved.

While Florensky, Krinov, and the highly reputable investigator V. Fessenkov continued to support the meteorite hypothesis, they also agreed that the meteorite had most likely exploded and disintegrated while still in flight, since there were no ground disturbances to suggest otherwise.

They further agreed that Kulik's oval bog "craters" were nothing more than natural bog formations, a conclusion that soil scientists had come to earlier.

Another important, and surprising, finding that came out of the 1958 expedition was that tree growth within the devastated area since 1908 had been much faster than tree growth outside the area. Trees that began to grow after the 1908 explosion should have reached heights of about 8 meters by 1958. Instead, they had towered to heights of 17 to 22 meters. Botanists and other investigators up to the present time still are unable to account for this accelerated growth, and they continue to search for its cause.

Around 1960, Fessenkov defected from the ranks of the meteorite enthusiasts. Meanwhile, many investigators had come to agree that if a solution to the Tunguska riddle was to be found, the effort would require experts of many different disciplines, including botanists, geneticists, geomorphologists, specialists in remote sensing and computer modeling, and physicians. Accordingly, a number of new and informal groups began to work on the problem. The most significant among them was the one formed in 1958 in Tomsk. Called the Interdisciplinary Independent Expedition (IIE), it led to the formation of the Committee on Meteorites and Cosmic Dust of the Siberian Branch of the Soviet (now Russian) Academy of Sciences.

The first IIE was launched in 1959-1960 and was led by G. F. Plekhanov. One of the goals was to verify, or refute, a nuclear cause of the explosion. For the first time, the soil and vegetation in the region of the epicenter were analyzed for traces of radioactivity. Plekhanov's group claimed that "in the center of the catastrophe, radioactivity is one and a half to two times higher than it is 30 or 40 kilometers away from the center." In addition, those who argued for the nuclear hypothesis cited eyewitness accounts of "radiation burns" found on certain of the reindeer in the form of "scabs that had never appeared before the fire came."

One of the IIE's major efforts, over a period of some thirty years, was the mapping of the area of forest destruction that Florensky had begun in 1958. This important work gradually enabled investigators to estimate not only the force of the explosion but its altitude and certain other aspects of the blast.

On expeditions conducted in 1960 through 1962, Florensky returned to the site in search of microscopic particles of cosmic matter that might lead to the identity of the Tunguska object. Assisted by several coworkers, among them the geologist B. Vronsky and members of the IIE, he collected more than 130 soil samples over an area of some 15,000 square kilometers. Two kinds of microspherule pellets were found —magnetite and silicate. When separated and counted, there were about fifteen silicate spherules for each magnetite spherule. In some cases a smaller magnetite spherule would be found embedded within a silicate spherule, which suggested that both were formed at the same time. But where did the spherules come from, and how were they formed?

When a meteoroid that is part iron and part rock burns down through Earth's atmosphere, its surface layers keep melting in a process called *ablation* until there is nothing left, or until what remains strikes the ground. During the fiery fall, the ablated matter—magnetite and silica—is blown off by strong air currents. It then forms a spray of microspherules that cool, solidify, and drift to the ground. Such microspherules make up the dust trails left behind those large exploding meteoroids called *bolides*.

Did the discovery of microspherules over the epicenter region provide evidence that the Tunguska object was a meteorite? Each year several thousand meteorites the size of golf balls and tennis balls fall to the ground. In addition, each day from 20 to 400 tons of meteoric dust and micrometeorites rain down on Earth. So virtually all of Earth's surface, including the ocean beds, contains a background concentration of microspherules. The question that immediately comes to mind, or that should come to mind, is "Did the Tunguska epicenter contain a higher concentration of microspherules than the normal background concentration found outside the epicenter region? And if it did, does that *prove* that the cosmic visitor was a meteorite?"

There is, however, a complication. According to Krinov, comet dust also sprays Earth's surface with the same kinds of microspherules that were dispersed unevenly over the Tunguska epicenter. So we must now ask the next and obvious question.

Could It Have Been a Comet?

As early as the 1930s, some astronomers had begun to wonder if what exploded over Tunguska in 1908 could have been a comet. Kulik had also considered this. Among them was one of the world's leading authorities on comets, Francis J. W. Whipple of England. Others were the American astronomer Harlow Shapley, the Russian comet authority I. S. Astapovich, and more recently the late Eugene Shoemaker. It was the American astronomer Fred L. Whipple who portrayed comets as "dirty snowballs," implying that they were mostly ices with elemental or molecular dust mixed in. Another astronomer has described these ghostly visitors as being "about as close to nothing as something can get." Space probe investigations of comets on the move have portrayed them as "frozen mudballs," since some appear to contain more dust than ice. During the 1996 Bologna, Italy international Tunguska conference, Shoemaker told me that "anyone who says he knows what a comet is, is talking through his hat." We know practically nothing about the inherent strength of cometary material, an important point we return to in a moment.

We currently regard comets as spongy ice mixed with rock dust, matter left over from the time the Solar System formed some 4.6 billion years ago. Billions of them are thought to be held in cold storage in an immense hollow sphere, called the Oort Cloud, which is wrapped like a fishbowl around the Solar System at a distance of a few trillion kilometers. Jan H. Oort, the Dutch astronomer after whom the cloud was named, thinks there may be 100 billion comets making up this balloonlike swarm. And there are an untold number of additional comets just out beyond the region of Neptune in another swarm called the Kuiper Belt, named after the University of Chicago astronomer G. P. Kuiper who predicted in 1951 that it must be there. There may be tens of thousands of Kuiper Belt objects as large as 80 kilometers across, real Earth crunchers. In fact, most astronomers now regard Pluto itself as a captured Kuiper Belt object. So there is a superabundance of cosmic missiles out there that have been targeting Earth and the other planets ever since the Solar System was formed.

Every once in a while gravitational perturbation flings a comet out of the Oort Cloud, or out of the Kuiper Belt, in toward the Sun. As the comet nears the Sun, the loose lump of rock dust and ice forming its nucleus is heated and some of the volatile ices boil off, forming a cocoon of gas called the coma. The coma swells into a ball extending up to a million kilometers or so out from the nucleus. The nucleus itself may be as small as only a kilometer or so in diameter, or it may be

100 kilometers across. In ages past, comets were called the "terrible stars," "death-bringing stars," and "hairy stars." They were "hairy" because of their long tails. The tails are composed of ionized gases and dust grains pushed out from the comet's coma by pressure from the Sun's solar wind, a continuous gale of atomic particles cast off by the Sun. As recently as about 100 years ago, people dreaded comets, thinking of them as messengers of doom that announce widespread disaster in the form of disease or war. Today we dread them for their potential of colliding with Earth and raising global havoc.

Such havoc was brought home to us in July 1994 when Comet Shoemaker-Levy-9's twenty-two fragments plowed into Jupiter and caused the most spectacular display of planetary fireworks ever observed in the Solar System. Any one of Shoemaker-Levy-9's fragments crashing into Earth would have wrought devastation beyond belief.

Added to the comets are countless millions of those rock-metal objects called asteroids, which range in size from golf balls to houses and small mountains. Most of the asteroids are held gravitationally captive between the orbits of Mars and Jupiter, where they never coalesced into a planet due to the influence of Jupiter's gravity. However, there are large numbers of rogue asteroids zipping around the inner Solar System that from time to time have near misses with Earth. There is more to be said about these objects—nature's interplanetary ballistic missiles—in the last chapter.

Could It Have Been an Asteroid?

In 1992 three respected American theoreticians—C. F. Chyba, P. J. Thomas, and K. J. Zahnie—designed a computer model implicating a stony asteroid, the most common asteroid type, as the Tunguska mystery object. They claim it was about 60 meters in diameter, or about half the length of a football field.

The model paints this picture of the asteroid's entry into the atmosphere and its disintegration: It enters at a velocity of about 15 kilometers per second Its great speed compresses and piles up the air ahead of it. But just behind the asteroid is a near vacuum, which sets up a huge pressure difference across the asteroid. The pressure difference increases as the object plunges into denser regions of the air. The rocky asteroid envisioned by Chyba would next tend to crumble and flatten out, or pancake, as it became unable to maintain its shape against the increasing pressure difference. This pancaking effect increases the atmospheric drag even more until suddenly the object has lost its physical integrity and explodes like a bomb.

Chyba dismissed the comet hypotheses, saying that comets are not dense enough to survive for long in the atmosphere and so they self-destruct at altitudes so high that "they are scarcely noticed at the surface." Astronomer Adnek Sekanina has supported this position, both in writing (in the September 1983 *Astronomical Journal*) and in a paper he gave at the Bologna conference in which he categorically dismissed any competing hypothesis. A comet fragment behaving as the Tunguska object behaved, he said, would have encountered almost 1000 times more air resistance than usually destroys cometary meteors—convincing evidence that the Tunguska object had to be a much denser object. But, as Shoemaker warned earlier, we know practically nothing about the inherent strength of cometary material.

41

How do Chyba and the rest of the asteroid model camp account for the well-documented "light nights" prior to and on June 30 and the following few days? They theorize that the fireball explosion hurled large amounts of water into the upper atmosphere. On cooling, the water droplets froze as ice crystal clouds that were then dispersed by the global circulation of the air. The resulting noctilucent clouds then produced the light nights.

H. J. Melosh, of the Lunar and Planetary Laboratory of the University of Arizona, calls the Chyba computer model "relatively crude" and adds that "there is still work to be done on the physics of Tunguskalike explosions."

Two other American researchers also favor the asteroid model. They are Jack G. Hills, of the Los Alamos National Laboratory, and M. Patrick Goda, of Wabash College. In the March 1992 issue of the *Astronomical Journal* they write that the Tunguska object was an asteroid fragment at least 80 meters in diameter that penetrated the atmosphere at 22 kilometers a second.

When Chyba's stony asteroid model was first published, it stirred considerable interest among astronomers. One thing the article failed to point out, however, was that the well-known Russian investigator V. P. Korobeinikov had pondered a stony asteroid model thirty years earlier, as had other Russian investigators in 1960, 1968, 1978, and 1989. In private correspondence with the author, Korobeinikov said that he found nothing new in Chyba's paper. He added, "In my opinion, we have to consider several suppositions—the object's flight through the atmosphere, its fracture, flight after fracturing and breaking up, shock wave system, radiation, ground effects, and so on. [I further feel that] the cometary hypothesis is one of the best from different scientific perspectives, although I do not reject the stony asteroid hypothesis." The fact is, he added, "the true study is not finished."

Astronomer Duncan Steel has been less kind to the Chyba model, calling it simplistic and chiding it for ignoring certain known parameters of the Tunguska object, e.g., its entry angle and velocity, and the modeling done by the Slovak astronomer Lubor Kresák. Based on work done several years earlier by the Russian investigator Igor Zotkin, in 1978 Kresák suggested, convincingly to many, that the Tunguska object was a fragment of periodic Comet Encke, which produced a meteor shower that peaked around the time of the Tunguska explosion. In his book *Rogue Asteroids and Doomsday Comets*, published in 1995, Steel writes, "I view it as being a poor piece of science to reject the observational information that one has available merely because the crude model that you have constructed does not agree with it."

Another criticism of the Chyba model is that it presumed that the exploding object was homogeneous, that is, of more or less uniform density throughout. A homogeneous object simply does not conform to observations reported by eyewitnesses of the Tunguska Event, who reported hearing a series of several explosions, not just a single blast. Such a series of explosions would tend to be characteristic of an object of heterogeneous composition. It is just such a heterogeneous structure that enables comet nuclei and asteroids to break apart.

Finally, some investigators say that if the object were a stony asteroid, there should be a swarm of loose gravel about 1 kilometer in diameter somewhere in the epicenter; but if the object were a comet, then you would not expect to find such deposits. Bronshten agrees, also calling the Chyba model "crude" and saying: "The asteroidal hypothesis is wholly invalid. No stony fragments have been found in the region of the catastrophe despite searches over the past decades. The cosmochemical data in particular, the results of an isotope analysis, and some other information confirm the cometary hypothesis. Furthermore, all the calculated altitudes of destruction in the Chyba model are excessive."

Could It Have Been Antimatter?

Most physicists will tell you that there is a lot of matter out there in space, the properties and behavior of which are unknown to us. That idea has led to a lot of pseudoscience, just plain bad science, and speculation.

The Russian geophysicist A. V. Zolotov echoed those sentiments in his statement that the Tunguska object "represents a new, yet unknown, much more complicated phenomenon of nature than has been encountered up to this time." But what kind of "complicated phenomenon"?

In 1932 Carl D. Anderson confirmed the existence of antimatter, or "opposite matter," as my young son used to call it. Could the Tunguska object have been an "opposite rock"? Antimatter is very interesting stuff. The English physicist P. A. M. Dirac first predicted its existence in 1928. The antiparticle discovered by Anderson turned out to be a positron, or an electron with a positive charge. We now know that when two protons smash into each other forcefully enough, they produce a shower of positrons, electrons, and certain other exotic subatomic particles. Then if a positron collides with an electron, or a proton collides with an antiproton, the oppositely charged particles destroy each other.

Dirac had imagined that every atomic particle had an antimatter twin. He further thought that antimatter particles could combine and form antiatoms. Antiatoms could further combine to form all kinds of antiobjects—antistars, anti-galaxies, and even antipeople. If a person shook hands with an antiperson, both would be annihilated in a shower of gamma ray greetings. The explosion would be powerful enough to destroy a small city. It's best that the CIA not be made aware of this. Although we can see the work of antimatter, so far no one has ever actually seen a quark or a lepton, two of the exotic particles created by an antimatter explosion. We have looked in the sea, on the Moon, and under the bed in our search for them, but all we have seen is their ghosts in the giant particle accelerators when a proton is smashed and broken apart. It is like seeing our favorite politician on television. We are seeing not the politician but an image of him traced out by a beam of electrons striking the inside of a glass tube painted with phosphorus. Evidence that quarks and leptons really exist is similarly convincing if you believe in such ghosts. Most physicists do.

So, could the Tunguska object have been a small antirock? In 1941 the American meteorite authority Lincoln La Paz became the first to suggest that it might have been. Kazantsev liked the idea, saying that his Martian spaceship's engine might have been made of antimatter. A number of American scientists, as late as the mid-1960s, also said they liked the idea. But antiarguments soon spelled doom for the antimatter idea. For instance, it was argued that a lump of antimatter wouldn't survive the journey down through the atmosphere without being annihilated. Another objection was that if the antirock did somehow manage to survive and reach a height of 10 kilometers above the ground before exploding, it would produce large amounts of radioactive carbon (^{14}C). Interestingly enough, several investigators have found traces of radioactive carbon in the 1909 ring of tree-ring samples from the epicenter region. However, the most probable cause for the radioactive carbon's presence is not an antirock but the occurrence of two periods of especially strong solar activity.

Could It Have Been a Black Hole?

In the late 1930s, physicists with a special interest in astronomy had begun to speak of a strange state of matter that eventually became known as the black hole.

Stars are kept shining as their hot core regions fuse hydrogen into helium and then helium into still heavier elements. The environment required for such fusion reactions to occur includes extremely high kinetic temperatures, extremely high pressure, and an extremely high number density of hydrogen nuclei, or protons. These fusion reactions produce enormous amounts of energy in the form of light, heat, and other radiation. After burning for millions or billions of years, all stars eventually use up their hydrogen fuel supply and must one day go out as their nuclear furnaces cool and shut down.

When extremely massive stars exhaust their nuclear fuels, there is no longer sufficient outward-pushing pressure in the core to keep the star's outer gas layers from tumbling into the core region because of gravitational infall. The giant star collapses and crunches all of its matter into a core only a few kilometers in diameter. Earlier its diameter had been more than a hundred million kilometers. Such a collapsed star becomes so dense and its gravity so strong that no energy— not even light—can escape from it. The star has become a black hole. A tablespoon of black hole matter is so dense that it weighs several billion tons. Black holes, British physicist Stephen Hawking tells us, come in many sizes—from the size of enormous mountains to that of a flea. The smallest black holes are called "goblins." A goblin the size of a small lemon is said to contain as much matter as planet Earth. A goblin the size of a speck of dust would weigh more than a billion tons.

If black holes seem to be exotic objects in themselves, their behavior is still queerer. A miniature black hole the size of a golf ball traveling 1000 kilometers per second could pass through millions of kilometers of solid rock before even considering slowing down.

By now you may have guessed that eventually someone would suggest that the Tunguska object was a black hole in the form of a nice little goblin. And someone did. The black hole supposedly smashed into the Southern Swamp and just kept on going until it passed right on through the planet and came out the other side, emerging out of the mid-Atlantic Ocean near the Azores. As in the case of antimatter, it was American scientists who, in 1973, proposed the black hole hypothesis, seemingly unaware of the masses of Tunguska data accumulated by Russian investigators over the years.

The Americans were A. A. Jackson and Michael P. Ryan, then of the University of Texas at Austin. They imagined a goblin-sized object with the mass of a large asteroid traveling fast enough to penetrate the last 30 kilometers of Earth's atmosphere in about a second or so. The shock wave pushed ahead of it supposedly caused all the damage. Writing in the British science magazine *Nature*, these researchers said that, "Since the black hole would leave no crater or material residue, it explains the mystery of the Tunguska Event. It would enter the Earth, and the rigidity of rock would allow no underground shock wave. Because of its high velocity and because it loses only a small fraction of its energy in passing through the Earth, the black hole should very nearly follow a straight line through the Earth, entering at 30 degrees to the horizon and leaving through the North Atlantic in the region 40 to 50 degrees N, and 30 to 40 degrees W."

There are so many objections to this hypothesis that the expedition scientists I worked with became irritated at the mere mention of the idea and shook their heads in frustration. Academician Vasiliev reflected their feelings and summarized their views: "If Jackson and Ryan had bothered to acquaint themselves with the geophysical materials published in Russia and America before publicizing their fantastic idea, they most likely would never have proposed it. Evidently the authors, in their naïveté, supposed that in 1908 such a cataclysmic event as a black hole exploding out of the north Atlantic Ocean would have gone unnoticed. However, the population of the eastern regions of Canada, Iceland, and southern Greenland was significant. Those people published newspapers and had meteorological stations and observatories, and there were dozens of vessels in the open ocean. Furthermore, a tsunami would have been generated. Under these circumstances the event could not possibly have gone unnoticed.

"If professional scientists indulge themselves in such liberties, you can imagine how readily such science fiction notions will be eagerly and gullibly seized by the mass media. For example, much publicity was given to the fantastic notion of Altov and Zhuravleva that the Tunguska Event was caused by a laser ray fired by inhabitants of a distant planet in an attempt to communicate with Earth. Too often the mass media try to clothe such pseudoscientific notions with the respectability of science. The sad results are disoriented public opinion and complications in the further study of this complex natural phenomenon," Vasiliev concluded.

A Man and His Comet

By about 1960, Fessenkov had written several articles that favored the cometary origin for the cosmic visitor of 1908, proposing that the "white nights" following the explosion were due to fragments of the small comet's tail mixing with the upper atmosphere. More recently, veteran investigator Yevgeniy Kolesnikov also has championed a cometary origin and continues to do so with the backing of, among several other major theoreticians, V. A. Bronshten, S. S. Grigorian, D. J. Asher, and D. I. Steel.

I first met Kolesnikov in 1992 when I visited him in his Moscow University laboratory and dined with him and his wife Nataly Kolesnikova, who is a member of the biology faculty of Moscow University and also an investigator into the Tunguska Event. Yevgeniy has done exhaustive field-work at the Tunguska site that has led him along the cometary path. He told me, "I became involved in the Tunguska investigations more than twenty years ago. At the time my colleagues and I were building devices to investigate the possible danger of radiation for cosmonauts in space. To do this our group investigated the radioactivity of meteorites. We measured the radioactivity levels of two different isotopes, or forms, of the element argon." In chemical shorthand the two isotopes are written ^{37}A and ^{39}A. The 37 and 39 indicate the atomic weight, or total number of protons and neutrons in the nucleus of an atom of argon. The most stable form of argon has an atomic weight of 39.948.

"It occurred to me that I could use these same devices to check the antimatter hypothesis as well as the nuclear hypothesis of the Tunguska explosion. Knowing the power of the explosion, and its height above the ground, it would be easy to calculate the level of radioactive argon 39 that should be found in the soil and upper layers of the basalt rocks of the epicenter region. My equipment was about 100 times more sensitive than it needed to be for this task, so I could be certain of my findings. Since I did not find argon 39 in any of the soil samples or basalt rocks brought to me, I was reasonably sure that the explosion was not a nuclear explosion, or one caused by antimatter."

He said, however, that he has a substantial body of data supporting a cometery origin of the Tunguska object. Part of that data includes comet matter found in peat from the epicenter region. He then described the peat samples he has been studying over the years. The sphagnum plant takes its nutrient elements from the air rather than from the ground through roots. So any minerals and microscopic matter falling on a plant's living upper parts are incorporated into the plant. Every year the lower part of the plant dies and a new segment of stem grows. After each year's growth a little knot forms and marks that year's growth region of the stem. So by counting the knots down the stem, the investigator can work all the way back to the 1908 layer in a sample block of peat. Chemical analysis of that layer of peat then reveals the abundance of this or that nutrient, or microspherules, that the plant concentrated in its tissues during a given year. Comparing one year's growth layer with that of a higher or lower layer then provides a year-by-year record of the amounts of matter the plant took from the environment.

"Although I didn't find any argon 39 in the soil and sphagnum samples I examined," Kolesnikov continued, "my colleagues [S. Golenstsky, for one] and I did find relatively high concentrations of silicate microspherules of unusual composition in the 1908 layer. At first we thought that these particles might be cometary matter released during the explosion, but it now seems more likely that the microspherules are not cosmic dust particles but were formed during the forest fires set by the 1908 explosion. In some places the 1908 layer also is marked by ash that settled on surviving vegetation during and after the fire."

None of the silicate microspherules appears to be composed of silicates found in any major meteorite group. So whatever the source of the silicate microspherules, in 1908 there was a marked increase of them in the Tunguska epicenter region.

Another of Kolesnikov's projects was a layer-by-layer study of peat samples to learn if the 1908 layer contained higher concentrations of certain chemical elements associated with cosmic matter. In the peat sample taken not far from the Suslov "crater" near Kulik's base camp, he and his colleagues found relatively high concentrations of a number of light and volatile elements, including bromine, zinc, rubidium, and lead. "Because comets contain many such volatile elements," he said, "we are convinced that fallout from part of a comet's nucleus enriched the peat where our Suslov 'crater' sample was taken." He said that there was further evidence of the cosmic origin of the high concentrations of volatile elements in the sample. That evidence was the presence of lead isotopes in the 1908 layer that differed from lead isotopes found in higher or lower layers of the sample, or in the surrounding soils or basalt rock. "Although extremely accurate," Kolesnikov added, "unfortunately, the kinds of analyses we did are very time consuming and labor intensive. For instance, for this one project we did about 3000 tests for different elements, and it took us more than two years."

Kolesnikov explained that you cannot dig just anywhere and expect to find telltale signs of cosmic dust at the 1908 level of peat samples: "My opinion is that the comet matter was dispersed unevenly," in a shotgun pattern rather than as an even rainfall. Krinov also supported a shotgun pattern of the blast, whatever its causes. As an example, he cited two sections of forest situated close to each other. While all the trees in one section had been felled, trees in the other section had not been touched by the blast. He also pointed out that within the larger epicenter area there are local and smaller epicenters of felled trees. Kulik had identified four such smaller epicenters, which would have been in keeping with the eyewitness statements that the explosion had sounded like a cannonade, a series of explosions, each creating its own mini-epicenter and local concentration of cosmic matter. "That is why I think it's necessary to explore many locations in order to discover places containing a large content of the dispersed cosmic matter," Kolesnikov said.

Despite the hard work involved, Kolesnikov feels that proof of the identity of the Tunguska object will come from a continued collection and study of cosmic dust dispersed over the epicenter region and a study of isotopes of various elements found in the 1908 peat layers. He says that the most telling isotopes are carbon 12 and carbon 13, hydrogen and deuterium, and nitrogen 14 and nitrogen 15, since comets contain those elements in especially high concentrations. He and his German colleague, Dr. Tatiana Boettger of Leipzig University, have measured isotopic anomalies of carbon and hydrogen in peat samples from the epicenter region. Additionally, Kolesnikov has found in peat samples "a very high carbon/iridium ratio . . . which points toward a cometary type impactor rather than a chondritic or achondritic asteroidal type impactor." In one peat analysis study, he found samples taken from the 1908 layer to contain isotopic anomalies of carbon and hydrogen "more probably explained by cometary matter presence" than by a stony (chondritic) asteroid.

Where Matters Stand Now

At the present time, many things about the Tunguska Event seem certain: First, the mystery has not been solved, despite misleading headlines that periodically appear in newspapers and popular science magazines. Here are some examples: "Study Finds Asteroid Leveled Siberian Area in '08" (the *New York Times*); "Scientists: 1908 Blast No Mystery" (Portland [Maine] *Press Herald*); "In 1908 a Small Asteroid Exploded Over Remote Siberia, Sounding a Warning Astronomers Are Just Beginning to Hear (*Astronomy* magazine). And from time to time scientists with only a superficial knowledge—or none at all—about the research conducted over the years at the epicenter site quote equally Tunguska-illiterate colleagues who have uncritically embraced Chyba's model categorically concluding that the 1908 object was a stony asteroid. Most investigators today favor either a cometary or an asteroid origin for the 1908 explosion, the cometary hypothesis being generally favored.

Had the Tunguska object come sailing into the atmosphere only a bit later that June 30 morning, it would have exploded over St. Petersburg and killed at least half a million people, by Vasiliev's estimate, and flattened the city virtually beyond recognition. But natural cosmic visitors immensely more massive and potentially more destructive than the Tunguska object have collided with Earth countless times in our geological past, and more such objects are bound to come crashing into us in the future—and very likely with devastating consequences to human life. Where is the evidence for cataclysmic events? For one, the giant impact crater of Popigai described in Chapter 6. For another, the even larger crater carved into the sea floor near Yucatan. That asteroidal object is generally thought to have contributed to the extinction of the dinosaurs some 65 million years ago. And although dozens more giant impact crater scars have been identified on Earth's surface, practically all have been seriously degraded by erosion. It is important that we investigate such sites before they are completely erased.

Recent research into meteorites recovered from the Moon strongly suggests that a swarm of cosmic debris heavily bombarded our one natural satellite some 3.9 billion years ago. Since the Moon and Earth were much closer together at that time, it is virtually certain that Earth was also targeted by that abundant meteorite storm. Lunar research going back to the 1970s strongly supports such a cosmic bombardment by either asteroids or comet nuclei. Considering Earth's closer proximity to the Moon then, and its greater gravitational tug on the cosmic debris, our planet may have sustained an impact rate ten to twenty times that suffered by the Moon. According to researcher Barbara A. Cohen, of the University of Tennessee in Knoxville, the cosmic bombardment probably was intense enough to boil Earth's oceans and pummel the rocky crust enough to pour untold tons of rock dust into the atmosphere where it would have lingered for years.

To place the Tunguska Event into a reliable context of cosmic intrigue will most likely take a combination of computer modeling and a continuation of current field work by teams of international investigators.

As Katya and I sit on our luggage at the landing site waiting for the arrival of the helicopter to take us back to Vanavara, she suddenly goes silent. "What's the matter?" I ask. "Give me an empty plastic bag, and make sure this one has a zip-lock," she says. "We can hike out if you want," I offer. "No," she says, "the bears will eat you. I'll just be sick and probably die."

During the flight back Katya drapes herself over a pile of luggage directly beneath an intimidating red handle that reads

"DANGER! Do not pull!" I tap her shoulder and point to it as a warning not to grab it whenever the helicopter bumps about in the unstable air. She shrugs indifferently and closes her eyes. For the remainder of the flight I alternately watch the landscape slip by beneath us and leaf through my notes filling in details here and there while they are still fresh in my mind. "MISSION ACCOMPLISHED!!!" I write at the end of the last page. Eleven rolls of 36-exposure color print and transparency film, more than two hours of videotape, and eighty-seven pages of notes. My self-congratulatory mood is interrupted by Katya catching my eye and smiling wickedly as she slowly reaches for the big red handle just above her head.

CHAPTER 2

Sikhote-Alin: Meteorite Shower of the Century

During my meetings with meteorite field investigator Valentin Tsvetkov in Moscow in 1992 just before my Tunguska expedition, he said that if I wanted to visit the world's most intriguing meteorite shower site, he would arrange a trip to the Russian Far East to the Sikhote-Alin crater field. In 1947 a massive meteorite shower thundered down near the mountain village of Meteority and left more than a hundred small craters. Tsvetkov, a member of the Russian Academy of Sciences' Astronomical Society, is the world's leading authority on the Sikhote-Alin site and earned a doctorate for his unprecedented investigative work at the crater field. "I'll show you several fine specimens," he assured me. But my chief interest was not to collect meteorites but to reconstruct the story of that fall and document the important role Tsvetkov had played in deducing exactly what had happened there.

At 10:30 A.M., February 12, 1947, untold thousands of pieces of iron-nickel rained down out of the sky as the famous Sikhote-Alin meteorite shower. Such voluminous showers are often termed meteorite storms. The Sikhote-Alin storm is the largest known such event and among the most thoroughly investigated of all meteorite falls, yet much of the information that continues to appear in articles and books about that spectacular storm is dated, and some of it is in error. The most often quoted, and dated, sources include E. L. Krinov's classic book *Giant Meteorites* published in 1966 and V. F. Buchwald's *Handbook of Iron Meteorites* published in 1975. Tsvetkov started visiting the crater field after these books appeared and has developed a number of methodologies that have provided significant details about the meteorite fall. His major findings are the extent and configuration of the crater dispersion field and the orbital elements of the asteroid fragment that parented the event.

The cosmic intruder streaked across the blue Siberian sky on that clear, cold morning as a monster bolide plunging through the atmosphere from north-northeast to south-southwest at an angle of about 45°. Trailing a dark dust tail about 35 kilometers long, at an altitude of about 4.5 kilometers, it broke up as a swarm of tiny fireballs that distant observers saw disappear in the foothills of the Sikhote-Alin mountain range about midway between Vladivostok and Khabarovsk. Eyewitnesses said the bolide was brighter than the Sun. It was observed over an area 300 to 400 kilometers in radius. A few minutes after the fireball first appeared, booming sounds like those from heavy-caliber guns were heard echoing among the mountain ridges.

Korney Shvets, one eyewitness I interviewed in the village of Meteority, told me he "saw blue flame sparkling in the sky because the meteorite was burning, and there were little fires trailing behind the main body. The windows of the bakery where I was working with my mother and brother trembled. A metal door of the oven flew open, and several hot charcoals fell out onto the floor. I was seventeen at the time. We were scared because we thought it was an atomic bomb from the Americans. It was soon after the bomb fell on Hiroshima."

Off on a New Adventure

Katya was as eager to visit the Sikhote-Alin site as I was, especially on learning there were 250 Siberian tigers roaming the area, along with two species of venomous snakes and gigantic brown bears. She "hmmphed" contemptuously when I suggested there might be an element of danger. "I'm more concerned about ticks and mosquitoes," she said closing the discussion.

To reach Vladivostok, where we were to team up with Tsvetkov, I flew to Seattle, then to Anchorage, and then across the Bering Sea first to Magadan, and then down to Khabarovsk, which is across from the old penal colony on the island of Sakhalin, which in turn is just west of the Kuril Islands off Japan. Meanwhile Katya traveled a roundabout way from her home city of Krasnoyarsk in the middle of Siberia to Novosibirsk and then east to Khabarovsk. Considering the uncertainties of Russian air travel and the vast distances the two of us habitually journey, I still consider it a wonder when I see her smiling and waving wildly at me from the customs doorway or passport control.

My large duffel bag carries three questionable pieces of equipment—a hunting knife with a 25-centimeter blade, which I have stuck into a lead-lined film pouch; a GPS navigational instrument; and a metal detector. My heart starts thumping as I watch the duffel bag disappear into the dark cave of the X-ray machine. When the duffel bag is halfway through, the carrier belt stops and the guard leans forward squinting into his monitor. This is it, I think. I have visions of being prodded along at bayonet point to the nearest gulag, never to be heard of again. But then he sits back and starts the belt again. My duffel bag thumps unmolested onto the concrete floor.

I grab it before the guard can change his mind and drag it through the exit where Katya is waiting all smiles and patting her head to call my attention to a new fur hat. "Sable," she proudly informs me. "You'll never believe how little I paid for it." Nearly the same color as her hair, which she often wears in a long braid nearly to her waist, it is hard to tell where the hat ends and her hair begins. She gives me a big hug and then waves authoritatively to her driver to load the American's luggage into the rear of the nice little van she has rented, neat as a pin and complete with purple curtains tied back with gold tassels. It even has a windshield free of cracks, miraculous in Russia. Eagerly rubbing her hands, Katya sits down amid bags of groceries, reaches into one, and holds up a bottle of champagne. "Extra dry," she says, "just the kind you like." Then out come a jar of black caviar and another of red. She exudes pride. "And wait till you see the apartment I have rented for us. It's great!"

It is in a new Korean enterprise building. There is an immaculate kitchen with an electric oven and a microwave, a big living room, a separate bath, even a separate toilet, and a large bedroom. The view is splendid, overlooking the broad Amur River into China with Vladivostok and North Korea off a way to the south. At $75 a day the apartment is a deal, especially in Khabarovsk. The van is $30 for Katya's half-day use. Prices have gone up since 1992 when a tin of black caviar was $5.50. (At the gourmet shop at the Frankfurt airport the same size tin has a price tag of $350!) In Khabarovsk it is $15. Red caviar, the best buy in the Russian Far East, is $10 for 450 grams (compared with the 1992 price of $2). Over the following years we will see prices climb still higher. In Moscow we had a car and driver for an eight-hour day for $10. Today a taxi from the Moscow airport to town is $60. A first-class hotel room, nothing fancy, can set you back $300. A martini costs $10.

Detour to Kamchatka

Since I am under contract to write a book about geysers, Katya has insisted that before starting our Sikhote-Alin expedition we spend a week on the Kamchatka Peninsula, a large Florida-shaped finger of land hanging off the end of northeastern-most Russia into the Sea of Okhotsk. She says it will be fun climbing around active volcanoes and skimming the mountaintops by helicopter. Most important, there will be the world's most impressive array of geysers, some 200 of them in the Valley of Geysers, or *Dolina Geizerov*. Little do we know that only three months after our visit to Mount Karymsky, one of the peninsula's most active volcanoes and a thirty-minute hike from our campsite, the mountain would blow up and transform the surrounding land into a sea of boiling lava. It has erupted twenty-one times over the previous 200 years. But, as the man says, "That's another story."

We leave the land of volcanoes at the end of August, flying from the capital city of Petropavlovsk-Kamchatskiy, the area from which the Russians shot down a Korean Airlines Boeing-747 passenger "spy plane" on September 1, 1983, killing all 269 "spies" on board. We are delayed from taking

61

off for three hours because military activities at the airport in Vladivostok where the flight originated have put all civilian flights on hold. With gear for two expeditions, our luggage is overweight to the tune of $42, but Katya slips the attendant a $10 bill and that settles matters. It also affords us the privilege of using the relatively comfortable waiting lounge reserved for foreigners, which usually costs $11 per person. After about an hour, the attendant smiles her way past us and tells the only other occupant of the lounge that he will have to pay an additional $11 because he has been sitting there for so long. He argues that it isn't his fault since the flight was three hours late. That doesn't matter, the attendant orders. He pays.

Back in Khabarovsk and in the comfort of our Korean apartment, complete with fax machine, we linger for four days sightseeing but mostly translating technical documents about the Sikhote-Alin site that later will be useful to me in my writing. Katya has even brought her laptop.

Khabarovsk was named after one Yerofei Khabarov, a wealthy merchant of the 1650s whose cruelty was legendary. He often bragged about the women and children he had killed along his various routes of travel. Although he eventually was dragged before a government tribunal, he was never punished. Later he was even awarded a noble title and made commander of a Siberian military garrison.

The town is relatively clean and attractive with tree-lined streets, parks, and cheerful-looking boutiques and food shops. By this time, in 1995, all the shops' shelves are swollen with goods—endless rows of tinned foods, displays of meat and salted fish, a wide variety of vegetables, alcoholic beverages, freezers of excellent Russian ice cream, and mountains of clothing. It is a contrast of abundance compared with the empty shelves in shops in 1992 and the long lines of grim customers hoping to buy bread before the last loaf vanished.

A stroll along the Amur River and through little wooded areas on these warm September afternoons is relaxing and tends to mollify anxiety. The walkway is adorned with numerous relics of the Soviet era. In addition to the ubiquitous statues of Lenin with his little cap and right arm with palm up extending into the future, there are life-size molded concrete figures that remind me of the grotesquely frozen figures of the victims of Pompeii's catastrophic A.D. 79 eruption of Vesuvius. But the riverside figures are Soviet patriots, a peasant worker bent over her hoe, rake, or sickle; a grim-faced soldier; a smiling factory worker; Russia's space hero Yuri Gagarin; and an athlete poised to hurl a discus. The spooky figures peep out from behind trees or stand boldly in open spaces as pervasive reminders of the glory of the Soviet worker and patriot and defender of the motherland.

During one of our strolls, Katya whispers that it is good to be free of the KGB for a while. In Krasnoyarsk they call her twice a week and summon her to half-hour "interviews" about what she does at her work for the Americans and whom she sees in her spare time. She was surprised to find that they knew about her planned trip to Kamchatka and Sikhote-Alin. "How did they know?" I ask. "Probably by listening in on our overseas telephone calls," she says. On one occasion in Krasnoyarsk when the two of us had met acquaintances from the American embassy for dinner, the KGB telephoned her the next day and wanted to know what we had talked about. To this day, whenever I mention the KGB, she winces and quickly changes the subject.

On September 4, we pack up and board a flight to Vladivostok where Katya's company has promised to send a car to meet us and take us to our hotel. For some reason I have yet to understand, in Russia you fly mostly by night, invariably departing and landing between midnight and six in the morning. Our flight to Vladivostok is no exception. We arrive at 2:00 A.M. Tsvetkov is there to greet us, obviously pleased to renew our friendship after a period of two years. He is enthusiastic about the week ahead. We find a taxi to drive us the 40 kilometers into Vladivostok for $50. The little car sags and sways under the weight of the three of us plus our mountain of expedition gear. Because of a fuel shortage for the city's power plants, there are few streetlights and most of the buildings are dark as we enter the city. Since Katya's company car has not materialized, we are left on our own to find a hotel. The Amuirski Zalief, or "Amur Bay," hotel is recommended by our driver. It overlooks the beautiful "Golden Horn" harbor and has rooms available facing the sea.

We manage our way around the hotel with flashlights and are surprised to find that our rooms actually have hot water, but that isn't to last. By noon the hot water tap simply exhales. In the gray light of dawn we count ten large ships at anchor a kilometer or more offshore, at least three of which appear to be war vessels. More than a dozen small sailboats are moored among the ships, and about the time we decide to get a few hours' sleep around 9:00 A.M. the small colorful craft are scurrying about the bay playing hide-and-seek among the gray iron behemoths.

Our stay in Vladivostok, "Lord of the East," is less than twenty-four hours. The city bustles with commerce and crime and has a reputation of being dangerous, although we never feel ill at ease or threatened. Though it is situated at the outer margin of the Russian realm, the city is very much westernized and every bit as Russian as Moscow with its odors of cigarette smoke and diesel fumes. Despite the Russian flag that flies above the city, its occupants are very much aware that the city has not always been Russian and that a billion Chinese live just across the river. Vladivostok was wrested from China a bit before 1860 and by 1900 had grown into the largest Russian city east of the Ural Mountains with virtually all its laborers and tradespeople being Chinese, Korean, or Japanese, including the prostitutes.

When the Bolsheviks took over in 1922, they demolished all the religious shrines and converted the cozy gambling clubs into political and cultural centers. Under Stalin, the city was further purged of its Asian flavor by the renaming of streets and squares. Korea Street, for example, was renamed Border Guard Street. By the mid-1930s Stalin's era of the Great Terror completed the purge by snuffing out private enterprise, by imprisoning nearly 65,000 Chinese in gulags and boarding up their buildings, and by deporting the entire Korean population to the steppes of Central Asia. Meanwhile, the Japanese wisely left of their own volition. Today Russians are everywhere guarding, exploiting, and smothering the motherland's great eastern gateway. As one writer has put it, today there is only one Vladivostok species: *Homo sovieticus*.

The Adventure Begins

True to temporal form, our Trans-Siberian train jerks us out of the Vladivostok station and heads north at the rude hour of 1:00 A.M. Katya, Tsvetkov, and I collapse into our berths and sleep soundly until 8:00 A.M. An hour and a half later we are jolted to a stop in a dreary outpost called Dalnerechensk.

We manage to carry and drag our duffel bags and backpacks down the metal steps with much tugging and pile them in a heap between two puddles. Despite its being midmorning, or perhaps because of it, not a soul is in sight except for a dog that eyes us warily, obviously wanting to investigate the luggage but not quite daring to. "Maybe he's looking for drugs," Katya says straight-faced. We are in an enormous dirt parking area along the far side of which and beneath some trees are a large wooden table and two benches. The three of us carry our gear over to the benches and pile it onto the table out of the mud. The only sound is a deep-toned bell resounding somewhere off in the distance. Our next task is to find transportation to the village of Ismailikha some 90 kilometers to the east.

"Stay here with the luggage while Valentin and I see if we can find a bus schedule or something," Katya orders. I salute, sit, and watch the dog while the dog sits and watches me. If there was an information board about Dalnerechensk, it would claim a population of some 36,000 people whose principal activity is logging and timber processing in the town's one sawmill. Most of the population is involved with logging, which could account for the scarcity of townspeople. Fifteen minutes later a jubilant Katya and Valentin proudly speed toward me, waving as they lean out the windows of a small red car with a roof rack. They have struck a deal with a local logger on his day off to drive us to Ismailikha.

The roads, if they can be called that, are a deplorable series of puddles, mud, and jaw-jolting potholes. Valentin rides up front barely able to see over his large red backpack which he holds in his lap. Katya and I are cramped in the back seat also with our backpacks on our laps. One duffel bag is stuffed into the trunk, another lashed onto the roof rack. Our progress is best measured in units of bounces and splashes. The driver tries to cheer us up by joking that the road is best negotiated by helicopter.

After an hour or so of alternately bumping our heads on the car roof and our bottoms against comatose springs and onto the car floor, we begin to see small, dilapidated log houses and signs of activity—meandering barriers of pigs, ducks, geese, and cows blocking the road and only with reluctance deferring to our overloaded *machina*. While Katya laughs and shouts at the cows, trying to pat them as we drive along, Valentin waves the driver on for two more kilometers until we come to a low rambling log building in the center of the small village of Ismailikha, whose human population numbers about 350. He pries himself out of the front seat and disappears inside the building. Ten minutes later he comes out with Alexander Vetrik, an old friend and the chief forester of the district. Ismailikha, along with Limonniki and a third village, Meteority, which most interests us because of its eyewitness observers of the meteorite shower, were built in 1948 as temporary villages to facilitate the district's sole industry of logging. Somehow their temporary status has dragged on into permanency, which accounts for the buildings' present shabbiness.

We planned to camp out in the Ismailikha area until transportation to the meteorite fall site could be arranged, but Alexander won't hear of it. He takes us to his house, directly across the street, and sets his wife and small daughter to work clearing a room for us. He says I am the first foreigner ever to set foot in his village and, to his knowledge, the first American to visit the meteorite fall site. Sanitary conditions are wanting. The toilet is a separate outhouse with a hole cut into the floor beneath which is a pit, or rather what had once been a pit. Excrement has piled up to within a foot beneath the floor and undulates with swarms of worms that form a living blanket. The odor is so bad and the sight so repulsive that even Katya refuses to squat. With me in one hand and a role of toilet paper in the other, she marches us down the main street until we run out of houses and eventually find a nice secluded patch of woods.

By eight the next morning, Alexander's wife and daughter are busy packing crates of fresh vegetables, preserves, and bread for our coming days at the meteorite crater site. Breakfast consists of tea; salads of tomatoes, onions, peppers, and cabbage; along with boiled potatoes and dark bread with two kinds of honey and preserves, all grown or prepared by his wife. They even make sure we have some homemade vodka to take along. So abundant are their gardens that what they grow during the summer and put up as preserves is more than adequate to last them through the winter. They will buy milk, meat, and fish from merchants in the village. Alexander wolfs down an enormous breakfast of six potatoes, three large servings of salad, and vodka. He says that he eats heavily at breakfast because he often has to spend the day in the forest and misses his midday meal.

By 10:00 we have packed selectively, leaving our money, Katya's computer, and much of our gear to be kept in the house while we are at the site. It is unthinkable that our belongings will be tampered with. Arranged for by Alexander, a large six-wheel truck, a Zil-131, picks us up to take us to the base camp site of the crater field. Katya and I ride in front while Alexander, Valentin, and the food bounce around in the back. "Isn't this fun!" Katya shouts above the engine as we narrowly miss a pig or cow or send a flock of chickens scattering. Within twenty minutes the road has narrowed as we enter dense forest and churn our way through water-filled, knee-deep ruts of mud. We dip into, splash through, and bounce out of two small rivers. Thick tree branches of young alders and birches are continuously and noisily pushed aside by the truck's sturdy mirror mounts. I lose count of the number of fallen trees the size of telephone poles the truck simply climbs over without a whimper. Now and then the driver clicks an electric switch that engages front-wheel drive, or another switch that inflates or deflates either front or rear tires. "It can't possibly get worse than this," I tell Katya at one stage, but it does. Gripping a brace bar fiercely with both hands she just keeps saying how exciting it is and how lucky we are to be here. And I keep saying that the next 50 meters can't possibly get worse than the last 50, but they nearly always do. Every so often we hear laughter or incoherent shouts and thumping from the back of the truck. Stony faced, the driver just steers and keeps clicking switches. After an hour, the punishment abruptly ends as we stop in a small clearing carpeted with grasses and moss. A fine mist has begun to fill the air and cloaks the forest in a ghostly haze.

"This has to be the end of the world," I say to Katya as I climb down onto our damp oasis. "I want to see the tigers," she says peering through the trees. Moments later we are greeted by a Russian man and woman who are startled to see us. The night before, Alexander told us that a party of seven meteorite "pirates" was at the site and had been there for three weeks. The woman cook quickly begins banging on an anvil that resounds through the forest. One by one, the other "pirates" appear and eye us silently and suspiciously. They are dressed mostly in military garb, and each carries a heavy and cumbersome metal detector. On learning Valentin Tsvetkov's identity, they suddenly are all obeisance and smiles. They are geologists from Moscow University moonlighting, they say, to supplement their meager and usually months-late salaries. They tell us that they are collecting meteorites despite being

denied authorization by the head of the Committee on Meteorites, a man named Shukolyukov. The group apparently
approached Shukolyukov and tried to make a deal that would
allow them to keep half of their prospecting finds in exchange
for turning over the remaining half to the Committee on
Meteorites. Shukolyukov reportedly had said, "No. You do
whatever you want, but that's my position."

They have a group of four tents and have erected a dining
shelter of poles lashed together and draped with sheet plastic.
A campfire is burning beside a large table. I am stunned to
see the table strewn with more than 100 meteorite fragments,
one weighing 45 kilograms. Serge, one member of the group,
says that in one day one person with a metal detector could
collect up to 25 kilograms of meteorites. I begin to calculate:
the work of five men per day equals 125 kilograms. Three
weeks of hard work per man ... Tsvetkov is visibly disturbed. As I leave to help Katya haul our gear over to the tent
site she has picked some distance away, Tsvetkov leads two of
the geologists over to the mess table, sits them down, and
begins to have what I presume is a serious talk with them.
Later he explains to me: "They should be recording the location and mass of the meteorites they remove. That information is important for many reasons—an improved estimate of
the original object's mass and more details about the object's
breakup in the atmosphere." You don't have to be an expert
to guess that many hundreds of kilograms of meteorite mass
pirated from a fall site most likely will never be recorded.

By 2:00 P.M. we have set up our two tents. First we have
to chop down numerous small trees and trim them to serve as
platforms for our tents. Then comes the task of weaving a
springy mattress of conifer boughs to top the platform. The
tent is then pitched on top of the boughs, an arrangement
that keeps us not only comfortable but above the water-

soaked ground and the critters that make it their home. And finally, we chop enough firewood to last through the end of the next day. By the time we are finished, the fine mist has turned to a heavy rain that drives us inside our tents. Our clothing, sleeping bags, everything is damp, despite our efforts to keep things dry. I am most concerned about condensation collecting inside my video camera and disabling it. I have used it almost continuously during the tortuous drive into the base camp area, and several times it has failed me. Both of my Nikons are sealed into zip-lock plastic bags. Over the following days, whenever the sky clears I open the video camera and expose it to direct sunlight to dry it out, so off and on I manage to keep it working but not always when I most want it. By night all three cameras go into the sleeping bag to be kept dry by my body heat.

The next morning breaks clear, but the forest is heavy and wet and its aromatic odor strong. The area is extraordinarily diverse in flora and fauna. There are many kinds of trees, including Manchurian chestnut, Mongolian oak, birch, fir, durian larch, spruce, three species of maple, aspen, and bird cherry trees with thorns. There are also Chinese lemon bushes with bright red berries; several types of orchids; tough lianas the size of small ropes that lace the forest floor and trip you up at nearly every step; a species of plant used as a blood pressure regulator; and zsen-sen roots which are useful as a medicinal potion. Katya says people grind the zsen-sen roots to a pulp, mix the pulp with alcohol, let it stand for a week or more, and then add a teaspoon of the solution to a cup of tea. The potion is supposed to bring about a feeling of "general well being." I could have done without the nasty plants similar to our poison ivy and a genus called *Aconitum*, a blue plant poisonous to touch. Among the animals in the area are 250 Siberian tigers, inhabitants of a nearby open preserve maintained by the Russian government. Some of the animals are tagged with radio collars to trace their movements. Although we think we hear the shy creatures from time to time, we never see one. There also are wild boars, two species of poisonous snakes, and numerous Siberian brown bears that leave footprints the size of a large dinner platter.

Two protections against intrusive bears are a gun and a flare, both of which require special permits. One night by the campfire Sergei demonstrates the startling effectiveness of a flare, which is about the size of a policeman's club. Scratch the end of the thing and it erupts with the roar of a welder's torch as it blazes explosively and continuously for about two minutes, long enough to frighten away a *Tyrannosaurus rex*.

The Tales Craters Tell

For the next few days the "pirates" go their way wielding their massive military metal detectors with heavy belt battery packs, and we go ours. Everywhere they worked they littered the area, leaving it pockmarked with holes made with their shovels. Katya works my lightweight, $200 metal detector with ease and productivity. Each time it beeps, Tsvetkov and I cautiously stomp around the area to scatter any snakes and cautiously kneel down to dig with our knives and our fingers. We could make off with bucketfuls of meteorite fragments, but that is not our mission. I am more interested in photographing and using my GPS to get position plots of several of the larger craters, nearly all of which still are very much in evidence with their rims of rock rubble but very much overgrown with saplings, vines, and other vegetation that has amassed over the past fifty years. Such plots would enable Tsvetkov to check some of the coordinates made earlier. We pin down the coordinates of one key marker at 46° 09′ N by 134° 38′ E. They agree nicely with measurements made decades earlier with less precise instruments.

The craters are numbered from 1 upward according to size, the higher-numbered craters being the smaller ones. Crater Number 1 is 26.6 meters in diameter and 6 meters deep. The bedrock is overlain by 2 to 3 meters of alluvium. During a 1970 expedition Krinov and a Moscow geologist named Larion Shkerin discovered that the bedrock walls of the craters were laced with visible fracturing caused by impacting. Despite its diameter of only 1.5 meters, Crater Number 65 interests me because it involved one of several disputes between Krinov and Tsvetkov. The 1947 expedition had found a 40-kilogram meteorite fragment in the crater. Years later Krinov told Tsvetkov that the meteorite had obviously formed the crater. But by that time Tsvetkov had investigated many of the craters and established a direct correlation between the size of a given crater and the mass of the meteorite that formed it. When he checked his graph for Krinov's 40-kilogram meteorite, he found that it fell way off the curve. He told Krinov that a more massive meteorite had to have made the crater. Krinov disagreed, expressing his suspicion of Tsvetkov's mathematical modeling. Then during a 1972 expedition, a team using a magnetometer detected a larger mass buried beneath the crater floor, one weighing 160 kilograms. It fell neatly on the curve of Tsvetkov's mass/crater-size diagram. Krinov reluctantly admitted that the larger-mass meteorite had probably made the crater and that the smaller-mass object impacted afterward. Nevertheless, Krinov continued to mistrust Tsvetkov's mathematical modeling of the crater field, especially of his application of probability theory, which Krinov referred to as the "theory of wonders."

Krinov was a highly respected and tireless investigator, meticulous in his work to the extent of examining virtually every square meter of forest floor and mapping every crater position and the exact location of meteorite fragments associated with each crater. He worked tirelessly with the precision and patience of a field archaeologist. Nevertheless, Tsvetkov described him as being "more in keeping with a natural historian of the late nineteenth century than as a man well versed in modern science."

It took investigators nineteen years to launch the first expedition to the Tunguska site in 1927. But only three days after the Sikhote-Alin strike, pilots spotted the fall site marked by a group of bright auburn patches in the snow-covered taiga. This revealed two important features of the fall—it was crater-forming, and it was multiple. The word "multiple" deserves a brief explanation. We now think that sometimes a large meteoroid traveling through space may be accompanied by a swarm of smaller ones. If the large object and its smaller attendants target Earth, then the larger object may shatter on impact as fragments while the smaller pieces retain their structure and simply burrow into the ground on impact. The Sikhote-Alin meteorite shower may well have been just such a multiple event, as will become clear later in the chapter.

Two months after the bright auburn patches in the snow were sighted, a team of investigators led by the well-known astronomer V. G. Fesenkov hacked its way through the dense taiga to the crater field. They counted 122 craters, the largest of which and first to be investigated was 28 meters in diameter and 6 meters deep. Additionally they counted seventy-eight smaller craters termed "pits." Four years later more than 20 tons of iron-nickel fragments were in the Soviet Academy of Sciences warehouse.

Krinov, the leader of later expeditions, concluded that the dispersion zone of craters, an elliptical area called a dispersion ellipse, measured 1 by 2 kilometers with a major axis suggesting that the swarm had rained down from north-northwest to south-southeast. Another investigator, N. B. Divari, disagreed, saying that his more than 180 eyewitness accounts of the smoke trail fixed the entry direction from north-northeast to south-southwest. Krinov said that the wind most likely blew the smoke trail off the bolide's true course. Tsvetkov's later work in 1975 was to prove Divari right, yet it is invariably Krinov's dated writings that appear in the English language scientific press. The 1975 expedition also was to cause a major conflict between Krinov and Tsvetkov.

Toward the end of that expedition, Tsvetkov suggested to Krinov that he, Tsvetkov, remain with a small group of ten workers and, instead of continuing the time-consuming examination of every square meter of the area, examine a grid of 25- by 25-meter plots with a distance between plots of 200 meters. In this way, Tsvetkov felt that he might get a more inclusive determination of the crater field boundary than Krinov had obtained and then firmly planted in the literature.

Tsvetkov's new search method quickly paid off. Indisputably it extended the dispersal zone some ten additional kilometers to the north-northeast. Not only did it extend the zone, but it reoriented the major axis of the crater field. Tsvetkov's work enlarged the dispersal zone to 12 by 4 kilometers. During our 1995 expedition, Tsvetkov told me that Krinov tried to explain away Tsvetkov's findings by saying that the meteorites he found outside the Krinov boundary had been driven away by the wind. However, the next day they brought Krinov a 43-kilogram fragment significantly outside his smaller zone. Such a massive object could not possibly have been driven several kilometers off track by wind. It was Tsvetkov's discovery of a significantly larger fall zone that settled once and for all the passionate and long-standing argument between Divari and Krinov.

Unlike the Tunguska Event, the Sikhote-Alin meteorite shower today is well understood, including the orbital elements of the parent asteroidal fragment as most recently calculated by Tsvetkov. According to Tsvetkov, this makes the Sikhote-Alin meteorite fall the world's first example of orbit calculation by analysis of the dispersion zone of impacting fragments. The Sikhote-Alin meteoroid is now known to have originated within the main swarm of asteroids located between Mars and Jupiter. Tsvetkov was later to apply his technique to another meteorite shower site, whose story is told in Chapter 5.

To date, more than 8000 iron meteorites weighing a total of some 28 to 29 metric tons have been collected at the Sikhote-Alin site. The expeditions of 1948, 1949, and 1950 collected 23 tons. Although there are hundreds of Sikhote-Alin meteorites in the cabinets of private collectors and in the inventories of meteorite dealers, most are in the collection of the Russian Academy of Sciences. Russia's official collection is controlled by the insular Committee on Meteorites, which will not sell specimens. It will lend specimens to research institutions or swap specimens with museums or scientific organizations. In rare instances the Committee has released specimens as gifts. The largest recovered specimen weighs 1745 kilograms and is kept in the Mineralogical Museum of Moscow University. The smallest fragment reported by Krinov was less than a millimeter across and weighed only 0.3 milligrams. In addition there is an abundance of micro-dispersed products of atmospheric melting, or ablation, mixed into the forest soil.

Krinov had estimated the postatmospheric mass of the asteroid fragment at some 70 metric tons. More recent estimates by Tsvetkov and others put the mass at around 100 metric tons. An additional estimated 200 tons of the entering mass, the lion's share, were presumably burned off and left behind in the atmosphere as the famous thick trail of black smoke. The Sikhote-Alin smoke trail lasted for some hours and was dense enough to block out the Sun. All meteoroid objects that enter the atmosphere lose mass as they burn brightly as meteors (or bolides) before reaching the ground as meteorites. It is the forward part of a falling meteoroid that incandesces and heats up the most. Pressure built up by the object's pushing against the air makes it so unstable that it shatters into thousands of pieces while still in the atmosphere. Fesenkov had estimated the meteoroid's velocity on impacting the atmosphere at 14.5 kilometers per second. More recent calculations by Tsvetkov put the entry velocity at 12.4 kilometers per second. Many meteoroids stream into the atmosphere at a velocity as high as 70 kilometers per second. The smaller the meteoroid, the sooner it loses its cosmic velocity and is drawn along the remainder of its journey to the ground by gravity alone. By the time it impacts, it may be traveling at only about 0.1 to 0.2 kilometers per second. A meteoroid with a mass of up to 1 ton loses all its cosmic velocity before impacting; but one of 10 tons or more retains much of its preatmospheric velocity as it impacts.

Fragments and Individuals

There are two types of Sikhote-Alin meteorites. The most common are called *fragments* and are the ones described so far in this chapter. They litter the major crater field at a depth of just a few centimeters and deeper in the soil. They are the result of relatively large-mass objects shattering on impact with the frozen ground and resemble pieces of shrapnel.

The second, and more valuable class, and these are harder to come by, are called *individuals*. They are pieces that did not break up on impact. Because of atmospheric heating and resulting ablation, the individuals developed smooth little indentations called *rhegmaglypts*. The first individuals recovered from the Sikhote-Alin shower were unprecedented since no museum in the world had such samples in their collections, Tsvetkov told me. To this day, collectors are eager to acquire individuals, although they are now commonly available.

All meteorites are classified according to their composition and structure. Generally, there are the stony meteorites, the irons, and a third intermediate group composed of part stone and part iron. The Sikhote-Alin meteorites are irons, which are further classified on the basis of their nickel content. There are the hexahedrites with a nickel content of about 4 to 6 percent. Next come the octahedrites with about 6 to 16 percent nickel, and finally the nickel-rich ataxites with 16 percent or more nickel. The Sikhote-Alin meteorites fall between the hexahedrites and the octahedrites with the following approximate composition:

Iron	84 percent
Phosphorus	10 percent
Nickel	6 percent

➤━◆━➤

Our next-to-the-last day at the site is the most rewarding, and most strenuous. The three of us slip out of camp so as not to be followed by any of the others. Tsvetkov says that he is taking us to an area where individuals can be found. It turns out to be a trailless four-hour trudge through dense taiga, swamps, and bogs complete with our friends the poisonous snakes, and across a small swift river to a remote mountain-side rich with individuals. To avoid being toppled by the strong river current, we form a tripod by grasping each other's wrists and inching our way across. It was a trip I have repeatedly told myself I would never undertake again but one so indelibly etched in my memory that I'm almost certain that I could find my way back there. My guess is that there are fewer than a half-dozen people alive who could find their way to the site. One hour on the hillside results in the recovery of five lovely individuals, each about the size of a shaving brush. By the time we arrive back at camp, it is 9:00 P.M. and we have covered a total of fourteen very difficult kilometers.

When I asked Tsvetkov if he currently had plans for more "official" expeditions to further study the Sikhote-Alin site, he said that like everything else in Russia the situation is very complex and discouraging. First of all, who is guardian of the site? The Committee on Meteorites claims that it is, but local officials in the district say they have the authority to regulate traffic into the site. So where does one apply for per-mission to visit the site? "Sometimes it is better not to ask," advised Tsvetkov. He said that anyone wanting permission could apply to the Administration of Promrye, the political district of the Russian Far East where the meteorite site is located. The Administration can issue an invitation to visit the site, but only with approval of the Russian Academy of Sciences. All applicants should be prepared to find them-selves involved in a catch-22 situation. One of my invitations had come in writing from St. Petersburg, which got my visa approved, and the other had come from Tsvetkov as a member of the Astronomical Society.

Will there be *any* future expeditions organized by the Committee on Meteorites? In 1994 Tsvetkov wrote a letter signed by the chairman of the Astronomical Society asking the bureaucratic Committee on Meteorites to authorize for 1997 a fifty-year international commemorative expedition, which Tsvetkov volunteered to organize and lead. He listed for the committee chairman, Mr. Shukulukov, several ways in which such an international effort would lead to further understanding of the Sikhote-Alin event and other meteorite falls. Further, it would give foreign investigators a rare opportunity to study the site, and it would be paid for entirely by foreign participants. The Russian government had everything to gain, not the least of which was the goodwill of the international scientific community.

On May 19, 1994, came the following reply, which in part reads: "Dear Dr. Tsvetkov: Details of the Sikhote-Alin meteorite site have already been exhaustively studied, and there is no need to further study the event. Further, I find it highly doubtful that your proposed expedition could contribute any new scientific data in the problem of the Sikhote-Alin meteorite. It is also doubtful that the study of microdispersed matter would contribute to further understanding of the event. Further, removal of S-A meteorites by foreigners decreases the opportunity [of the Committee on Meteorites] to exchange samples with scientists who have meteorites from other sites. In response to transferring part of the recovered fragments to the Russian Academy, there is no need since the Academy already has enough recovered samples, and they are well studied. We further think that all future visits to the site should be restricted."

Does this scientifically unsound decision mean that the remaining 70 tons of Sikhote-Alin meteorites, oxidizing away in the ground, will never see the light of day? Probably, but then there will always be pirates.

CHAPTER 3

Chinge: Gold, Greed, Murder, and Dumplings

In the 1980s, astronomers were surprised to find certain regions in the asteroid belt that seem to act as escape hatches through which asteroids are from time to time propelled on courses through the inner Solar System. Asteroids that dwell in those regions seem to be especially subject to gravitational tugs from the planetary giants Jupiter and Saturn, with the result that the asteroids' orbits are elongated. The new stretched-out paths then may intersect with the orbit of Mars, Earth, Venus, or Mercury. Those asteroids then become cosmic missiles that periodically rain down on Earth's surface as a shower of rock-metal fragments that may or may not command attention. Meteorite hunters are unusually pleased when such falls are made up of irons with an especially high component of nickel. My 1996 expedition to Chinge (pronounced *"ching-geh"*) was to the site of just such a fall.

Off to a Fabled Land

Barely had I completed writing two articles, filed away my slides, and put the final touches on a paper about my 1995 expedition to the Sikhote-Alin meteorite site in the Russian Far East than I found myself once again stuffing my duffel bags with tent, sleeping bag, and some 50 kilograms of supplies in preparation for an expedition to Siberia's Chinge meteorite site. My Russian colleague and friend Valentin Tsvetkov, who had done pioneering work at the Sikhote-Alin site as well as at the Chinge site, assured Katya and me that we would find the Chinge site more than mildly interesting and worth every ruble of the cost to get there. The site is 1675 meters up in the Tannu-Oola Mountains in the Russian Republic of Tyva (formerly pronounced Tuva) not more than a spitball throw away from Outer Mongolia when the wind is in the right direction.

I first visited Tyva in 1992 and have returned twice since then. It is an exotic land of shamans, native inhabitants of Mongoloid stock, incredibly beautiful vistas, and a history extending back to the Mongol khans. It is rimmed off from the rest of Russia by the Sayan Mountains and is accessible from the north only by air or by its one major road. After a long climb by car of half an hour or more up the northern slopes, you pass through a narrow notch and find yourself in an alpine ecosystem adorned with a profusion of wild flowers and walled in on two sides by jagged walls of rock. A gorge plunges 1000 or so feet out of sight into forest. Several years ago an avalanche swept a passenger bus down the slopes of that yawning chasm. The pass is the only major thoroughfare linking Tyva with the rest of the world. So treacherous are these mountain passes that even the Cossacks of old chose to avoid them and to take long routes through gentler terrain, as did the silk and fur caravans that linked the Manchu and Russian empires in trade centuries ago. In 1992, when our car reached the pass and then made a roller coaster pitch down the southern side of the mountain, there suddenly was Tyva spread out far below, a broad, flat, and fertile land stretching to the horizon— a gigantic checkerboard of a varitextured landscape. Few Westerners have been blessed with that sweeping view of a land at once exotic, mysterious, and overwhelmingly beautiful.

Czarist Russia in 1914 and then the Soviets in 1944 annexed Tyva as part of Russia. The country, formerly known as Uriankai, existed uneasily under the tutelage of the Mongol khans Genghis and Kublai. A number of words in Tyva's language, which is Turkic in origin, have Mongol roots; and many of the inhabitants practice a brand of Tibetan Buddhism that worked its way into Uriankai from Mongolia in the mid-1500s. In the mid-1700s, Uriankai was part of the Oirot Empire commanded by several warring Mongol chieftains. Troops of the Chinese Manchu dynasty found the disjointed chieftains easy prey and are reported to have slaughtered a million Mongol and Turkic tribespeople in 1755–1756. In the early 1920s, with the end of Chinese control and the arrival of the Bolsheviks, Tyva found itself divided between one group that wanted an independent Buddhist republic allied with Mongolia and a group of younger people who had found sweetness in the taste of Marxism-Leninism.

Then over the next three decades, the younger generation watched helplessly as its faith in Soviet-style socialism soured. First, Tyva's written script in the Mongolian alphabet was changed to Russian Cyrillic. The people, traditionally nomadic and stubbornly independent, were herded under Stalin into collectivization and impotently watched their cattle, sheep, and reindeer rounded up and locked into the confines of state farms. Additionally, they equally helplessly looked on in horror as the rich topsoil of their unused steppe lands was plowed up by Khrushchev's tractors, in his "Virgin Lands" crusade to boost agricultural production, and just as quickly blown away. Economic and ecological disaster followed as the starry-eyed young Marxist-Leninists wondered what had happened.

In the early 1990s, a number of anti-Russian demonstrators began to vent their discontent. The older generation had stubbornly preserved its identity by clinging to Tyva's traditions. Today the country has a strong measure of cultural independence as a republic of the Russian Federation; nevertheless its purse strings are still in the clutches of Moscow.

Ordeal to Krasnoyarsk

It's 9:30 P.M., June 24. Katya, Tsvetkov, and I are at the airport in Moscow to catch our flight to Krasnoyarsk. Each of us has a well-stuffed backpack; in addition, I have my bulging black duffel bag. Since my ticket shows that I am a foreigner, I am obliged to check in at the in-tourist end of the terminal while Katya and Tsvetkov with their Russian identities have to check in at the opposite end "miles" away. But Katya soon persuades a female ticket agent to let her check in with me.

Tsvetkov's backpack weighs the limit of 20 kilograms, so he is all right. But Katya and I have an overweight problem: the black duffel bag weighs 23 kilograms, one backpack weighs 24 kilograms, one wheeled bag another 23 kilograms, a second wheeled bag comfortably under the limit, plus Katya's backpack that teeters at the weight limit. What to do? There is no assurance that they will even let us through with so much luggage. As usual in such circumstances, Katya springs into action, determined not to be done in by the Russian bureaucracy.

"Now just let me handle this," she says grabbing one end of the black duffel bag and strapping on one of the backpacks. "You stay here and pretend you don't understand Russian. I'll be back soon." She is off at a trot, dragging the heavy duffel bag through the multitude of travelers and soon is swallowed up in the crowd. With one less bag in my inventory, I wait and wait, shrugging and smiling whenever someone comes up to me and asks in Russian for directions. Ten minutes pass; then I see Katya elbowing her way through the crowd toward me, skirt flying, stepping over luggage, and with a thumbs-up sign.

"Here's what I did," she begins to explain triumphantly. "I found Tsvetkov in line and studied the situation. I told him to give me his backpack and left the overweight duffel and my backpack with him. I then scanned the line until I spotted a nice man without luggage. With my best smile I asked him if he would check through my (Tsvetkov's) backpack, and he said yes. Then I told Tsvetkov just to pay the overweight and save us seats on the airplane. How's that!" Telling Tsvetkov to save us seats was wise for two reasons. First, foreigners are always held back so that Russians can board the airplane first, even though foreigners pay a heftier fee; and second, seat assignments in Russia often are ignored by passengers and flight attendants alike. Seating is a free-for-all affair, often with heated disputes over who is to get a window seat.

Katya uses the same ploy in our line to pass off my legal-weight-limit wheeled bag. Her questionably close wheeled bag plus my overweight bag are weighed together and we are waved through without as much as a nod. We soon discover why.

We next enter a little dimly lit room with our inventory of one backpack, Katya's wheeled bag, and my reclaimed wheeled bag. Ah, ha, I think. Now we get rid of the heavy backpack. But no, the uniformed woman at the exit door only wants to examine our tickets. We then climb down two flights of poorly lit iron stairs that lead into a long room and which, to our dismay, contains luggage scales attended by four *bábushka* types, fat, glum, and very authoritarian appearing in their pinched uniforms. "You're overweight" the most overweight of the four announces as she slides my backpack off the scales and onto a belt carrier. Katya looks crushed.

Bábushka number two tells Katya she will have to go to the other end of the room to pay the overweight fee. I see her march off and then watch as she waves in anger at the invisible woman behind the thick glass of her cage. Some sort of dialogue of waving and shouts goes on for several minutes. Katya returns furious. "Here's what happened," she says, removing a shoe and rubbing her foot. "You are supposed to pay 1 percent of your ticket cost per kilo overweight. But what did that idiot try to do? She tried to include my ticket from Krasnoyarsk to Tyva as well as my ticket from Moscow to Krasnoyarsk. I tried to tell her that only part of the luggage was going to Tyva, but she said we'd have to pay anyway. I insisted no and demanded that she recalculate the fee. Finally she did. We had to pay twenty dollars."

Back at the gate guarded by the four musketeers, we are ordered to "Go through that door and down two flights to the tarmac where a bus will take you to the airplane." We go and wait and wait and wait. Katya says nothing except that she will never wear high heels again. Finally the bus comes and takes us to the huge airplane, an airbus IL86. The jet engines are roaring as the last few passengers mill about beneath the wings waiting to climb the boarding stairs. One of the passengers is smoking. After another ticket check on the stairs, we deposit our two wheeled bags in the carry-on luggage compartment before climbing up to the cabin area. Our assigned seats, of course, are occupied, and the flight attendant simply shrugs when Katya shows her our tickets. But far down near the tail section we spot Tsvetkov waving energetically and indicating two empty seats beside him. Long live Tsvetkov!

For those readers who may still be determined to travel by air within Russia, I include the following in-flight menu:

One piece of cold, overdone, unchewable steak with cold, dry white rice
Four slices of cold, greasy sausage
One tiny cup of tepid tea
Two slices of dark bread
One small piece of cheese
Butter and jam

We land in Krasnoyarsk right on time, and it is a beautiful day. Katya's company car and driver are nowhere to be seen after a wait of twenty minutes, but we manage to hitch a ride Russian style, that is, by simply standing beside the road and holding one arm slightly raised. Twenty dollars sees us the forty-five minute drive into town and to Katya's apartment. We have crossed four time zones from Moscow. I have crossed twelve from Boston.

Solace in Kyzyl

It's 7:00 A.M., June 26. Tsvetkov, Katya, and I carry and drag our backpacks and duffel bag down the five flights of stairs of Katya's apartment. Dimitri Yurkovsky, the fourth member of our expedition, is waiting for us as he chats with the driver of our taxi to the airport where we will catch our flight to Tyva's capital, Kyzyl, 450 kilometers distant. "Dima," as he is familiarly called, is in his early thirties, easygoing, a hard worker, and every bit as eager to visit the Chinge site as Katya and I are.

Within weight limits, at 8:45 A.M. we go through security baggage check before boarding a thirty-four-passenger Yak-40 aircraft to Kyzyl. But there's a problem. The guard scanning baggage on her monitor doesn't like something she sees in Tsvetkov's backpack, a hunting knife. "Give it to me," she orders. "It's a deadly weapon."

"It's my hunting knife that we'll need on our expedition," Tsvetkov pleads in Russian.

"Keep quiet," she barks, "or I might write up my report in such a way that you will go to jail." And she begins filling out a long form. My duffel bag goes through unchallenged. I had carefully tucked away my big knife with its 25-centimeter blade inside two lead-lined film bags. Katya tells Dima and me to board the bus to the airplane while she stays with Tsvetkov. We save two seats, and the loaded plane waits . . . and waits. "*Niet karashaw*" (not good), I say to Dima. He frowns and nods. Just as the flight attendant is shutting the door, there is a rapid thumping. Katya and Tsvetkov pile their luggage in the storage area and fall into their seats. A woman sitting behind me holds a cat that begins to meow plaintively as the plane starts to taxi.

In Kyzyl a car driven by the branch office manager of Katya's company meets us and whisks us to what was once the Communist party guest house, the "Cottage Hotel," where I had stayed in 1992. But this time Katya and I are given Yeltsin's luxury apartment. It has a huge office, with a desk nearly the size of a pool table, a dining room with a table that can seat twelve, cabinets with elegant china and crystal, and drawers filled with heavy plate silver. The only thing in the desk drawers is a ground-out cigarette butt. There is a large sitting room, and an equally large bedroom with two enormous hand-carved beds made especially for Yeltsin and his wife. "Let's just stay here," Katya says shaking her head in disbelief. "You should be glad that you travel with me." There is even a balcony that overlooks a garden and small river. Across the street is a dour four-story gray stone building, KGB headquarters, which is hard to miss since in virtually every city they all look alike. And across from that is a store with a sign reading "Gallant's Store." Katya can't stop laughing and accuses me of trying to introduce capitalism to Tyva.

The next morning the 90-kilometer drive to Bai-Haak over a paved but dreadfully neglected road takes an hour and a half. Bai-Haak is the small village where I am to be issued a permit to be in the area. The official, Sergei Sapelkin, then director of the Tandinski Forest District, is the husband of one of Katya's old school chums. In 1992 he had led Katya and me on a demanding three-day horseback climb up the Sayan Mountains and along a ridge that descended into Mongolia. We still talk about it.

After lunch, we set off for the Chinge site, an abandoned and depleted gold mining area some 20 kilometers and about two hours distant. Along the way we stop in a nearby village to buy bread and fresh vegetables. Sergei has provisioned us with potatoes, carrots, beets, and salted fish. Our transportation is a Gorkey all-terrain van with seven double seats. At one stage Sergei leaves us. He is armed and in full major's uniform, and accompanied by a militia man who resembles Pancho Villa in ferocity but turns out to be kindly and polite in the extreme. They mount horses and set off at a canter along the road, capes flying, while we shop. Sergei had expressed some doubt about the Gorkey's ability to make it over the steep mountain pass and over the tongue of a mountain glacier. At one stage, the end of a birch tree leaning into the trail comes crashing through my window with the force of a thrown spear and misses my head by inches. When we come to the glacier, we all get out and study the situation. The problem is a yawning deep chasm about a meter wide. After conferring with Sergei, the driver tells us all to wait as he climbs up into the cab and then backs up the Gorkey, revs it, and attacks the crevasse with determination. One bounce in and another out does it.

The mud then begins to fly as we churn our way up the long steep approach to the pass. At times our progress seems hopeless as the Gorkey churns and moans to a stop with its wheels just spinning and digging in deeper. But each time, the thick tire treads catch on a piece of rock ledge or a large tree root and the Gorkey lurches another few meters up the slope. Eventually we make it to the top and begin to pitch down the other side, at times skidding almost out of control. I don't see how the truck can possibly make it back up the slope. To make matters worse, within minutes the sky clouds over and darkens enough for us to need our headlights. Then we are being pelted with a profusion of hail stones the size of marbles, a reminder that we are in the mountains, at an altitude of 1600 meters. Within five minutes the storm passes and we are once more under blue sky but skidding along a skating rink. As we round a hairpin turn, our campsite comes into view below. One tiny intact log cabin, a larger dilapidated one, and a serviceable outhouse are all that was left by the gold miners. The area had been worked off and on over the past 200 years or more. I was prepared to see pristine forest with a river of crystal-clear water. Instead I gaze over an expanse of ecological devastation.

The last time Tsvetkov had been here was in 1986. The 27-hectare-, 1-kilometer-wide Chinge River valley was then a green carpet of lush vegetation with the clear stream a few meters wide locked in along either side by steep, 245-meter-high conifer-clad slopes. Tsvetkov had described it as a mountain paradise. But no more, and the expression on his face when our Gorkey drives up to the miners' cabins reveals his shock as he quickly surveys our surroundings. The gold miners had been back for one final assault on the unspoiled valley and had abandoned it a year ago. This time they dug into the land with the most modern and destructive mining equipment. In place of the carpets of wild grasses and myriad small shrubs are heaps of boulders, then rocks, then sand, and finally a large mud pool. About a 1.5-kilometer stretch of the valley to the edges of the steep slopes on either side of the stream is utter ruin.

First the giant bulldozers had scraped away all living matter and the alluvium. Then the draggers scraped up a mixture of underlying rock, gravel, sand, and mud. The dragger first spit out the heavy rock rubble, heaping it into piles. Next it spit out the coarse gravel into still more piles. Then it washed the gold out of the finer sand and mud. The gold was caught in a fine-mesh grid, collected, put in portable vaults, and then taken to Bai-Haak. About fifty miners had worked the area in consecutive twelve-hour shifts, Sergei tells us. In their last year here they collected about 40 kilograms of gold. Then they left as suddenly as they had come. They also left their litter of rusted and discarded machine parts, fuel containers, broken bulldozer tracks, and any other equipment that was no longer serviceable. We pitch our tents not far from the stream and set up a makeshift table and cooking area near the old cabin. Our carpet is sorted rocks the size of tennis balls, rotting planks with nails sticking through, and strewn tree stumps. Tsvetkov just keeps shaking his head in disbelief.

When Sergei and his assistant's horses trot into camp, the mood changes. Both are grinning as Sergei holds up a sack of freshly caught trout which he hands over to Katya. While she and Dima clean the fish and Tsvetkov and I get a fire going, Sergei gathers bunches of scallionlike plants with the Russian name of *cheryemtsa*. Thirty minutes later, we are indulging ourselves with vodka and a delicious fish soup with chopped up potatoes. After our midafternoon lunch, Sergei and his assistant slide their rifles into their saddle holsters and wave good-bye, but not before leaving a short-wave radio transmitter/receiver with us. He says there are bears in the area but that they probably won't bother us. The real danger is ticks. We are to be on our own for the next four days. Tsvetkov and Dima then set out on a half-hour hike along the river and into "Meteorite Valley" to search for a likely place to dig the next day.

Tale of the Meteorite

While the scientific aspects of the Chinge iron shower are intriguing in themselves, the background cultural aspects surrounding the event are equally absorbing, for they abound with gold, greed, politics, violence leading to murder, and dumplings.

The time is around 1900 in the present Republic of Tyva, then a loosely organized region known variously as Uri-ankhai and Uronhi. The story's pivotal figure is one Nicholai M. Chernevich, a Russian engineer about whom we know little, except that by the early 1900s he had settled in the region as the first Russian property owner and was buying up small parcels of land from the Uronhinites. A few other Russians—merchants, adventurers, and gold miners—along with their counterparts from neighboring Manchuria also sought their fortune in Uronhi from time to time. At the turn of the century Uronhi was a resource-rich plum waiting to be plucked by one or the other of the two competing major powers to the south and north—Russia and Manchuria.

During his expeditions in the late 1970s and 1980s, Tsvetkov took every opportunity to talk with elderly villagers in and around Bai-Haak who had known Chernevich, or known about him. Bai-Haak, with its one main street and a population of only a few hundred, is the largest village near the Chinge site. Some remembered this cultured Russian of about age sixty as an imposing figure with a shaved head and a large moustache. He was reputedly a kind man with a fondness for children, to whom he habitually gave candies that kept his pockets bulging whenever he visited the village. Legend had it that he knew members of the czar's family, but a falling out in that relationship resulted in his being sent into exile in Uronhi on the southern edge of the Russian Empire. But, unexplainably, he apparently was permitted to visit the capital of St. Petersburg whenever he wished.

That Chernevich had money cannot be doubted. By 1911 not only was he buying up land but also employing laborers from Bai-Haak to work his newly established gold mines on a 4-kilometer-long segment of the Chinge Creek, a four-hour or more horseback ride from Bai-Haak. The creek is an 11-kilometer-long waterway that feeds a tributary of the mighty Yenisei River.

In addition to digging into the streambed and washing the gravel and sand rubble for gold, Chernevitch's workers also collected many gold nuggets lodged in depressions around boulders and elsewhere in the streambed. From time to time they found other heavy "nuggets" of iron, sometimes deposited in association with the heavier lumps of gold. The workers usually tossed these unwanted nuggets onto the heaps of discarded rubble, or sometimes they were fashioned into tools.

Each time one of Chernevitch's miners called his attention to an iron fragment, Chernevitch would put it aside. Before long he had a sizable collection. Early in 1912, he brought thirty of the specimens, which he was convinced were meteorites, to the czar's Academy of Sciences in St. Petersburg. The masses of the specimens ranged from 85 grams to 20.5 kilograms. True to his training as a mining engineer, Chernevitch provided Academy scientists with a detailed map showing exactly where each meteorite had been found, a map that later was to prove useful to Tsvetkov. In confirmation of his belief in the origin of his iron "nuggets," Chernevich had named his gold mining area Meteority.

Two specialists went to work on the samples, cutting and examining them in cross section. One was O. O. Backlund, an astronomer, the other a chemist named V. G. Khlopin. Three years passed before they published an article stating that the samples were of iron-nickel composition but "did not reveal any positive signs of belonging to the class of iron meteorites." Their opinion appears to have been based on the octahedrite crystal structure of the then known irons, which didn't match the cross-sectional crystal pattern of the nickel-rich (16 percent) Chinge irons. Despite their negative conclusion, Chernevich's interest in what he stubbornly believed to be meteorites continued and his collection grew. In September 1915, he returned to St. Petersburg, this time with a 10-kilogram specimen, the second largest meteorite from the Chinge site.

A year earlier, the Russian government had sent an official to Uronhi to establish the territory as a Russian protectorate. In his initial report home, he wrote that the only man of culture and education in all of Uronhi was one Mr. Chernevich.

As our story unfolds, the year 1917 takes on triple significance. Two individuals from Finland, identified simply as Sederholm and Haussen, visited the Chinge site and returned home with three meteorites with masses of 988, 883, and 103 grams. These were examined by one G. Pehrman, who tentatively declared the specimens as having a cosmic origin. On what he based his conclusion we do not know.

The year 1917 was notable also for the revolution which rocked Russia in civil war. Even remote Tuva (Tyva) felt the shock as control of the little region was passed back and forth between the Red Guard and the White Guard. It was said that a force of only 200 soldiers was enough to keep the region under control. During one raid a group of what Chernevich at first supposed to be Red Army guards burst into his office in the village of Argolik. They were not Red Guards but bandits who set about abusing Chernevich to force him to reveal where his gold was hidden.

At some stage in a person's life there may come a time when a decisive show of character is required. That stage in Chernevich's life had come with his determination not to give the bandits satisfaction. One can only imagine his resolve in defiance of his tormentors. The more insistent they became, the more determined was Chernevich. Beyond endurance with his resistance, the bandits resorted to torture. Chernevich still refused to yield. In utter desperation the bandits cut off both his ears, bound him, dumped him into a cart, and took him to Bai-Haak. His loss of blood during those hours of jostling must have weakened him terribly.

In 1979, Tsvetkov was lucky enough to find an elder of the village who as a young man had driven that cart. Yes, he remembered the event well, he told Tsvetkov. How was it possible to forget such heinous behavior? For when the cart was about to pass the cemetery, he was ordered to stop and then he watched in horror as the bandits drew their sabers, hacked Chernevich to death, and left him for the dogs.

Following the revolution, what is now Tyva became an independent state, although with close ties to Russia. Meanwhile the gold mine had continued to be operated and more meteorites continued to surface, several finding their way into museums not only in Tyva but in several Russian cities as well. In 1929 a worker named Tikhonov was given nine of the twenty meteorites found in the Chinge Creek by a fellow worker, one S. Ivanov. The nine meteorites were given to the museums of Kysyl, Irkutsk, Minussinsk, and Alma-Aty. Two of the specimens had masses of 2846 and 1405 grams. In 1948 the St. Petersburg geologist A. L. Dodin found a specimen weighing 7580 grams. Although the largest part of the Chinge meteorite collection today is locked up in the Russian Academy of Sciences, specimens now can be found in museums in the United States, Britain, and Australia. Specimens can also be found in the cabinets of private collectors and in the stores.

By the 1930s, the loose gold of Chinge became too scarce to be recovered economically by the crude equipment then in use. According to Sergei, during one or more winter seasons of the productive years a female cook for the gold mining camp was left behind at the mines to fend for herself. Her job over those bleak and cold months was to make dumplings and freeze them in the snow in preparation for the miners' return in the spring.

The 1938 discovery of several Chinge meteorites by the Leningrad geologist A. L. Dodin helped rekindle interest in the site. One specimen weighed in at 7580 grams. But it wasn't until the 1960s that the Committee on Meteorites decided to seriously look into the Chinge site. Russian interest in meteorites had been given a boost by the work being done by E. L. Krinov and others at the Sikhote-Alin site to the east near Vladivostok.

In 1963 the Committee on Meteorites sent a three-man expedition to Chinge to search for impact craters. The large number of fragments recovered up to that time suggested a crater-forming impact, possibly similar to that of the Canyon Diablo meteorite. But a thorough search of the surrounding area turned up nothing.

The next expedition sent to Chinge by the Committee was in 1978 and was led by Tsvetkov. In view of the high success of metal detectors at Sikhote-Alin, Tsvetkov decided to use them at Chinge. But some were doubtful about just how useful they might be, considering the 3-meter depth of alluvium in the Chinge Creek and the presence of magnetite ores. While the alluvium depth would render the metal detectors useless, the magnetite would simply produce spurious signals. Despite advice to keep his expedition small and to bring only a few metal detectors, Tsvetkov mustered a group of twenty-two researchers and twenty metal detectors.

Chernevich's map of sixty-six years earlier now came in very useful. It enabled Tsvetkov to survey the creek bed along 3.5 kilometers and locate the exact positions where Chernevich's gold miners had recovered meteorites. The fact that those and other meteorites recovered before 1978 lay at a depth of from 2.5 to 3 meters within the alluvium indicated that the meteorite fall was an old one. The first day his team of twenty-two combed the creek and its shores with no luck. But the second day produced beeping that was to be more significant than they realized at first. One meteorite was discovered in the creek bed at the outlet of a small valley tributary to the creek, "Meteorite Valley," as it became unofficially known. The next day four more meteorites were found in the same area.

At this stage Tsvetkov began to wonder if the meteorites had been washed into the Chinge Creek from the small valley tributary. A methodical search of seven other similar valley tributaries in the area revealed nothing. Only Meteorite Valley turned out to be a real beeper; three return expeditions over the next ten years produced some 200 meteorites. Those expeditions took place in 1979, 1981, and 1986.

Mishap in a Glacial Stream

The next morning, June 27, with backpacks, shovels, and cameras, the four of us hike downstream for about 3 kilometers. Two-thirds of the way the rock rubble abruptly ends where the bulldozers stopped fashioning their moonscape terrain. The remainder of the hike takes us up and over the stubborn remnant of a small mountain glacier and then into the unspoiled landscape that Tsvetkov remembered. Ten minutes later we are standing at the junction of Meteorite Valley and Chinge Creek, the point where Tsvetkov's first expedition had found meteorites.

Our target area is another two or so kilometers up the narrow V-shaped valley. It is an old glacial valley carved out during the last ice age. Its steep, thickly wooded slopes are inclined some 20° to 50°. In some places the stream is only a trickle; in others it is a meter or more broad but rarely more than half a meter deep. Along the way, while inching along an especially steep-walled section, I lose my footing and start to plunge down the slope to the valley floor about 10 meters below, but I manage to grab a shrub that holds long enough for Dima to pull me back up. My souvenir from that fall is a 15-centimeter-long scar on the inside of my left wrist.

The most likely places to find meteorites in the valley, Tsvetkov tells us, are at the heads of the small pools that proceed in steplike fashion up along the streambed. His reasoning goes like this: In ages past when the meteorites came to this valley, some may have been deposited at random along the stream, as was the case with the Chinge Creek. But others most likely were washed down in postglacial times by swiftly flowing spring melt water. They were tumbled downstream along the then exposed bedrock of the new valley and, like gold nuggets, became trapped in depressions at the bases of miniature waterfalls that fed the numerous small pools.

The digging is not easy, for over the centuries debris of rocks, alluvium, and dead trees has clogged the stream and in places even hidden it from view. Dima, our digger-in-chief, hacks away at one dead tree at the head of the first pool we excavate while Tsvetkov, Katya, and I dig and tumble boulders and smaller rocks out of the way to clear the head of the pool. Hour after hour of this work, with constant monitoring of our piles of debris with a metal detector, brings only fatigue, hands numbed by the cold water, and bruised fingers. Katya looks with disgust at her once polished nails. Other than the sharp rocks, the only other natural enemies are the bears and ticks. Of the two, ticks are the most worrisome, for a bite can bring on encephalitis. So at the end of each day a thorough examination of our clothes and bodies is in order. The problem is that the ticks are too tiny to be easily detected, especially on dark clothing. The first pool is not rewarding, so we call it a day and drag ourselves stiff and cold back to camp. After a supper of steaming hot fish soup, rain pelts us and drives us into our tents. With a full stomach and warm in my sleeping bag, I welcome the dark and coziness of my microenvironment. A steady tattoo of raindrops drumming against the tent is somehow soothing and relaxing. "Surely, no sensible bear would be out in weather like this, would he?" Katya asks. As I feel myself drifting off into a deep sleep, I sense a secret smile come over me: I think it is the knowledge that we are in the wild, alone and uncontaminated by civilization.

The next morning it is still raining, but our spirits and hopes are high as we slip our ponchos over our heads and troop off again like four of the seven dwarfs, shouldering our shovels, crowbars, and tripod.

Pool Number 2 is farther upstream and larger than Pool Number 1. Soon after we begin digging and prying out rocks, we realize that we'll have to build dams to hold back the water from another pool above. No sooner do we marvel at our newest and improved dam than it too breaks and again floods our neatly excavated section of exposed stream bottom. "I'm shoveling more water than rocks," Katya laments. Tsvetkov says not to fret. Rarely does the first day of digging a pool produce results, he tells us, but doesn't bother to reveal the statistics underlying his observation. Sometimes you have to dig through a meter of rubble before reaching the bedrock where the meteorites are found, he says stoically. "A whole meter?" Katya moans, still shoveling water.

The next day finds us back at Pool Number 2. After two hours of digging and my trying to get a fire started with wet wood, I hear a trio of cheers go up amid a rapid series of beeps. Dima is removing a fine fragment specimen from a pile of rubble. About the size of a hand, it weighs 864 grams. A half-hour later we find a second, but smaller, fragment.

Katya is beside herself with excitement, and I think we'll have to take the shovel away from her before she breaks it.

At one stage the metal detector starts beeping at something lodged beneath the edge of an enormous boulder at one side of our pool. Although we can reach it underwater, and even wiggle it slightly, we are afraid to dislodge it for fear of the large boulder above slipping down and entombing our prize forever. Finally, we manage to prop up the large boulder. Then with very cautious digging, prying, and wiggling, Tsvetkov triumphantly withdraws the prize and with difficulty holds it high over his head. We all cheer as Katya caresses the meteorite as if it were gold. It is a large fragment that weighs in at 7900 grams and, like the other Chinge specimens, is 83 percent iron and 16 percent nickel with cobalt and other trace elements. Wow!

Each time we return to camp, instead of resting, Katya wanders off to the part of the creek where we wash and brush our teeth. This ritual is repeated each day, and all I can think of is that she has lost her toothbrush or an earring among the rocks. When my curiosity gets the better of me, I ask what she is doing each day on her little ventures. "Looking for gold," she says.

A Mystery Waiting for a Solution

The origin of the Chinge meteorites has yet to be learned. In 1947 Krinov was the first to propose that it might have been a crater-forming object. Although the 1963 expedition failed to find any evidence for large impact craters, it was nevertheless felt that smaller impact craters with diameters of several dozens of meters might exist. Evidence for this comes from morphological studies of the many fragments, although their long storage in the ground has resulted in deformation. The most likely region to search for such small craters was in Meteorite Valley where most of the meteorites so far recovered have been found. But the preservation of craters seems highly unlikely because of active slope processes. Then it was argued that possibly the stream's bedrock would reveal impact fracturing. Although bedrock deformations similar to deformations typical for well-known impact craters were found in Meteorite Valley, firm conclusions about them cannot be made.

As with the Sikhote-Alin shower, it's possible that the Chinge object first broke up in the atmosphere and then further fragmented as relatively large pieces impacted the ground. In such a case we would expect the morphology of the meteorites to be revealing—that is, some would be "individuals" with characteristic rhegmaglyptic features due to ablation; and others would be "fragments" with sharp edges, although in this instance noticeably dulled by long-term chemical erosion in the soil. Both subclasses of the meteorite have been identified for the Chinge fall. Krinov even included a third subclass—fragments from the interior of the meteorite as well as outer region fragments.

Has it been possible to determine a trajectory of the fall? The closest Tsvetkov has come to suggesting one is based on the occurrence at the northern region of meteorite finds of lots of small meteorites while at the southern region several relatively large pieces have been found. This mass distribution could suggest a hypothetical rough trajectory from north to south.

In 1982, the Russian mineralogist Vera Semenenko published her findings on the inner structure—crystal structures and fractures—of Chinge specimens. She said that the absence of internal crystal distortions suggested a meteorite shower with atmospheric fragmentation rather than impact fragmentation—as evidenced in crystal distortions of the Sikhote-Alin fragments, but not in the individuals.

In 1981, at the All Union Meteorite Conference held in Moscow, the Estonian geologist Yulo Kestlane was the first to hypothesize that the Chinge meteorite fall was prehistoric and fell on glacial ice. Presumably, the greatest number of fragments were carried along with the glacier as it carved out Meteorite Valley, eventually were deposited on the bedrock of the resulting glacial stream, and then over the ensuing millennia were buried beneath rubble of rocks, sand, and layers of alluvia.

Three years later at another All Union Meteorite Conference, N. V. Lukina gave a paper putting a possible age of the Chinge meteorite at from 20,000 to 25,000 years. The age was based on the geology of the valley and the depth of meteorites beneath the alluvium. A younger date of from 10,000 to 12,000 years also has been proposed.

To date, a total of some 250 meteorites have been recovered from the site, although the exact number cannot be known because of the undocumented history of meteorite finds between Chernevich's death in 1917 and the 1978 expedition led by Tsvetkov and commissioned by the Committee on Meteorites. The last two expeditions of 1981 and 1986 were authorized by the Geochemical Institute.

Most of the Chinge meteorites recovered to date are in the Academy of Sciences in Moscow. Like the uncertainty of the total number of meteorites recovered, there is equal uncertainty about an estimated total mass of recovered objects, although it must be considerably more than 350 kilograms. It would be sheer speculation to attempt to attach a number to the mass of the preatmospheric object.

The Chinge meteorite story is a fascinating one, and one waiting to be resolved. For the present, however, the Geochemical Institute's lack of funds prevents the Russians from organizing future expeditions. But that may change. Until only recently both the Tunguska and Sikhote-Alin sites were off limits to foreign scientists. But now the Russians are quite willing to admit foreign scientists to work at certain sites, Tunguska being notable among them. So don't be surprised if one day Chinge, too, will be beckoning.

CHAPTER 4

Pallas: The Fall and Rise of the Pallas Nugget

I t's the world's most famous meteorite and granddaddy of that class of meteorites known as pallasites. It has been variously known as the Iron Nugget, the Pallas Iron, the Gift from the Sky, and simply the Lump. A number of things make it an exceptional cosmic visitor—its discovery, identity, and destiny; its role in the founding of the science of meteoritics; and its becoming the world's first meteorite to have a 1.5-ton mountaintop monument dedicated to it. The first meteorite in the Russian Academy of Sciences' collection, it fell out of the sky—no one knows when—and seemingly landed like a marshmallow dropped onto a featherbed, at least judging from the lack of any trace of an impact crater. Its story could just as well be called "A Man Named Bear and His Meteorite," because it all started with a blacksmith, Yakov Medvedev, in the year 1749. In Russian, *medvedev* means "Son of Bear."

Medvedev was a retired Cossack soldier who supplemented his pension income by hunting for and collecting valuable metals. One day while climbing the heavily wooded slopes of south central Siberia's 900-meter-high Mount Bolshoi Imir in search of gold, red elk, or anything else of value, an outcrop of iron ore beside a huge rock caught his eye. He most likely hefted and examined several lumps of magnetite ore lying about, dreamed of riches, and made a careful mental note of the outcrop's location by the big rock.

On returning to his village on the Yenisei River some 20 kilometers from Mount Bolshoi Imir, Medvedev informed government mining authorities in Krasnoyarsk, some 200 kilometers downriver, of the outcrop, hopeful that it might also contain gold. If a sizable metal deposit that turned out to be of commercial value were reported to the government, the discoverer was paid a finder's fee.

The Krasnoyarsk authorities promptly sent Johann Mettich, a German mining engineer, to examine the site, which turned out not to be of commercial value. While there, he and Medvedev decided to have a look around the broad ridge sloping down from the peak of the mountain and further explore the area. Some 150 lachters (an old Russian unit of measure equivalent to 300 meters) from the outcrop, they were startled to see an object resembling a rather large potato some 70 centimeters in diameter just sitting there on the forest floor as if it had been gently lowered by a crane. When struck, the object gave off a pleasant ringing sound. At first supposing it was an iron nugget of terrestrial origin, Mettich soon became puzzled when he was unable to find any other samples that resembled the mysterious nugget among rock specimens along the ridge. Mettich returned to Krasnoyarsk, and Son of Bear returned to his own village.

There can be no doubt of Medvedev's preoccupation and fascination with the iron potato, for the following winter he somehow managed—probably by horse and sleigh—the Herculean task of hauling, rolling, and sliding the 700-kilogram nugget down the mountain and over the frozen bogs and streams to his village and into his backyard. As a blacksmith, he tried to work the metal but found it too malleable to be of use. Further, on being heated it lost its ductility and became hopelessly brittle. We have no idea whether Medvedev suspected that his nugget was of a cosmic origin.. However, the thought might have been suggested to him by local shamans who had conducted mountaintop rituals in worship of "the Gift from the Sky." The name should have suggested the possibility of someone having seen the object fall.

Stones from Heaven?

At the time, many members of the scientific community regarded the notion of meteorites coming from space as sheer fantasy, or at least highly questionable, including such luminaries as the U.S. scientist-president Thomas Jefferson, who had entered office in 1801. That Jefferson categorically dismissed the possibility of meteorites falling from outer space is uncertain; however, he scoffed at the notion that they could be hurled from volcanoes or generated in the atmosphere. In 1802, we find one anonymous critic who was scornful of those who believed in stones falling out of the sky:

"The rarity of these phenomena, however, which has not allowed of their being seen at a short distance by observers possessed of intelligence, and at the same time worthy of credit, and which seems hitherto to have reserved them for the eyes of the vulgar, so much inclined to exaggeration, has prevented the learned from believing in the existence of these stones."

Nevertheless, since ancient times, meteorites had been seen to fall and were collected by the Chinese and Egyptians. According to Britain's D. W. Sears, "the hieroglyphic symbol for meteoritic iron found in [Egyptian] tombs means literally 'heavenly iron.' . . . Many meteorites were worshiped, and one was given a royal procession into Rome."

Pliny in his *Naturall Historie* (Holland's translation) reports of "stones falling downe from the skie" in the year 468 B.C. "That stones fall oftentimes downe, no man will make any doubt," he writes. He goes on to say that "in the publicke place of Exercise in Abydos, there is one at this day upon the same cause preserved and kept for to be seene, and held in great reverence."

What seems to have been the earliest authentic meteorite fall is that of the Ensisheim meteorite, in Ober-Elsass, Germany, in 1492. According to a literal translation of one account:

"On Wednesday, Nov. 7, the night before St. Martins deay, in the year of our Lord 1492, a singular miracle happened: for between the hours of eleven and twelve a loud clap of thunder took place, with a long-continued noise, which was heard at a great distance: and a stone fell from the heavens in the Ban of Ensisheim which weighed 260 pounds: and the noice was much louder in other places than here. . . . It did no hurt, except that it made a hole there. It was afterwards transported thence: and a great many fragments were detached from it. . . . It was then deposited in the church with intention of suspending it as a miracle: and a great many people came hither to see this stone. . . . But the learned said they did not know what it was, for it was something supernatural that so large a stone should fall from the atmosphere: but that it was

Among Russia's diverse ethnic groups is a southern Siberian people from the Republic of Tuva. Of Mongoloid stock, their culture dates to the time of the Mongol khans Genghis and Kublai. This family photograph was probably taken in the early 1900s. (*Courtesy of the Minusinsk Museum, Tuva*)

Lenin's study in the village of Shushenskoe, where he was exiled for three years before the October 1917 revolution. (*From the author's collection*)

Rusting remains of a railroad engine abandoned in one of the notorious Russian gulags established under Stalin's reign of terror in the 1930s. Called the "railroad to nowhere," it was little more than a project of forced labor to help settle Siberia by employing untold thousands of "enemies of the state." (*From the author's collection*)

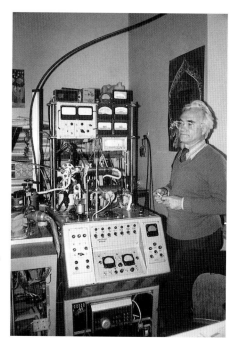

Evgeniy Kolesnikov, a Russian isotopic cosmic chemist of Moscow University, is the leading supporter of a cometary origin of the object that exploded over central Siberia in 1908. He has been involved in Tunguska investigations for more than twenty-five years. (*From the author's collection*)

Leonid A. Kulik, photographed in November 1928, probably by ethnographer Innokenty Suslov. Kulik wears a typical goatskin coat and is armed for possible encounters with bears and wolves, both of which are common in the epicenter area today. (*Courtesy of Yuri Kandiba*)

Lyuchetkan's wife Maria and three children near their tepee. The antennalike object is the skin of a sacrificed young deer displayed to appease the god Havokee and persuade him not to send his iron birds to destroy their home. This photo was taken in October 1928 by Suslov. (*Courtesy of Yuri Kandiba*)

This 1928 photograph taken by Suslov shows the "telegraph pole" forest near the Tunguska epicenter. Those trees directly beneath the point of explosion were stripped of most of their branches because of the downward pressure wave. The bark was seared away by the following firewind. (*Courtesy of Yuri Kandiba*)

In June 1927, before reaching what he believed to be the epicenter region of the 1908 Tunguska explosion, Kulik built The Dock, the first of his two camps. It consisted of a log cabin with a raised platform for sleeping, a shelter area with a hearth for cooking, and a storage hut. Later he added a banya, or steam bath hut. Here, Katya whittles a fishing pole. (*From the author's collection*)

This rare photograph of Kulik (*right*) and Suslov shows them working over a magnetometer. The photograph was taken in March 1927 by Suslov's wife, Vera. (*Courtesy of Yuri Kandiba*)

Sand Dune Hill strewn with dead tree trunks felled in parallel by the 1908 Tunguska blast that reduced about 2000 square kilometers to rubble, as photographed in October 1928 by Suslov. (*Courtesy of Yuri Kandiba*)

Most of the world authorities on the Tunguska Event attended the Bologna, Italy conference in 1996. A few are identified here: (1) W. H. Fast; (2) V. P. Korobeinikov; (3) R. Gallant; (4) G. Longo; (5) Caroline Shoemaker; (6) S. S. Gregorian; (7) N. Vasiliev; (8) B. Marsden; (9) E. Shoemaker; (10) E. Rossovskaya; (11) E. Kolesnikov; (12) N. Kolesnikova.

Smoke trail of the Sikhote-Alin meteorite shower of 1947 was painted by Yakov Medvedev and hangs in the Mineralogical Museum of the University of Moscow.

In his first painting, done several years after he witnessed the event, Yakov had the smoke trail going in the wrong direction and later had to redo the painting. (*From the author's collection*)

Prize meteorite of the Sikhote-Alin shower is this 1700-kilogram iron specimen with several hundred indentations, called *rhegmaglypts*, caused by surface melting as the meteorite was heated during its plunge through the atmosphere. (*Courtesy of E. Rossovskaya*)

The author catching up on his notes while waiting for the van to take him to the airport for the helicopter trip to Popigai's northwest crater wall. The pins in his cap are tokens of his various Siberian expeditions. (*Courtesy of E. Rossovskaya*)

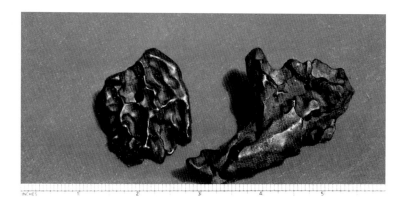

Sikhote-Alin iron meteorites come in two varieties—fragments and individuals. The fragments look like pieces of shrapnel. The two specimens shown here display the small melt indentations characteristic of the individuals. (*From the author's collection*)

During my Chinge expedition, our van was temporarily stopped by this mass of permanent ice until we examined it and decided that the small crevasses could be negotiated without endangering either us or the vehicle. Nevertheless, I chose to walk across. Katya and Dima stand by. (*From the author's collection*)

Dima, Tsvetkov, and Katya dig in the Chinge streambed of clay and rock rubble in search of meteorites. This site proved to be sterile, producing nothing but bruised and nearly frozen fingers. (*From the author's collection*)

Katya displays the first meteorite find of our Chinge expedition, a nice specimen that weighed 851 grams. Tsvetkov, seated, is credited with the find. (*From the author's collection*)

The prize of the Chinge expedition was a specimen the size of a loaf of bread, which later was cut and the section faces polished. The chromelike shine of this 1537-gram slice is due to the unusually high nickel content (16 percent) of the Chinge meteorites. (*From the author's collection*)

In 1976 Russian historian of astronomy Alina Eremeyeva determined to rediscover the fall site of the famous Pallas Iron and arrange for a 1.5-ton cast iron monument to be built in pieces and then carried to the mountain-top fall site and assembled as the first known monument to a meteorite. (*From the author's collection*)

Expedition geologist Alexander Andreev poses by the Pallas Iron monument at its dedication in 1981.

From left, Lida Nikiforova, Tsvetkov, Katya, and the author with the 4.3-kg Tsarev stony meteorite that Tsvetkov discovered hidden in an old accordion case and locked away in a shed by Lida's husband years earlier. Lida had not known about the treasure. (*From the author's collection*)

Rumors about the Tsarev meteorite abounded soon after it struck. Some said it was the size of a two-story building. Others said it was solid gold. The local newspaper *Communist* published this sketch showing the meteorite as a giant potato resting easily on the ground.

The Tsarev stony meteorite belongs to a subclass of chondrites designated as L5. A cut and polished section reveals a dark interior with flecks of metal visible. The mineral olivine is abundant in the L subclass of chondrites. The lighter colored section is an end piece of the meteorite and shows chemical erosion and the effects of weathering. (*From the author's collection*)

This section of the northwest wall of the Popigai impact crater is a geologist's dream come true. It displays a mixed variety of rock types including granite gneiss, light-colored carbonates, and a denser rock type called *tagamite*, which contains tiny diamond impactites. (*From the author's collection*)

Derelict buildings mark a former settlement of an indigenous group called Dolgans who inhabit the far-north region around Popigai. Decades ago the Soviet government tried to turn the migrant Dolgans into permanent settlers, but the experiment failed and all but destroyed the Dolgan culture. (*From the author's collection*)

John Anfinogenov (*left*) and the author examine two suspect specimens, one of which we were able to identify as a shower meteorite remnant of the 1904 Teleutskoye fall. (*Courtesy of E. Rossovskaya*)

Microscopic examination of the Teleutskoye stones revealed them as chondrites with about 30 percent natural meteoritic iron with a large component of olivine. (*Courtesy of Sergei Parshikov*)

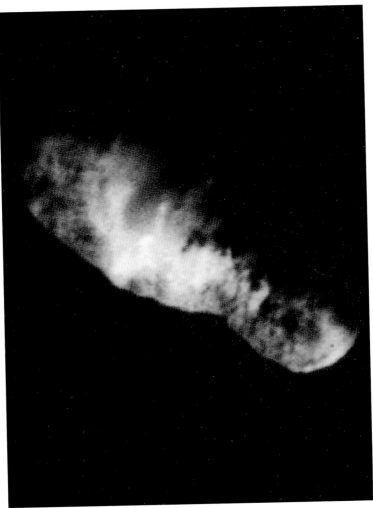

Potato-shaped, 10-kilometer-long nucleus of comet Borrelly photographed by NASA's Deep Space 1 probe in late September 2001. (*Courtesy of NASA/JPL/Caltech*)

a miracle of God: because, before that time, nothing of the kind has ever been heard of, seen, or described. When this stone was found, it had entered the earth to a depth equal to the height of a man. What everybody asserted was, that it had been the will of God that it should be found. And the noise of it was heard at Lucerne, at Villing, and many other places, so loud that it was thought the houses were all overturned. . . ."

There are a number of scriptural references to what appear to have been meteorite falls:

"And the stars of heaven fell unto the earth, even as a fig tree casteth her untimely figs, when she is shaken of a mighty wind." (Rev. vi, 13)

and

"And there appeared another great wonder in heaven; and behold a great red dragon, having seven heads and ten horns, and seven crowns upon his heads. And his tail drew the third part of the stars of heaven, and did cast them to earth." (Rev. xii, 3, 4.)

Among those of the scientific community around 1800 who admitted to the possibility of stones from the sky were four groups. One said the stones were the products of volcanoes or hurricanes. Another believed they were terrestrial rocks fused by lightning, a third that they were atmospheric "concretions" of matter degassed from Earth, and a fourth, that the stones were masses foreign to our planet. Among the fourth was the famous French astronomer and mathematician Simon Laplace, who supposed—correctly, as it turns out—that some meteorites originate from the Moon. This idea seems to have been given credence by the equally famous English astronomer William Herschel's alleged observation in 1787 of lunar "volcanoes." The idea of lunar volcanoes was lent credibility by Wilhelm Olber, of "Olbers' paradox" fame, around 1795. One observer remarked that "the moon was an uncivil neighbor for throwing stones at us." The lunar volcano views of Laplace, Olbers, and others can be summed up as follows:

Since the Moon's gravity is only a sixth as strong as Earth's and since the Moon lacks an atmosphere, explosive volcanic action might well hurl projectiles well beyond lunar "gravimetric recall" and become satellites of Earth. Eventually, such castoffs would be pulled into Earth's environment where friction with the atmosphere would slow the objects and send them flaming to the ground as meteors and meteorites.

Olbers carried the cosmic origin of meteorites to still greater heights when he proposed that some meteorites most probably come from the larger asteroids Ceres, Juno, Pallas, and Vesta as a result of collisions of these objects with smaller asteroids, all of which trace orbits between Mars and Jupiter. All the asteroids, he supposed, were the fragmented products of some unaccountable explosion of a planet that once orbited in what is now the asteroid belt, the larger of those objects being the asteroids and the smaller ones being termed meteoroids.

Astronomers today deny that such a planet ever existed. The asteroidal rubble is simply primordial matter that was never allowed to coalesce because of the effects of Jupiter's strong gravity.

Enter Pyotr Simon Pallas

Medvedev's backyard curiosity remained just that until 1771 or 1772. At that time, an extraordinary natural historian of German descent named Pyotr Simon Pallas was conducting a wide range of scientific investigations across Siberia for the czar's Academy of Sciences in St. Petersburg. At the time, the origin of meteorites was still up in the air, so to speak. Pallas's interests ranged from mountain formation to the variability of animals and paleogeographic interpretations of fossil animal remains. He discussed these subjects with the teacher of the future Emperor Alexander I and his brother Constantine. And he acquired all of this knowledge while still in his thirties. Pallas was so highly regarded that he was given the honorary title of Academician for his numerous research projects, which also included studies in botany, geology, and ethnography.

While in Krasnoyarsk, Pallas dispatched his servant Yakub on a mission that happened to take him to Medvedev's village. Yakub, also a former Cossack, possibly knew Medvedev. In any case, he was shown the famous backyard nugget. Sensing the unusual nature of the object, Yakub asked Medvedev to hack off a sample to take back to Pallas. When Pallas examined it, he strongly suspected that here was something unusual indeed, but not from the sky, rather a natural by-product of terrestrial geological transformations. Pallas was resolutely in the no-stones-from-heaven camp. His position might have been reinforced by the 1772 publication of a report by a committee of the French Academy of Sciences that had performed the first chemical analysis of a stone that reportedly had fallen from the sky. The committee, which included the famous French chemist Antoine Lavoisier, concluded that the stone was simply a piece of terrestrial pyrite that had been struck by lightning. Such stones consequently came to be known as "thunderstones" and were considered as nothing especially unusual. Says Sears: "The scientific fraternity are said to have 'made merry over the credulity of people who imagined the stones to have fallen from the heavens.'"

The Lump Gets Smaller

Pallas lost no time in making arrangements for the nugget destined to be named after him to be shipped to St. Petersburg for detailed examination by Academy scientists. It was sent overland across the snow during the winter to the nearest port of the next river. There it remained until summer and was taken across the river by ship, only to remain there on the opposite shore until the following winter and its next overland journey by sleigh to the next river, and so on to St. Petersburg. Wherever it went, it generated curiosity, especially among the Kolyvanovoskresensky mine management authorities in the capital city of Barnaul, who, among others, chipped off samples. Finally, in May 1776 the Lump arrived in St. Petersburg, lighter by many pounds. The total travel time was four years and three months.

Samples continued to be chipped off the Lump and found their way into the laboratories of numerous scientific societies and museums in London, Paris, Vienna, Berlin, Jena, and Stockholm, not to mention dozens of private collections. Some European scientists expressed alarm, saying that if samples continued to be cut off, soon there would be nothing left of the Lump. Accordingly, in 1787 Russian authorities stopped distributing samples. Sometime before 1830 the Pallas Iron was moved from St. Petersburg's Kunstkamer to the Academy's Mineralogical Museum. In 1835 the Russian chemist G. I. Hess determined the official weight of the meteorite to be 31 poods (522 kilograms). The "pood" is an old Russian unit of weight equivalent to 16.38 kilograms. The original mass of the Pallas Iron was probably between 41 and 42 poods (670 and 688 kilograms), according to the Russian historian of astronomy Alina Eremeyeva, who will soon enter our story. Eremeyeva insists that the original weight of the Pallas Iron is controversial. She feels that the 687-kilogram figure found in M. H. Hey's *Catalog of Meteorites* published in 1966, and the Soviet Academy of Sciences' catalog of its meteorite collection published in 1978, is groundless. So during its travels, and later in St. Petersburg, about 10 poods (165 kilograms) got hacked off, the largest weighing 1.5 poods. That sample disappeared without a trace. From 1778 to 1866 the Pallas Iron lay mute. Not a single paper was published by the Russian Academy about the, by then, world-famous iron nugget.

By 1776, a small sample of only a few grams of the Pallas Iron had fallen into the hands of the German chemist E. K. F. Meyer. He became the first person in Europe to do a qualitative and quantitative chemical analysis of a Pallas fragment. He identified the crystal structure and fracturing of the stony component of the meteorite (later to be identified as olivine) and listed other components as iron oxide, silicon dioxide, and manganese oxide. Meyer's work showed that the sample could not have been an artifact of human activity or volcanic in origin. Further, the ductility of the iron component convinced him that an extraordinarily slow cooling process had been involved. On examining several other mysterious nugget-iron masses, he discovered that three also had yellowish, translucent olivine components. Here was a glimmering of the foundation of a new science of meteoritics.

In 1794 the German physicist Ernst Chladni summarized his extensive work on bolides in a book in which he made the unpopular assertion that the "stones" that fall from the sky come from outer space. He went even further by claiming that meteorites are the remnants of cosmic matter out of which the Solar System formed. Since space was considered by many to be "empty," such a notion seemed untenable. Chladni believed that the earliest known fall of a meteorite on record dated back to 1478 B.C. in Crete, but that date, if not the fall itself, seems somewhat doubtful. He included the Pallas Iron as being of cosmic origin, arguing that the iron nugget had to have been formed only in great heat and could not have been formed atop Mount Bolshoi Imir, or have been made by humans or electrical discharges or condensations in the atmosphere, and could not have been volcanic in origin. He, therefore, concluded that the Pallas nugget had come from outer space. Sears, however, took issue with Chladni's assertion, saying that "what Chladni lacked was a definite link between [the large masses, including the Pallas Iron, he cited] and the stones that were actually seen to fall." We will return to the simultaneity of two such related events later.

Nevertheless, as if to reinforce Chladni's supposition, in 1794, the same year that he declared the Pallas Iron to be a cosmic intruder, a meteorite shower rained down on Siena, Italy, and the following year a 25-kilogram stone from heaven barely missed a laborer near Wold Cottage in Yorkshire, England.

The real hero in establishing the identity of meteorites as objects from space, says Sears, was not Chladni but the English chemist Edward Howard. With the help of the French mineralogist Jacques-Louis Compte de Bournon, Howard analyzed more than a half-dozen large meteoritic masses, including the Pallas Iron, which Chladni had never examined himself, by the way. Howard's chemical analysis showed a remarkable similarity among the objects, but even more remarkable was that they all contained nickel, a unifying aspect missing in Chladni's work. Howard's work showed the significance of the similarity among meteorites that had fallen at widely different locations. Since the country rock at the fall sites differed widely but the chemical composition of the meteorites themselves was nearly the same, a common origin was implicated.

The year following Howard's work of 1802 a spectacular event brought into even sharper focus the likelihood of meteorites coming from the heavens. On April 26, 1803, out of a clear bright sky more than 3000 stones rained down onto the neighborhood of L'Aigle, Normandy, France. They formed an elliptical oval fall zone characteristic of shower meteorite falls, such as the dispersion field of the Sikhote-Alin fall (Chapter 2) and another that will be described in the next chapter.

One eyewitness account of the L'Aigle fall is in order here for its description of acoustical properties accompanying the fall, noise similar to that reported by eyewitnesses of other major falls, including Tunguska and a lesser fall of the Teleutskoye shower (see Chapter 7):

"At about one in the afternoon [I observed] a fiery globe of a very brilliant splendour, which moved in the atmosphere with great rapidity. Some moments there was heard at Laigle, and in the environs of that city to the extent of more than thirty leagues in every direction, a violent explosion which lasted five or six minutes.

"At first there were three or four reports like those of a cannon, followed by a kind of discharge which resembled a firing of musketry; after which there was heard a dreadful rumbling like the beating of a drum. The air was calm and the sky serene, except for a few clouds. . . . The noise proceeded from one small cloud . . . about half a league . . . to the north-north-east of Laigle. . . . In the whole canton over which this cloud hovered, a hissing noise like that of a stone discharged from a sling was heard, and a multitude of mineral masses exactly similar to those distinguished by the name of meteoric stones were seen to fall at the same time."

So it was Chladni's work bolstered by the vigorous chemical analysis of Howard in 1802 and other investigators, plus a thorough investigation of the spectacular shower of L'Aigle by the highly respected French scientist Jean-Baptiste Biot, that caused most of the European scientific establishment to do a flip-flop and come to accept the extraterrestrial origin of meteorites. But not all scientists were won over. As late as 1819 a number of museum curators either hid away, or actually discarded, meteorite specimens in fear of being made a laughingstock for their belief in stones from the sky. The Swiss geologist J. André de Luc reputedly said that even if he saw a meteorite fall he would not believe it. But such doubters by then were the exceptions.

After the mid-1800s, virtually all of the scientific community had come around and further had shifted from a lunar origin of meteorites to an origin in the asteroid belt. The first asteroid was spotted in 1801. By 1870 more than a hundred were known, and by 1890 the number had grown to some 300. Since the discovery of asteroids, which showed that "empty" space was not at all empty, it seemed easier to believe in meteorites as cosmic visitors. By the time thirty asteroids had been identified, some in the scientific community assumed they might be pieces of that mythical planet torn asunder by Jupiter's strong gravitational force and that commonly dropped in on Earth. In 1849 we find the illustrious German geophysicist Friedrich Wilhelm Heinrich Alexander Baron von Humboldt calling meteorites "the smallest of all asteroids."

Valid Status for the Pallas Nugget

Although Howard's work may have given meteorites in general a respectable name, it did not cinch the case of the cosmic origin of the Pallas Iron. Despite Biot's study of the L'Aigle fall, in 1872 the general mining inspector of France, addressing a meeting of the Paris Geological Society, denied the cosmic origin of the Pallas Iron in particular. Investigations on an island off Greenland had revealed that suspected meteorites found there actually were of the same composition as local ore deposits and, therefore, most probably did not have a cosmic origin. The Pallas Iron, he argued, most likely would be found to have the same iron composition as the iron ore outcrop discovered by Medvedev and so would revert to its humble status as a mere terrestrial artifact of normal geologic processes.

To settle the argument, in August of the following year the St. Petersburg Academy dispatched mining engineer I. A. Lopatin to do a thorough analysis of the outcrop so that its composition could be compared with that of the Pallas Iron. In his 1874 report Lopatin said he could find no inclusions of nugget iron in the ore outcrop that even closely resembled the Pallas Iron. So the Lump regained its cosmic respectability.

There is one more historical persona in our saga of the Pallas Nugget who should be included. He was the Berlin mineralogist Gustav Rose who in 1825 had investigated the crystalline structure of olivine in the Pallas Meteorite. Some of the crystals had thin little pipelike structures, sometimes empty, other times filled with material of a color different from the yellowish translucent color of the olivine crystals. On the basis of his work, Rose became the first to introduce a new class of stony-iron meteorites, all of which were similar to the Pallas Iron and so came to be called *pallasites*. It was the Russian geologist P. N. Chirvinsky (1889-1955) who then classified pallasites as intermediary between irons and stones.

If a specific time and place could be given for the occasion of the Pallas Meteorite earning its wings, it might be July 1, 1902, near St. Petersburg. On that day anyone who happened to be looking up saw a bolide burn its way across the sky and crash onto the shore of Ladoga Lake in the region of Marialachti Bay. When it struck, it shattered and splashed fragments over a radius of 50 meters. The largest fragment weighed 22.7 kilograms and when analyzed was found to virtually duplicate all the previous findings of the structure and composition of pallasites. By the mid-1900s there were some forty known pallasites, but only two had been observed as bolides that were later recovered.

After the Pallas Iron was cut and one surface polished, it became an object of public interest for its rare beauty. However, with its detailed analysis and classification complete, the scientists had finished with it. But the end of its story had yet to be written.

Meet Alina Eremeyeva

Author of the final chapter, or at least an "afterword," to the story of the Pallas Iron is Alina Eremeyeva, historian of astronomy of the Russian Academy of Sciences and a former member of the prestigious Committee on Meteorites. Determined, dedicated, stubborn, at times inflexible, immensely likable, scholarly, highly emotional, energetic, and spunky are some of the terms that describe this remarkable woman of sixty-eight when I interviewed her in 1997. Her courage and resolve were demonstrated when, during the years of Stalin's reign of terror, she openly criticized him. She was lucky not to have been sent off to a gulag as a dissident. Instead, she was kicked off the Committee of Meteorites but allowed to retain her academic appointment.

In the 1970s Alina was shown a letter from Yerphin Vladermov who wrote to the Committee suggesting that some sort of memorial be established at the meteorite's fall site. Alina liked the idea and decided to do something about it. But where, exactly, was the fall site? It had not been visited in more than 100 years. Who knew the way?

Mining engineer I. A. Lopatin's 1873 detailed account of the site, along with his map, could not be found in the archives. All Alina had to go on were the less precise accounts of Pallas and Mettich. Although some suspect that Pallas himself had never visited the site, Alina thinks he probably did, since he was not known to describe any site he had not first visited. Amid the difficulties of penetrating the remote and dense mountainous country, as I was to experience on my expedition there, Alina led three search expeditions over three years before narrowing the fall site down to a few square meters.

On her first expedition in 1976, all she had was Mettich's description of the site and an old map that lacked coordinates. Her party of four first had to locate the Ubei River, a tributary to the Yenisei, which they found without difficulty. Next they had to find the Maliy Izhat River, a tributary to the Ubei. Following the Maliy Izhat upstream and then climbing a ridge would, presumably, bring them to the iron ore outcrop by the big rock described by Medvedev and Mettich. Then walking southwest uphill a distance of 150 lachters (315 meters) would bring them to the site where Mettich and Medvedev had found the 700-kilogram lump of iron.

It seemed simple enough to Alina. The only thing was that she led her group past the Maliy (meaning "small") Izhat and directed their route instead up the Bolshoi (meaning "large") Izhat, a few kilometers beyond. On making the steep climb up to the ridge, they found neither the ore outcrop nor the big rock, and they were unable to identify any rocks with revealing signs of magnetite. Discouraged, the little group returned to Moscow. Alina decided she needed a better map, and maybe a geologist.

The 1977 Expedition

The following year she was back again, this time with Alexander Andreev, a mineralogist, as part of her troop and a map that at least showed distances. It was Alexander who would lead my 1997 Pallas expedition and join me on an expedition to the Arctic in 1999. Because of a particularly heavy spring runoff from melting snow, small tributaries to the Mali Izhat were swollen and once again Alina, in the lead, went right past it to the Bolshoi Izhat and the wrong valley leading to the ridge. Consulting his map, Alexander began to be suspicious. Nevertheless, Alina led the group up the Bolshoi Izhat where they pitched camp.

"The local geography simply didn't match certain markings on the map," Alexander told me. "Now Alina can be very emotional and stubborn," he explained, "so I had to trick her to show her that she was wrong." He convinced her to stay in camp for the rest of the day to review her detailed notes of the previous year's expedition while he and two others explored the area. With only a compass and the poor map, Alexander was able to show that they had indeed bypassed the Maliy Izhat by several kilometers and instead had gone up the Bolshoi Izhat. His proof was the caves indicated on the map. At first Alina refused to believe him, saying, "What kind of a geologist are you. You can't even tell the difference between the Bolshoi Izhat and the Maliy Izhat!" Alexander next asked Alina to please check her diary of her earlier trip against distances shown on the map. Then he asked her how it could possibly have taken them seven hours to hike from the mouth of the Ubei to the mouth of their river if the distance were only four kilometers. And what about the caves? Alina reluctantly agreed that she had been wrong.

After hiking back down along the Ubei and finding the mouth of the Maliy Izhat, they made their way upstream, climbed to the top of the ridge, and began looking for the ore outcrop. But there was no outcrop. By then their expedition time had run out, and they were forced to return to Krasnoyarsk.

Once back in Krasnoyarsk, Alexander advised Alina to look through every geological report she could find for the 1700s and early 1800s to identify the exact location of the outcrop described by Mettich and Medvedev, and later by Lopatin. Meanwhile Alexander took up the search and found just what he was looking for, a topographic map of the area with coordinates.

The Outcrop and the Rock

The summer of 1978 found their expedition of seven back at the base camp at the foot of the ridge on the Maliy Izhat. The next day Alina and Alexander, armed against bears, climbed the ridge. At one point they saw a beautiful red elk motionless and staring at them. "Oh, shoot him, shoot him," Alina urged. "We have no meat on the expedition." Alexander didn't have the heart, and they watched the animal vanish into the forest with three great leaps.

Before long they came to a tree that Alexander had marked with a cross the previous year. Then they came to a big rock. Alina felt it must be the rock described by Mettich and that the magnetite outcrop must be right beside it. "You are the geologist, so now find the magnetite," Alina commanded. Alexander examined every centimeter of ground around the rock while Alina waited impatiently. "There is no magnetite here," he told her. "How come there is a rock but no magnetite?" Alina demanded. Alexander said they should search further.

About fifteen minutes later they came to another big rock. Again, Alexander carefully examined the ground all around the rock but found nothing. An annoyed Alina asked, "What kind of a geologist are you anyway? Have you never seen magnetite in your life? How come two rocks and still no magnetite?"

Alexander said they should keep looking. Before long they came to a small ditch that made Alexander suspicious. He recognized it as the kind of ditch dug by prospectors to sample ore specimens. He climbed in and began examining the rocks. He tossed one up to Alina and told her to hold her compass against it. The needle spun wildly. "There's your magnetite," said Alexander. "OK," she said, "there's magnetite here, but where's the rock?" Alexander climbed back out of the ditch, looked around, and then made his way to what appeared to be a large mound of vegetation. As he tore away at it, he exposed the face of a very big rock. "And here's your rock!" he exclaimed. Alina clasped her small hands beneath her chin and beamed.

They next cut off a 25-meter length of rope and measured their way the 150 lachters southwest uphill. Alexander marked the spot with two crosses, and since then the spot has been known as the Peak of Two Crosses. Next they measured off a 25-square-meter plot, which they felt confident would include the fall point of the meteorite, as described by Mettich.

The plan was to take core samples at nineteen locations within the plot in hopes of finding trace substances of the meteorite. The first three samples came from locations several meters apart. On washing and screening them, they found tiny flecks of shiny metal in all three samples. Could it be nickel? While taking a fourth core, Alexander became suspicious as he worked his aluminum digging tool and noticed numerous tiny nicks. Could the flecks of shiny metal be shavings from his small shovel? When evaluated back in Moscow, not one of the nineteen core samples contained anything that could be associated with the Pallas Iron. At the clearing where they took their samples they erected a 3-meter-high larch pole with a small sign bearing the initials for the Pallas Iron (ПЖ), and Alina heated a nail and burned the year "1978" into the pole.

In preparation for the design of a monument for the Pallas Iron, the following year they returned to the fall site, this time with one of Russia's best-known sculptors, Yuri Ishkanov. He had told them that in order to design a monument, he would first have to see the site.

Once again, this time because of a particularly heavy spring runoff from melting snow, small tributaries to the Maliy Izhat were swollen beyond recognition, and the group mistook one for the Maliy Izhat. This led them up the wrong valley toward the ridge. When Alexander realized their mistake and said they should turn back, Alina decided to "do a little research." Alexander told me, "Climbing down from her horse, our energetic Alina said, 'I'll just go up that mountain and have a look.'" Alexander said they would wait for her, but "Please come back," he pleaded.

Alexander continued, "So she dismounted and began climbing and climbing until she was swallowed up by the dense vegetation, reeds, and grasses in places being well over her head. The climb was steep, but she made it and nearly reached the location of the pole without realizing it. She decided not to rejoin us, thinking our group would soon follow and find her. We waited and waited, becoming more and more anxious. Meanwhile, Alina was up there waiting for us, and it would soon begin to get dark. What to do? She didn't have a gun, or matches, or food, or water, and we were afraid that she might meet a bear. That could mean real trouble."

Alexander decided that he and one of the guides would wait for Alina in case she decided to come back down. He sent the rest of the group back to the Maliy Izhat and told them to build a big fire so that Alina might see it if she were lost. Before night set in, Alexander and the guide decided to join the others, fearing that the horses might break a leg in the difficult terrain. There was no Alina all night.

Early the next morning they climbed up to the ridge and after much yelling found her at the previous year's campsite. "She was wet with dew, cold, hungry, and thirsty. We were so happy to find her alive," Alexander recalled. When Alina related the event to me, she said, "I was so miserable. I was without rations, without a knife or matches or a gun, and I had only moss for a pillow and bears for companions."

"We were so overwhelmed with joy to find her that we decided to punish her," Alexander said. "Yuri poured her half a glass of vodka and made her drink it down 'so you won't catch a cold,' he told her. Then I admonished, 'When you are on your horse, I am going to bind your feet together under your horse's belly. Next I will tie the reins of your horse to the tail of my horse. Then see if you can escape from us again!'"

When they arrived at the fall site, Yuri examined the location and made a sketch for the monument. It was to be a large disk that included streaks forming an arched trajectory of the meteorite. Alina said no. Meteorites don't fall that way. They fall in straight lines, so make the trajectory straight. Yuri said that for artistic reasons the trajectory must be curved. They argued. "My attempts to make them find a compromise were not quite successful," said Alexander. Later, when the monument was completed, the trajectory was represented by straight lines. The group retraced their steps down the mountain, back to the village of Kulcheck, then to Krasnoyarsk.

My 1997 Expedition

I've been told that probably fewer than fifty people have ever been to the fall site of the Pallas Iron, and it's no wonder considering the obstacle-course nature of the terrain that has to be navigated to reach the site. The expedition of six that Katya organized for July 1997 was the first to visit the site in sixteen years. It began in Moscow where I spent several hours interviewing Alina at the History of Astronomy Institute at Moscow University and the Fersman Mineralogical Museum where two slices of the Pallas Iron rest in a glass case. Only a few feet across an aisle from the famed meteorite, and a papier-mâché replica of the intact meteorite, was the beautiful 1745-kilogram iron from Sikhote-Alin with its wavy surface deeply pitted with rhegmaglypts. To be in the presence of two such magnificent treasures was a moving experience. And there on an adjacent wall hung the famous Sikhote-Alin oil painting by Yakov Medvedev. Although the museum was officially closed for renovation, its curator Dimitri Belakovsky was kind enough to let us visit for as long as we wished. He spent some two hours enthusiastically describing many of its mineral treasures and removing prized specimens for us to examine.

Late in the evening of July 7 a car picks us up at our Moscow apartment and takes us to the Domodedovo Airport for our 11:00 P.M. flight to Krasnoyarsk. Domodedovo is for domestic flights, while Cheremetyevo Airport is for foreign flights. The two are 100 kilometers apart. As usual, we are overweight with my two duffel bags, my big backpack, and Katya's carry-on bag. But not to worry (*niet problema*), as I have come to learn from Katya. As we wait to be weighed in, she scans the line ahead and behind us and says, "Stay here. I'll be right back." Minutes later she returns smiling and saying, "I found a nice lady without luggage who said she'd check one of your duffels through for us," whereupon she drags one duffel bag away.

The cavernous waiting area where we check in is dirty, inadequately lit, and packed with overheated and grouchy humanity impatient to board the plane, cool off, and go to sleep. After a forty-five minute wait in front of an unmarked gate that we all presume to be for Krasnoyarsk, the iron gate clanks open and the cattle stampede through, shoving and groaning. We go down an unlit iron stairway and then sprint to the airplane. The route takes us under one of its wings and only feet away from one of its jet engines roaring with ear-splitting intensity and flooding the area with noxious jet fuel fumes. If it hadn't been hot enough to keep you away, you could have reached out and touched the engine. After the final stampede up the boarding stairs, through the luggage compartment, and up another flight of stairs to the passenger compartment, we find seats together and collapse into them.

"Give me the baggage claim checks and your passport," Katya says. "I just want to make sure everything will be OK in Krasnoyarsk." I hand over my passport with the tickets and claim checks and watch as she examines them. "Oh, oh," she says, pointing to a line in my visa. The Russian consulate in New York had made a mistake. Instead of typing Krasnoyarsk as one of the cities I would be permitted to visit, someone had typed "Krasnodar," which is some 4000 kilometers eastward in the Crimea! "This could be a serious problem," Katya says frowning. "When we register you with the Krasnoyarsk KGB, we will have to ask for a reauthorization. It might be easy, or they could cause trouble. It depends on the KGB agent we get and what mood he happens to be in." Four hours later in flight time and eight hours later by clock time we touch down uneventfully at the Krasnoyarsk airport, where by now I am beginning to feel at home.

Two days later, at 10:00 A.M., Alexander and the crew pick us up at Katya's apartment. We are fortunate to have Alexander as our leader. There is also Alexey Kovalyov, a major in the militia who is to be our armed guard and expedition assistant; Dima Yurkovsky, digger-in-chief of the Chinge expedition; and Sergei Kovlov whose Jeep Cherokee will take us the 250 kilometers from Krasnoyarsk to Kulcheck, which is located at 54° 54′ N and 91° 25′ E. The car is full. Two duffel bags and four backpacks are wrapped in a tarp and tied onto the roof rack. The rest of the gear is stuffed inside. I'm in front with Sergei while Katya, Alexander, and Alexey are squashed into the back seat with supplies underfoot. We have what must be a field of potatoes, onions, a huge box of tomatoes, cereals, four chickens, lots of cheese, cucumbers, milk, macaroni, canned corn, smoked fish, meat, boiled eggs, a dozen loaves of excellent Russian brown bread, tea, and coffee. At the last village before we start our climb into the mountains, we'll take on more supplies as needed.

Our first stop is Krasnoyarsk's KGB office, where the agent on duty fortunately is in a good mood and reauthorizes my visa for only a small fee. Another stop to get a popped-out lens of my glasses fixed and the frames realigned in a state-operated optical shop, which costs me 34 cents, a welcomed remnant of some of the beneficial aspects of socialism. Our final stop on the way out of town is to pick up Dima, who makes a nest among the luggage and supplies in the back. A few kilometers beyond the city is a famous steep climb with a very long switchback section of road called the Mother-in-Law, so named, according to Katya, "because it never seems to end." We follow the mighty Yenisei for much of our journey. Sergei's style of driving is typically Russian, meaning reckless by American standards. The centerline is simply a decoration to be ignored. You drive all over the road as it suits you, pass on hills or on the right or left, speed as fast as you can on the straightaway and up hills, and then coast down the other side for as long as you can to a crawl to save fuel. All Russian cars have spiderweblike windshields from rocks being flung by the tire treads of the car you happen to be tailgating. Police barricades, even in the remote countryside, are common. You are forced to slow down to a crawl in order to funnel through a narrow section of road where usually two police officers with tightly gripped batons eye you suspiciously as you pass through. Sometimes, if it suits them, they stop you and search the car.

Four hours after leaving Krasnoyarsk, most of the time through heavy rain, we reach the Yenisei River ferry crossing at the village of Novosyolovo just after 3:00 P.M. We have missed the ferry, which runs on a schedule of sorts, by half an hour and will have to wait six hours for the next one. This means that we'll be setting up our first camp on the other side just before midnight. The ferry ramp is a rugged iron affair like those iron mesh bridges that make your tires hum. It looks strong enough to support a military tank or two despite its being perched partly on a fairly steep incline and partly on the gravel beach. The ramp itself is about 10 meters long and 6 meters wide. Out of the blue Katya announces that the next ferry is at 7:00 P.M. When I ask how she knows, she just shrugs. I nap in the car and get poked by Katya at 7 o'clock. The sun is shining, and several cars ahead of us in line have begun to spin their tires up the iron grid ramp and bounce onto the deck of the ferry. I wonder how many tailpipe assemblies get tossed overboard each week. I count thirty cars and trucks by the time a man with a red flag waves off three remaining cars that can't be accommodated.

Several days of heavy rains in the area have turned the 12 kilometers of narrow dirt road from the ferry to our first village, Koma, into deeply rutted mud with hidden potholes. We never know just how deep the next mud pond will be. Alexander invents a new unit of measure called "bps," for bumps per second. Two hours of creeping our way along, mostly in four-wheel drive, take us through the villages of Koma and Chonya Koma, and around midnight to the village of Kulcheck, where we will stay overnight and in the morning try to find transportation into the mountains. But where will we stay? There are no hotels.

"I kind of like that house over there," Alexander says jokingly. Alexander looks at Alexey, Alexey looks at Alexander, and the two climb out, approach the house, and begin knocking on the door. A few minutes later lights come on and a sleepy young man appears, very surprised to see someone in uniform carrying a gun and wearing a knife. It takes a few minutes to reassure him. He turns out to be the geography teacher in the local school. Alexy explains that the late-night visit is unofficial and humanitarian, that we are humble travelers in seek of shelter. He quickly dresses and rides with us to the schoolhouse, which he unlocks and where we are permitted to sleep in the gym with large exercise mats as sleeping pads. After twenty minutes, we even have running water.

The young teacher was Victor Ivanovich Evmenov, who would be the pride of any middle school anywhere. Born in Kulcheck, he went through teacher training at the Krasnoyarsk Pedagogical Institute and chose to return to his small village. At his own expense, he had recently painted his geography classroom, which was immaculate in every detail. Stubs of chalk were frugally clustered in the chalk tray, and the six student tables gleamed with fresh paint. He had made all of the teaching aids, including detailed topographic maps and charts showing the local terrain, rainfall, soil composition, and agricultural productivity. He had even painted a 5-meter-long ecological profile of soil types, elevation, and other geographical features across Russia from west to east. Surely, this was a gifted and devoted teacher, attested to by the $50 award he had earned for being the best geography teacher in the region. Before leaving his school, I presented him with another "award" of $50 for classroom supplies. He was extremely embarrassed, and grateful.

Our first task the following morning is to find some kind of vehicle that can take us into the forest and as close as possible to what will be our base camp at the foot of Mt. Bolshoi Imir. This, by the way, is not the route Alina and Alexander had followed on their expeditions along the Ubei River and then up the Maliy Izhat river valley. The local logging collective has a Gorkey 166 truck, a marvel of Russian automotive engineering, but to rent it and a driver we first need permission from the mayor of the territory. When reached by telephone, he shouts, "What? An American in my territory? Why wasn't I informed?" Apparently, no foreigner had set foot in Kulcheck in living memory. It turns out that the mayor isn't angry, but surprised and delighted to have his first American visitor. "Of course, he may have the truck and Nickolai will drive him," the mayor says, "and I wish to welcome him on his way back." My experience has been that once out of the large cities and away from your typical rude bureaucrat the village officials and people bend over backward to be accommodating, especially if you have a militia man with a gun. That has been the case virtually every place I have traveled throughout rural Russia, even without a militia man as a companion, from Estonia in the west to the shores of the Russian Far East.

The morning is cloudless with the cleanest air and clearest visibility imaginable. The little school is situated on a small hill overlooking the village and surrounding countryside. We are in a land of rolling hills and sprawling fields of wheat and oats rimmed by distant, low, forested mountains, among which we are soon to be. Farming, cattle breeding, and small dairy industries are the main means of livelihood in the region. I am surprised to see a small group of men chatting with Alexey and Alexander outside the gym. Two of them had been guides on Alina's and Alexander's expeditions. They are interested to see what the American looks like and to renew Alexander's acquaintance. By then everyone in the village knows that I am in town. There is only one telephone number for the entire village, and many had surely listened in on Alexander's conversation with the mayor.

The next leg of our journey is by the Gorkey. We spend about four hours going through dense forest, up and down numerous steep hills, and through thick reedlike growth up to 2 meters high. We make fourteen river crossings. The waters are deep and swift enough to cause me more than passing concern, especially whenever my side of the truck is facing downriver, which means that I will be pinned to the bottom if the truck is toppled over by the strong current. But not once does the Gorkey even teeter threateningly, although the current snarls above the wheel tops and water splashes up through the floorboards. I am beginning to think that if we will it to, that the Gorkey will swim. Several of the river crossings are of the wildly meandering Ubei Ozera ("Kill Lake"), so named in a legend dating back to before 1749. It seems that gold was discovered in the river, and when word spread, gold miners began to come to the region from far away. Since the villagers wanted the gold for themselves, they simply killed the outsiders one by one as they appeared.

There is no road as we continue to crash our way through the forest, follow river valleys, and slosh through endless bogs. Sometimes the Gorkey bounces over fallen trees; other times it just bulldozes them out of the way. At one stage while crossing a bog, with giant mosquitoes, even larger biting flies, and other insects that probably haven't even been classified by taxonomists, the Gorkey's wheels lose their grip and simply moan as they spin, and the truck starts to sink into the mud. Everybody climbs out, and I can see us abandoning the truck and hiking through God knows what is ahead for six hours or more. The truck has settled into the bog to about three-quarters of its wheel height, and its wheels are very big. As if this were routine, Nickolai gives Sergei a long-handled shovel and tells him to start digging out the front left wheel. He then gives Alexey an axe and tells him to chop down two birch trees that he points out.

With one of the trees serving as a log support running along the side of the Gorkey from front to rear wheels, the end of the other tree is tucked under the large front wheel hub. The rest of us then line up along the tree angled up in the air and first pull and then push it down, using it as a lever with the support tree serving as a fulcrum. As we hold the wheel suspended high out of the mud, Sergei begins stuffing broken limbs and branches under it and then with more branches makes a ramp in front of both front wheels. After jacking up the front left wheel twice in this way and building a log base under it, we then attack the other three wheels in the same manner. An hour and a half later, exhausted and left nearly bloodless by the hordes of insects, we pile back into the Gorkey and, miraculously, proceed on our way through the bog. I welcome another river crossing, which at least will wash off the mud, but I do not welcome the bog on the other side. Once again my heart sinks as the Gorkey does the same. Stuck again. Where is my cell phone so I can call the AAA? By now experienced in such trivial inconveniences, we dig and chop and stuff and free the Gorkey, this time in less than an hour. "Nothing to it," Katya says, rubbing the dripping mascara from her face.

About two hours later we emerge from the forest, which by contrast seems like a respectable secondary road, and into another bog. Five minutes later the Gorkey squishes to a stop, stuck for the third time. It is nine thirty and the light is just beginning to fade. A conference with Nickolai determines that we will set up camp in a nearby cluster of trees on relatively dry ground and face reality in the morning. A campfire, several rounds of vodka, and hot soup make life better, except for the bugs, which in Siberia never go to bed. In addition to the mosquitoes there are large flies that leave a visible pit in your flesh where they eat you. Nobody had told them about insect repellant. When I am snug and warm in my sleeping bag, I review the events of a day I will be unlikely ever to forget. I also wonder what new adventures tomorrow will bring.

I am awakened by what sounds like someone chopping down a tree. When I emerge from my tent, I find the camp vibrant with activity. Katya has a breakfast of hot cereal, tea, and bread toasted over the coals waiting for me. Like ants, Sergei, Nickolai, and Alexey are trooping back and forth between the Gorkey and the forest carrying large lengths of birch logs and branches, and Victor, the geography teacher, is busy shoveling out from under one wheel. Alexander has already taken down his tent and is packed. The plan is for Alexander, Katya, and me to hike the remainder of the way, about three hours, to the foot of Mt. Bolshoi Imir and a small cabin that will serve as our base camp. Once the Gorkey is free ("Hah, nothing to it!"), Nickolai and Victor will drive back to Kulcheck while Alexey, Sergei, and Dima will follow our trail and join us at the cabin. Alexey has given Alexander the gun in case we have unwanted companions. Wherever there is a cabin in the wilderness, bears have learned that there may well be a store of dried food, crumbs, or tin cans to lick.

The hike to the cabin is one I do not relish repeating, much of it through bogs where the weight of our backpacks makes us sink into the muck to the top of our Wellingtons (calf-high rubber boots) or over. Every now and then one of my Wellingtons stays stuck in the ooze and I am left staggering for my balance with one soaked stocking foot waving in the air. Alexander once gets so stuck with both boots that we have to pull him out. The small flies, similar to Maine's black flies, are so thick that as soon as I remove the lens cap from a camera at least 200 of the tiny critters swarm on the lens, making it impossible to take a photograph. Another 100 or more hover around my head. We would be miserable without our net hats. Alexander leads our march to clear the way for any venomous snakes that we might encounter. Katya insists on bringing up the rear so she can keep an eye out for ticks on my clothing. So the three of us slog our way through tall grasses up to our shoulders, sometimes over our heads, sloshing through three streams from which we gratefully drink. The cold mountain stream water feels good as it trickles down my throat and flows over the tops of and into my boots, which from time to time I empty, leaning against one of my companions for support. There is a profusion of wild flowers, none of which, except for giant purple thistlelike plants, I can identify. There are also large blue lupinlike flowers and among the grasses next to the ground a profusion of small flowers resembling violets. Color is everywhere, and all is beautiful.

As soon as we arrive at the cabin we start a fire and feed it with wet branches to maintain a smoke signal to guide the others, although you don't have to be a Boy Scout to follow the trail we must have left. Every fifteen minutes or so we use our hatchet to vigorously beat on a large scrap of iron hanging by a length of rope from the cabin eaves, a gong that serves as an audible beacon in case the others fail to see our smoke or lose our trail through the woods. When they arrive, they report seeing many bear tracks and one viper. The bears apparently have picked up our scent on the trail and are curious. Alexey, Sergei, and Dima have been carrying backpacks stacked higher than their heads and weighing at least 20 kilograms each; Sergei's probably weighs closer to 27 kilograms. How they managed them through the bogs I can't imagine. The backs of both of Dima's hands, the thumbs of which he kept hooked in front of him under the backpack straps to ease the load, are bloody and swollen from insect bites. Dripping wet with sweat, they laugh at seeing us huddled around the fire. With a choice of inhaling insects or smoke, Katya says, we have chosen the smoke.

Alexey, Sergei, and Dima had worked until 3:00 P.M. prying the Gorkey out and seeing Nickolai and Victor on their way back to Kulcheck. The plan is for the Gorkey to return for us at our first campsite in two days, or if Victor can locate a caterpillar track vehicle, he will try to make it all the way to the cabin. The boys have been hiking for four and a half hours. It is nearly 8:00 P.M. by the time someone breaks out the vodka and the three join us around the fire. At one stage Dima asks me how old I am. I tell him seventy-three. He says they have been discussing how courageous and fit someone my age has to be to undertake such an expedition, which would discourage most people half my age. I tell him that if I were half my age I'd probably have enough sense not to be here. We all laugh.

The cabin, which is to be our home for two days, was built in 1981 by one of the guides we met back in Kulcheck. It is made of 23-centimeter-diameter aspen logs with moss caulking. Inside is a raised pine plank platform wide enough for four people to sleep on.

The following morning before we began the climb up the mountain, we find ourselves in a near blizzard of butterflies, beautiful black creatures with orange markings and wingspans of some 8 centimeters. They are not Monarchs. They fill the air and follow us partway on our climb. While I am taking notes by the cabin, one butterfly lands on the knuckle of my index finger and just stays there, aspirating for three lines of notes before flying away. "Maybe it didn't like what you were writing," Katya observes. There must be a thousand butterflies dancing around me and delightfully clouding the air.

Despite no trace of the tracks made by the bulldozer that carried the 1.5-ton cast-iron monument to the Pallas Iron up the mountain sixteen years earlier, Alexander remembers the way. I carry only my video camera, big knife, and two Nikons. I always keep slide film in one camera and print film in the other, often duplicating shots. As the foot stomps, it is a three-hour, 5-kilometer trek, but it is probably much shorter as the crow flies. The climb is steep all the way and made especially difficult by many areas of vegetation so dense that we have to hack our way through. How on Earth Medvedev managed his way down this mountain with the meteorite I'll never know, and with each step my admiration for Alina on her solo climb, "with only moss for a pillow and bears as companions," grows. At one stage, Katya senses that Alexander's pace is becoming too much for me and takes the lead. Another reason for her taking the lead is to serve as a tick trap for my protection. Her instincts for such things are remarkable, and her chief concerns are for my comfort.

After two and three-quarter hours, a beaming Alexander leads us into the small clearing where he and Alina had planted the ПЖ pole on their 1978 expedition, at the spot where Mettich and Medvedev had discovered the meteorite. From there it is a short walk to the site of the monument that had been designed by Yuri Ishkanov. It is a cast-iron disk 2 meters in diameter. It had been hauled up the mountain in four pieces by a bulldozer in 1980 and was then assembled and erected atop a concrete base poured by a small group of students from Krasnoyarsk.

Neither Alina nor Alexander was present at that historic event. However, both returned the following year to take part in the dedication ceremony, complete with a television correspondent from Krasnoyarsk. According to Alexander, everyone was chatting happily, patting the monument, and congratulating each other, except Alina who sat silent and glum on the base of the monument, chin in hands and near tears.

"She was very sad," says Alexander. "Nearly six years of continuous efforts, extremely difficult trips to this place, and now it was over."

On reaching the monument, we celebrate with a bottle of Russian champagne that Dima has secretly carried all the way from Krasnoyarsk, and we toast Alina. Sergei, with a triumphant grin, produces a tin of sliced pineapple. Alexander then ceremoniously presents each of us with a Pallas Meteorite commemorative pin in honor of our achievement. It is a proud moment, and I am deeply moved.

By the time we have built a fire and are cooking lunch, it has begun to rain buckets. After lunch, Alexander takes us to the famous rock and pit where he had found the magnetite. Climbing in, he starts tossing up souvenir chunks to us. Mine now sits on a coffee table by the fireplace, and I often heft it with fond and vivid memories.

The way back down the mountain takes nearly as long as the climb up because of mud and slippery rain-soaked tree limbs hidden underfoot by the tall grasses. It is around 7:00 P.M. by the time we reach the cabin and our tent to find paw prints the size of a large frying pan and bear excrement by the cabin door. Alexey smiles, shrugs, and pats his gun, which, by the way, always stays wherever Roy is.

By the next morning the rain has stopped and we climb into our backpacks for the trek back to our campsite where the Gorkey had been stuck. Our clothes are still damp despite our attempts to dry them by the fire. The hike back takes about three hours, with Alexander getting stuck again and our first having to pry him out of his backpack and then tug and drag him out of the mud. As we break out of the tall grass near our old campsite, there is a grinning Nickolai leaning with arms folded against the front bumper of the Gorkey. Our initial exuberance fades to moans when we realize that the Gorkey is stuck. Immediately Sergei grabs the shovel and directs the others to start to work with the two birch logs. Meanwhile, Katya and I get a fire going with wet wood, and in about an hour we are all enjoying a late afternoon lunch with bread baked only a few hours earlier by Nickolai's wife. She has also sent along a jar of delicious red currant preserves. By 5 o'clock we are all packed into the Gorkey and begin a slipping, sliding, and bouncing journey through bog and forest and across rivers back to Kulcheck. Nickolai had come a different way this time, a bit longer but less grueling. It is comforting to have tracks to follow for a change. It is even more comforting to find that Nickolai's wife has fired up the banya for our return.

Recipe for Taking a Banya

A banya is a Russian version of a sauna, where water is splashed onto hot rocks to create a steam bath. Sometimes, instead of splashing water on the hot rocks, beer is used. Inhaling the fumes can be interesting, and "therapeutic," Katya adds. It is supposed to improve respiration and provide comfort to anyone suffering from bronchitis. She says it has the same effect as breathing deeply in a pine or spruce forest, where many Russian sanatoriums for people suffering with respiratory ailments are located.

1. Enter the banya and sit on the highest-level platform you can endure for fifteen minutes or more. This opens the pores of the skin.
2. Go outside to cool off and drink plenty of cranberry juice and water.
3. Go back in; then splash water onto the stones to create more steam. As the air is heated and the humidity rises, you begin to feel as though

---

you're on fire. You then begin to gently whip yourself and rub your body all over with birch branches with leaves that have been soaked in hot water for an hour. According to Katya, rubbing the soaked birch leaves over the body not only stimulates circulation but causes the skin to absorb through the open pores vitamins along with other "microelements" and volatile oils of the birch leaves. You then wash your hair with the water in which the birch leaves have been soaked.

4. After you feel that you can stand the heat no longer, you rush outside and, if winter, jump into the snow and thrash about, or, if in summer, jump into a lake or river or a large tub of cold water, the colder the better. This causes the heart to beat faster and the surface blood vessels to contract. The open skin pores cause heavy sweating, which cleanses the body.

5. The final step is a soaping down in a shower (if available), a vigorous towel rubdown, and then a rest in the banya's dressing room with tea.

Although I cannot vouch for the claimed therapeutic benefits of a banya as described here, I nevertheless heartily recommend the experience.

One thing that had bothered me about the Pallas Iron's fall site was later cleared up by Alina. How could she be certain that their 25-square-meter patch accurately marked the site? She said that in 1979 she finally managed to track down in the Academy archives the long-missing papers of Lopatin's 1873 expedition, complete with a detailed map.

The site she and Alexander had marked off agreed perfectly with Lopatin's account, she said, banging her little fist into the palm of her hand.

The Pallas Iron Today

In 1825 the Berlin mineralogist G. Rose had suggested that the Pallas Meteorite be sliced and one surface polished and etched to reveal a crystal pattern, called the Widmanstatten structure. The effort took seemingly forever but was finally completed in 1919 with breathtaking results. According to Alina, "At one time it amazed observers to see the remarkable spectrum of colors of pure olivine, from light green to purple, the drops of which were like gemstones in a setting of sparkling nickel within a sponge matrix of nickel-iron."

Although I had visited the Russian Academy of Sciences' Fersman Mineralogical Museum in Moscow and seen the Pallas meteorite before my expedition, I don't care to see it a second time, but instead let linger in my memory Alina's beautiful description of it. Today the meteorite rests in its original display case, dull and rusting.

CHAPTER 5

Tsarev:
The "Fiery Snake"

My 1998 exploration of the Tsarev (pronounced Tsar-ray-*yov*) meteorite shower impact site in south central Siberia grew out of a suggestion of Valentin Tsvetkov, a long-time friend and colleague and the leading field investigator of Russia's meteorite impact sites. Based on his examination of meteorite fall dispersion fields—the elliptical area where the shower meteorites landed—he has calculated the orbits of fourteen celestial objects that have ended as meteorite shower fragments. His work at the remote Sikhote-Alin and Chinge sites helped earn him his stony-iron "wings" and international recognition. The other member of our three-person team is Katya, my friend, colleague, and organizer of my previous expeditions to Siberia.

On August 13 the three of us board our 2:00 P.M. train from Moscow for the overnight journey of about 1000 kilometers southeast to the city of Volgograd (formerly Stalingrad), which was all but reduced to rubble and ashes by the

Nazis during World War II. Except for the toilets, the train is clean, the *prahvadneetsah* polite and accommodating. She even brings magazines, orange drinks, and four box dinners, all included in our first-class ticket prices. This is a marked and welcome change from our 1992 Trans-Siberian trip from Moscow to Krasnoyarsk. The train is slow due to a combination of stops at numerous villages and a roadbed badly in need of maintenance along many sections of track. At 5 o'clock Valentin comes into the compartment and asks if we want hot boiled potatoes and warm milk that is being sold by *bábushkas* on the station platform. Despite it being mid-August, there is enough of a chill in the air that the people on the platform are bundled up in long coats, sweaters, and heavy jackets.

Tsarev: A Fallen Village

The next morning finds us in Volgograd, named for Europe's longest river, the Volga, which flows through the heart of the city and terminates in the Caspian Sea after a journey of some 3700 kilometers. At the station we engage a friendly taxi driver who agrees to take us the 80 kilometers east to the village of Tsarev in the district of Leninsk. The driver is to return for us in four days.

Leninsk is a region of seemingly endless and featureless fields browned by the summer drought, a sprawl of hundreds of thousands of hectares of once-lush collective farms, steppe country now all but abandoned since the fall of communism in the early 1990s. That event was calamitous for the formerly thriving villages that gained their sustenance from the state farms. Today, what few farm machines remain are broken and rusted relics. There are no mechanics to repair them, and replacement parts are unobtainable. Even if the parts were obtainable, the villagers have no money to maintain or fuel the huge machines. So they just sit there, industrial tombstones of a former age of plenty.

At their peak, the 110,000 hectares of farmland of the Tsarev State Farm supported 36,000 sheep, 3000 milk cows, poultry, and large herds of beef cattle. Tending their fields of barley, rice, corn, wheat, and mustard plants kept more than 5000 villagers fully employed and happily prosperous. Then came the fall of communism and the economic collapse of the farm collectives. In 1992 and 1993 each family of the state farm workers was given 19 hectares to "own" and work. But with the distribution of free land, most of the farm machinery in working order quickly disappeared, so few of the new landowners had the means to work the land, and the new privatization laws did not permit a family to sell their acreage. Today, like the fields, the villages have grown fallow with their aging and diminishing populations mostly in their late sixties and seventies. Few young people bother to hang around.

When we drive into the center of town, we pause by a monument that relates high points in the long history of the village. One inscription reads:

"At one time this place was the city of Sarai-Berke, capital of the Golden Horde. A hundred people lived here, and the village was visited by many Russian dukes. Then came the Khans with their ferocious clan battles between Khan Takhtamysh and Khan Timur. The latter Khan captured and then demolished the city of Sarai-Berke in 1395."

There is not a car, tractor, wagon, motorcycle, bicycle, or dog in sight, only dust raised by our car as we creep along the unpaved streets. Small houses, virtually all in disrepair, and virtually all painted with blue trim like virtually all the houses in virtually all Russian villages, line the streets. Beside and in the rear of each house is a vegetable garden, manicured and nurtured with the care that comes of necessity. Its yield will support its owners not only through the summer, but through the coming winter. Dozens of jars of preserves line the small front porches and hallways and fill the corners of every room. Where there is not a garden, there are squealing and snorting pigs, and hens scratching and pecking the hard ground. There are gaggles of geese and paddlings of preening ducks in dirty ditch water. Behind each house is a large mound of hay and a shed housing one or two cows. In most kitchens is an electric cream separator and a tub for making butter. By most houses one or two goats, tethered to an iron pipe carelessly driven into the ground, nibble at the dusty ground.

Looking down the long brown streets for those who tend these houses and their animals, I spot only two large women sitting in the dilapidated shelter that was once a bus stop. One appears elderly—but it's sometimes hard to tell with Russian farm people—and the other is probably in her twenties. Despite the heat, their heads are shawled, and their fat fingers work meaningfully as they talk in hushed voices, foreheads nearly touching.

Tsvetkov points to them, and our driver, Alexi, slowly turns the wheel and approaches their bench. As Tsvetkov climbs out, they stop talking, eyeing us more with suspicion than curiosity. But after listening to Tsvetkov for a few moments, they are smiling, gesturing, and drawing a street map in the air. Tsvetkov climbs back in and jerks a finger, indicating one of the hushed streets. We bounce along and splash through two deep puddles made by a leaking water pipe until we are forced to stop under a large larch tree beside an aging fence that encloses a compound of huts, neglected shrubbery, an apple tree, and a weed-choked yard. Seeming to know exactly where he is going, Tsvetkov disappears into a small house with a whitewashed clay exterior. We climb out of the car and maintain a respectful distance from the gate.

Five minutes later, Tsvetkov, smiling broadly, walks toward us in the company of the female owner. Like so many Russians of her generation, she displays several large gold teeth that flash in the sunlight. Some say that most of Russia's mineral wealth is stored in the mouths of its socialist citizens. In her sixties, she is very much overweight and exudes an abundance of friendliness as she greets us.

She is Lida Nikiforova, widow of the collective farm worker, Boris Nikiforov. (Russian wives take the last name of their husbands and extend them by adding the feminine "a" or "ya" ending.) It was Boris who first discovered Tsarev meteorite fragments and later invited Tsvetkov to stay in his house during Tsvetkov's 1982 expedition to the strewn field. Lida's modest compound of two small houses, two sheds, one outhouse, and a shelter for her two cows and a pair of goats is to be our home for the next several days as we sweep the hot fields a few kilometers distant with our metal detectors. I am the first American ever to visit the village, and within an hour the word is out: "An American is staying in Lida's house!" For Lida, it means instant fame. She makes sure that she is conspicuously by my side during every promenade through town.

While I unpack, Katya and Valentin walk to the village square and post notices advertising our interest in acquiring meteorites and historical information about the Tsarev shower. When Lida is not looking after our immediate needs, she is preparing breakfasts, lunches, or dinners—Russian blintzes with homemade black and red currant preserves, freshly separated cream for our coffee, churned butter for endless servings of dark bread, borscht made with lamb and with thick gobs of heavy cream, fried fish and fish soup from fish just caught by her fifteen-year-old visiting grandson, a bull of a youth who fishes with only his bare hands. And there are elaborate salads of lettuce, tomatoes, chopped potatoes, peas, cucumbers, and other ingredients laced with fresh herbs.

On the first day of our search for meteorites, we hire a local driver who happens to have been born in Chechnya. When he finds out that Katya's home province had been neighboring Ocetia, he refuses to accept money from such a close neighbor, although I manage to hide some in his glove compartment on our last day. We drive to an area of broad flat fields parched from drought. The grass is so brittle that it is like walking on Rice Krispies, snapping, crackling, and popping with every step. Off in the distance I can make out the rusting remains of a water irrigation system long abandoned. Valentine leads us to one of several long median strips of brush and small trees that separate one field from the next. The hunting is best, he says, along the edges of these strips because it was there that the farm workers would deposit "bothersome stones" that interfered with their plowing. During several sweeps with my metal detector over a period of about four hours, I record some thirty "hits," but not of meteorites. All are bits of wire, nails, and broken tractor parts. The next two days are equally unrewarding, and I become convinced that most of the missing Russian tractors of that state farm were long ago reduced to bits and pieces and planted in the fields with hopes of growing new tractors.

Although we do find a sizable meteorite, it is in a most unlikely place. One afternoon, while playing mosquito badminton in Lida's yard, overseen by her dog Bill, named for Bill Clinton, Tsvetkov asks if he can look through a nearby padlocked shed. Lida nods yes and leaves to find the key.

When she returns, she shrugs, shaking her head no. The shed has been locked since her husband's death in 1992, and the key is nowhere to be found. Will it be all right to pry the lock open, Tsvetkov asks? *"Da, da, da"* ("Yes, yes, yes"), she replies, waving encouragingly toward the door. Russian padlocks can be of monumental proportions, and this one is no exception. No available tool will remove either the lock or its hasp. Tsvetkov and Lida's grandson finally manage to detach the hinges from the door and enter the dark shed that way. While we are waiting, I ask Lida why she keeps Bill Clinton tied up; he seems a very friendly dog. She explains that she let her previous friendly dog loose one day and he dispatched seventy-one chickens before she could catch him. Ten minutes later Tsvetkov comes out into the light, holding high before him a large chunk of meteorite that he found hidden in an old accordion case. It had been sectioned and one surface polished. Lida is astonished, and we all cheer. We weigh it on an old set of hanging scales and photograph it. It weighs in at 4.3 kilograms.

Although we had posted one "Meteorites Wanted" notice on a telephone pole by the small shop in the center of town, only the shop owner comes forth with a prize. It turns out to be about the same size as the specimen Tsvetkov found in the shed. We tell her that we don't want to buy it, only examine and photograph it. I'm sure, however, that I could have had it for $50 or less.

Classifying Meteorites

In earlier chapters I mentioned iron meteorites and stony-iron meteorites without adequately distinguishing among the main meteorite groups. Here is the time and place to draw some lines of distinction among at least the three broad classes of meteorites, because in the Tsarev story we are introduced to the stony variety, a breed quite different from the high-nickel-content irons of Chinge, for instance, and the stony-iron pallasites. The bulk of these objects seem to come from the asteroids, that belt of rock/iron rubble in countless orbits largely between Mars and Jupiter.

In the early days, stones that fell from the sky were given a variety of names, or classes, based on not very useful characteristics, and certainly not on their mineral content, which modern meteoritics looks to. They were shooting stars, bolides, fireballs, thunderstones, uranolites, and skystones. Not until 1863 were the present major three divisions proposed—siderites (iron meteorites), siderolites (stony-iron meteorites), and aerolites (stony meteorites).

The Irons

The irons are relatively easy to identify since they are heavy to heft and pull a magnet strongly to them. They are the most likely of space debris to survive their journey through the atmosphere and reach the ground as meteorites, since their ability to resist breaking up or burning up is greater than that of the stony-irons or the stony varieties. The irons contain, as their name implies, mostly iron, but they also have a relatively high component of the element nickel—from about 5 to 50 percent. Such a blend of iron and nickel is rarely found in Earth rocks and so serves as one reliable means of saying whether a random lump of iron found by the seashore is a meteorite or a chunk of discarded ballast from some freighter. Many samples brought to me for identification at my planetarium have been just that—ballast, to the disappointment of their finders. Only the rare mineral Josephinite occurring among Earth rocks might be mistaken for an iron meteorite because of its relatively high nickel content.

The irons also contain compounds called *phosphides* and *sulfides*. This class of meteorites resembles the iron-nickel core of Earth.

When a meteoroid blazes down through the atmosphere, it ablates and casts off tiny particles of melt material that add to the smoky trail it leaves behind. Some of this material, however, is left clinging to the meteoroid and forms a dark coating called a *fusion crust* of the recovered meteorite. Most fusion crusts are very dark, but some stony meteorites with only a little iron have light-colored crusts. The degree of lightness or darkness will depend on the meteorite's composition.

The Stony-Irons

These are a spongelike structure of iron-nickel with the spaces filled in with silicate minerals of igneous rock. The stony-irons are not all that common and are much sought after by collectors for their beauty when cut and a surface polished. Recall Alina's description of the Pallas Iron (Chapter 4), which is a stony-iron. The two most common subclasses are the mesosiderites and pallasites.

Pallasite slices are incredibly beautiful, a mixture of crystalline olivine within a matrix of iron-nickel. Olivine is a rather dense mineral, characteristic of Earth's mantle region that sits just above the core. Because the olivine crystals show little signs of being broken owing to collisional forces, we assume pallasites were formed gently as the molten iron-nickel component flowed among the olivine crystals before cooling. But that is not always the case. Some olivine crystals of pallasites do exhibit signs of shock.

The mesosiderites are different. They tend to have just about as much metal as silicate rock, whereas the pallasites may have twice as much olivine as metal. The mesosiderites have highly fractured and broken pieces of different silicate rocks. It's as though they underwent forceful collisions with other objects, melted, and then resolidified as a jumbled mixture.

Because of their high olivine content, the stony-irons can be thought of as mantle material of a planetlike body. Astronomers envision Earth and the other planets being formed originally from a cloud of iron-silicate lumps of matter called *planetesimals*, Asteroid Eros being a prime candidate. As gravitation pulled the planetesimals together as a sphere and packed them, they melted. The densest materials—iron and nickel—sank into the core region, while the somewhat less dense olivine formed that middle region called the mantle, and the lightest materials of all—the silicates—floated to form the crustal surface rock. In this model, the stony-irons represent the mantle material of such a planetlike object.

The Stony Meteorites

If the irons represent the core of a planetlike body, and the stony-irons represent the mantle, then the stony meteorites represent the rocky crust. Three minerals make up the majority of the most common members of the stony group by weight—olivine makes up nearly half, a mineral group called *pyroxenes* a quarter or less, and iron-nickel grains a few percent. Accessory minerals include iron sulfides and oxides, for example.

It was Gustav Rose who in 1862 classified the stony meteorites according to their mineral composition and structure, dividing them into chondrites and achondrites. The chondrites are the most common, making up some 85 percent or more of *all* meteorite falls. Little spheres of olivines and pyroxenes only a few millimeters wide, called *chondrules*, are what give the chondrites their name. They are curious little structures, quite pretty when sectioned, polished, and viewed under a microscope. They occur as tiny droplets that can be pried out of their matrix. If we could scoop out a handful of the Sun's material and get rid of all the hydrogen and helium, we would be left with a handful of chondrule matter. Although we don't know exactly how chondrules formed, we do know that they don't occur in terrestrial rocks, so they can serve as a reasonably reliable means of distinguishing a stone from the sky from a stone found in your local gravel pit.

Rarest and most primitive of the chondrites are the carbonaceous chondrites, which look more like something you'd use as fuel for your charcoal grill than a prized museum piece. Chemically, they are much like chondrules except that they contain lots of carbon. They also contain water, which indicates that they have not been significantly heated since they formed. Additionally, they contain curious structures that are somewhat larger than the chondrules and that appear white in contrast with their dark gray matrix. These calcium-aluminum inclusions are now thought to be among the earliest minerals ever formed, predating Earth's formation, and probably originating as granular material forged during a supernova explosion more than about six billion years ago. It's a rare treat to hold one of these treasures in your hand—a piece of the Universe older than Earth.

The second main group of the stony meteorites is the achondrites, which are very different from the chondrites. Meaning "without chondrules," the achondrites constitute between 5 and 10 percent of the fewer than 2000 stony meteorites in collections around the world. So they are also considered rare.

The achondrites seem to be chondritic material that underwent heating to the melting point, at which time the chondrules and other material melted. On cooling, a recrystallization process took place, but with the absence of chondrules. Since just such a melting, cooling, and recrystallization process is what produces Earth's igneous crustal rocks, it's no wonder that achondrites so closely resemble Earth rocks. The achondrites are the igneous rocks of another planet.

History of the Tsarev Shower

The Tsarev stony meteorite shower is the largest known stony shower in Russia and one of the largest stony showers in the world, after the Jilin (China) fall of 1976, the Norton County (Kansas) fall of 1948, and the Allende (Mexico) fall of 1969. The Tsarev fall rained down some 1300 kilograms of about eighty recovered chondritic meteorites, dispersing them over an area of some 65 square kilometers. The biggest specimen recovered so far weighs 284 kilograms; the smallest, 50 grams.

Initially, the spectacular shower of Tsarev became better known for the fanciful rumors it generated than for any new light it shed on the study of chondritic meteorites. And it wasn't until more than fifty years after the shower was first reported that Russian investigators examined the fall site. We might well wonder how the fallout fragments from such a bright bolide seen by so many eyewitnesses, and so widely reported in newspaper accounts, went undiscovered for so long. The event occurred in the dark, which contributed to the difficulty of estimating the distance and presumed landing point of a bright object streaking groundward. Although the local people made many searches, they were all looking in the wrong place. Also, it was nearly impossible to distinguish observations that could be considered reliable from those that bordered on the fanciful.

According to the newspaper *Communist,* in early December of 1922 rumors circulating around the city of Astrakhan said that a giant meteorite struck and shook the ground. Another rumor said the meteorite was "the size of the city of Astrakhan and was made of solid gold."

Aside from erroneous facts, exaggeration, and malicious or naïve rumor-spreading, a number of early accounts show the distorting roles ignorance and superstition can play.

In 1997 the Russian newspaper *Znamya* published an extraordinary article written by one S. Monikov, a member of the Russian Geographical Society. In it he comments on the random nature of large meteorite showers and our inability to predict them and then goes on to describe an account entitled "An Unusual Meteor" published in the December 24, 1922, issue of the newspaper *Bor 'ba.* The article related that a citizen of the Leninsk region named Comrade Kuznetsov showed up one day in the district's Provincial Department of Political Education of the People. Kuznetsov reported that about two weeks earlier, on the date of the meteor fall, eyewitnesses heard a loud noise like that of several cannons all the way from the city of Leninsk to the village of Vladimirovskya. The report said that some of the windows of houses in Vladimirovskya were broken and that, according to rumors, the meteor could be seen from a distance of seven versts (the verst is an old Russian unit of distance equal to about 1 kilometer), and for several hours one could feel its heat quite far away from the meteor's flight path.

The Provincial Department of Political Education of the People decided to send Comrade Kuznetsov to the fall site to investigate the facts and take photographs, but for reasons we are never told he never returned. Nevertheless, to feed the insatiable curiosity of its readers about the event, *Bor 'ba* continued to publish accounts, but mostly rumors, which, according to Monikov "occasionally contained fantastic science-fiction details about the meteorite fall that did little more than feed the superstitious bent of the public."

Then, apparently after running out of reliable information about the event, the January 17, 1923, issue of *Bor 'ba* published a plea for help and a letter from a reader identified only as M. G. Ch. from the village of Proleika who demanded that the silly rumors, "spread largely by religious fanatics," be exposed. "We must reveal this dark force as soon as possible," said the letter writer, "but we don't have sufficient intellectual resources locally. Is it possible that someone from the village of Dubovka can help us?" he asked.

Monikov reported that the villagers from nearby Solodcha also appealed to Dubovka for help, but he does not tell us what intellectual resources Dubovka might have had. Nevertheless, a letter writer from Solodcha laments that, "darkened by illiteracy, the following is all the people of my village know as 'fact': A big stone was torn away from a cloud and fell near the village of Kamyshin. It burned for an entire week, and it rolled a distance of 75 versts until it reached Balykly, where it struck something and sank 6 sazhens (an old unit of length equal to 2.13 meters) into the ground. When the meteorite struck, fragments flew off and destroyed three houses."

"Correspondents from the newspapers rarely visit us in Solodcha," the letter writer continued, "neither do regional authorities, so who will expose all the incredible rumors that are being fueled by different dark personalities who use them for their own purposes?"

Bor 'ba was not alone as a juicy source of rumors. The following report appeared in the newspaper *Krasnaya Gazeta* for November 1, 1923: "The meteor fell with noise that was heard six days before the actual fall. It dug itself into the ground to a depth of 4 arshins [an arshin is an old Russian unit of length equal to 71 centimeters]. The main body of the meteorite was left sticking out of the ground to a height of 4 sazhens. It weighs about 200,000 poods [3,276,000 kilograms]. The meteorite is the size of a two story building." An illustration in one newspaper showed a sketch of a gigantic potato-shaped object resting in a shallow pit and towering above several people with arms raised who were dwarfed by the stone. According to other rumors, the meteorite was so hot when it landed that one could not approach close to it and the soil around it was molten and later turned into a black, anthracite-looking mass. As soon as it cooled, people from neighboring villages supposedly came to it, as if on a pilgrimage, and broke off pieces, calling them "Saint Stone."

Despite such accounts, one expedition conducted by scientists from Saratov University and another from Rostov University failed to locate the "uranolite" visitor from the sky. Meanwhile, news of the spectacle quickly spread to many distant parts of Russia. At one stage, the Soviet Academy of Sciences printed fliers offering an award of 100 golden rubles to anyone who could lead them to the meteorite. The fliers were mailed out to Astrakhan and Tsaritsin (later renamed Stalingrad and then Volgograd) provinces for posting, but one of the distributors, head of the local meteorological station, said that "hardly any success should be expected, due to the people's illiteracy." He was right. Eyewitness accounts of the bolide collected over the years proved somewhat more helpful than newspaper accounts in the initial investigations into the cosmic stone's size, mass, trajectory, and fragmentation.

According to Roman Khotinok, of the then Soviet Academy of Sciences, one eyewitness identified only as Safonov said, "at two o'clock in the night in the last days of October, or during the first days of November of 1921, when I was nine, I happened to be out of my house and all of a sudden there came an unusually bright light as if 100 thunderstorms were occurring together. At the same time I saw in the back of the village a flying fireball, and then I heard a very loud explosion. The ground trembled and then everything went still in the darkness. I definitely knew that it must have been a meteorite fall."

Another eyewitness was A. G. Gerasimova from the village of Tsarev and born in 1912. She reportedly told Khotinok the following, recalling the event from the time she was about ten years old. It was "very late in the fall or very beginning of winter close to nighttime, because they had not yet gone to bed. Her father was still at work mending boots by a little candle. Then all of a sudden it became so bright that everything in the house looked as if it were daytime. 'I saw through the window a very bright fireball and I cried: Look, a dragon, a fiery snake is flying with a tail.' Next she said that there was one very strong explosion. Several days later, people would come to her house to tell her father that a big stone fell in his nearby field.

"She said that she remembered very clearly that the house window faced east, and that the fireball was flying from the right to the left, that is from south to north and at a slight angle to the horizon."

These and other eyewitness accounts, plus the many newspaper reports, put the time of the Tsarev shower at some evening in late fall or early winter of 1921 or 1922. But other eyewitnesses provided wide discrepancies, by as much as ten or more years earlier or later than 1922. After a hiatus of more than fifty years, which was when eyewitness accounts began to be systematically collected by Tsvetkov, Zotkin, and others, just how reliable could the accounts be regarded? Although a sufficient number did point to 1920, 1921, or 1922, the Academy's archives of reports of meteorite sightings, fragments of which had never been discovered, held the most likely answer. One "problem case" file card listed a bolide reported to have fallen on December 6, 1922, between 1700 and 1800 hours. It was listed as the Tsaritsinsky Meteorite. That date and time then became official. The time agreed nicely with eyewitness Gerasimova's and others' recollections.

A Welder Finds Some Stones

We now jump ahead to 1979 and to the state farm near Tsarev. The electric welder Boris Nikiforov wrote a long letter to the Academy's Committee on Meteorites and reported that in the spring of 1968 farm workers began to find big rusty stones in the fields of the state farm. This in itself was puzzling because the surrounding land was not rocky and lacked any native large stones. Every time a tractor driver came across one of the stones, he would either push it out of the way to the edge of the field or load it onto his plow and use it as a weight.

Having worked with oil geologists and having a keen interest in astronomy and meteorites, in 1978 Nikiforov became suspicious of the stones. They were nothing like anything he had ever seen. Their heft relative to their size made him especially suspicious. In his letter he said that he thought they might be meteorites. Committee members were skeptical. It seemed unlikely that the stones, which had been lying in the field for so long in the open where everyone could see them, could turn out to be meteorites. Nevertheless, as a routine matter, they wrote back and asked Nikiforov to break off a sample and send it to Moscow for analysis. To the Committee's surprise, the 324-gram sample turned out to be a subclass of chondrite known as an L5, which designates its petrologic type, and a new addition to the Academy's collection.

Committee member Khotinok was immediately sent to Tsarev. Carrying a briefcase to bring the specimens back to Moscow, he walked through the fence gate to Nikiforov's yard and froze in disbelief on seeing a heap of large rusty stones, each measuring about half a meter in diameter. Nikiforov said there were four more even larger ones back in the field, but they were too heavy to be moved by hand. Examination of seven of the meteorites in Nikiforov's yard established their masses at several dozen kilograms each. They were rusty as a result of long-term oxidation, and they had a dark fusion crust indented with rhegmaglypts formed by ablation during their searing flight through the atmosphere.

According to Khotinok, the internal structure of the meteorites showed traces of impact metamorphism. "Most probably, after millions of years in interplanetary space, the original unfragmented meteoroid underwent a very forceful collision," he reports in an article, "New Meteorites of the USSR: The Stony Meteorite Shower at Tsarev."

While many of the meteorites most likely remained where they originally had fallen, the locations of most of those that had been moved could be reasonably well reestablished since the state farm was relatively new, and the workers accurately knew how the fields had been worked and where the removed stones had been found. Four of the largest meteorites remained in their original locations, and Nikiforov could show exactly where he had found the seven large stones he had moved to his backyard. In October 1979 a fifteenth meteorite with a mass of 50 kilograms was found.

In April and August of 1980, thirteen more were found and their data recorded.

Recovered fragments provided at least a start for estimating a mass for the original meteoroid. Direct chemical and physical analysis provided the stones' composition and structure. Fieldwork provided a start in mapping the orientation, size, and shape of the strewn field. It also showed dispersal of the fragments by mass. During a meteorite shower, the fragments are sorted in the atmosphere according to mass. The lesser-mass fragments are slowed more during their flight through the atmosphere and so fall out of the swarm before the larger-mass fragments do. Examination of the ellipsoid strewn field clearly confirmed eyewitness accounts of the bolide having a trajectory from south to north since the larger-mass fragments were found in the northern region of the strewn field. This provided an azimuth of 140°, or trajectory from southeast to northwest.

An important unknown was the entry velocity of the bolide, which would help establish the meteoroid's orbital elements when in space. A study of the strewn field configuration, and mapping of the position of each meteorite's location within the strewn field, can provide an estimate of the unfragmented object's entry velocity. Tsvetkov's 1982 expedition to Tsarev filled in many details of the mapping of the strewn field when twenty-five new fragments weighing a combined total of 100 kilograms were located. A second strewn field analysis confirmed an azimuth of 140° for the bolide.

More exploration of the Tsarev meteorite shower site remains to be done, especially at the low-mass end of the strewn field. By now, however, many of the very low mass meteorites have most likely been eroded away. Although the meteoroid composition of largely olivine with some pigeonite and iron and the meteoroid density of from 3.3 to 3.5 grams per cubic centimeter are established, refinements of the strewn field can still be made. This would further refine the object's estimated entry velocity of 9.4 kilometers per second and, hence, its orbital elements among the asteroids.

For interested collectors, many more fragments still await discovery.

CHAPTER 6

Popigai: Mosquitoes, Diamonds, and a Very Big Crater

It all started with a wild suggestion from my intrepid Siberian colleague Katya during the train ride back from our 1997 expedition to the Chinge meteorite shower site down near Mongolia: "Next year let's go to Popigai," she said. It came out as casually as, "Let's go to the market and buy a fish."

The Popigai impact structure is a petrological plum that many a geologist would give up his hammer to visit. Around 36 million years ago a chunk of cosmic debris came crashing down and blasted out a crater some 80 to 100 kilometers wide and raised havoc with the rock down to a depth of about 10 kilometers. Untold thousands of cubic kilometers of rock and earth were hurled thousands of meters skyward and then tumbled back as allogenic breccia fragments more or less sorted out according to mass. The resulting rubble was a scrambled eggs mixture of boulder-size to golf-ball-size pieces of carbonate rocks, granite gneiss, and sandstone.

In addition, there were reconstituted melt rock masses of a rock called *tagamite* and a lower-density rock type called *suevite*. The tagamite contains rich stores of impact diamonds, but just how rich, the Russians aren't about to tell. According to geologist Keenan Lee, "Popigai probably exceeds all the world's known diamonds combined."

At least two conditions have made the Popigai impact structure unique in the annals of geology. According to Russian investigators V. L. Masaitis and O. N. Simonov, the Popigai impact event marked the first time that diamonds were discovered in impactites and the first time that conditions of impact metamorphism of crystalline rocks were studied.

Unless you are a lemming or an Arctic fox, the only way to get into the site is by helicopter. From Khatanga, it is about a two-hour flight to the northwest crater wall, which offers the best exposure. Khatanga is about an eight-hour flight by turboprop aircraft from Krasnoyarsk; Krasnoyarsk is about a five-hour flight from Moscow; and if you want the big numbers, Popigai to New York City is about 13,000 kilometers.

As our train clatters on, Katya's suggestion to visit Popigai seems more and more out of the question when the kilometers—and the dollars—begin to add up. And what about permits to enter the Popigai region? Money-hungry bureaucrats might well be a problem in that remote part of the world. And we will need support staff and equipment—rubber boats, food for about ten days, gallons of toxic liquids, sprays, pastes, and clubs to beat off mosquitoes.

"No, Katya, we'll have to find another site," I say, rattling my newspaper. She then goes all silent, biting her lip, knitting her brow, and staring off into the distant landscape as it slips past. I know that look, and I don't like it. It means that we will be going to Popigai.

Early Planning

Over the next year Katya crunched numbers. Meanwhile, I was concentrating on plans to visit the remote site of the famous Pallas Meteorite, which we did in the summer of 1998. On our return from the Pallas site, Popigai e-mails from Katya began to clog my computer. We would need to raise about $40,000 and hire a support staff of about six, and should we bring along a doctor? And there would be the rubber boats and mess tent rentals, and several hours of helicopter rental at $800 an hour. Those were just the basic needs. There would also be airline flight costs, transfer fees in Moscow and Krasnoyarsk, and hotel and dining expenses in Krasnoyarsk and Khatanga. "No!" and "*Niet*," I added in Russian for emphasis. It was too much and too complex, and perhaps even *dangerous*. Maybe there would be polar bears. Possibly the word dangerous would bring her to her senses, even though I knew polar bears wouldn't. A few days later she e-mailed back and said that she had a cook lined up, a nice biophysicist friend, and she was pretty. And Alexander Andreev, the mineralogist who had led us on our Pallas expedition, and Alexey Kovalyov, a military lawyer also on that expedition, both said they wanted to come. Katya said it might come in handy to have a nice strong lawyer along, and he would bring a gun. Also, would I please get in touch with Dr. Keenan Lee of the Colorado School of Mines. He had visited the Tunguska site and most likely would jump at the chance to visit Popigai. He did, explaining that "geologists are just beginning to recognize the significance of impact structures and the role they have played in Earth's geologic history. It wasn't until fairly recently, with Mexico's Chicxulub Basin event, that geologists have really started to pay attention to these astroblemes."

He could have added that the uniqueness of the Popigai site has prompted UNESCO (United Nations Scientific and Cultural Organization) to include it as an area to be preserved and studied in all details for the future.

A School of Mines colleague of Lee's, Dr. John Warme, also was eager to sign on, saying: "Popigai is important because it's one of the biggest craters on Earth, one of the top ten. Not very many people get to see something like this, a truly fabulous exposure. From a personal standpoint, I'm studying an impact deposit in Nevada that's about ten times older than Popigai, but the Nevada site has been tectonically disturbed by faulting and subsequent events. Popigai is in much better condition because it's in a stable area of Earth's crust. This expedition will give me a chance to see different impact phenomena in their proper position, and I'm hoping that we can apply what we see in Popigai to better understand and reconstruct the Nevada crater."

A colleague of Warme's, Dr. Jared Morrow, another impact crater specialist from the University of Northern Colorado, also wanted to join us. He said that Popigai was important to him for two reasons: "First, for my own research interest in the Devonian-aged Alamo impact structure in Nevada; and second, in my teaching I've found that students have a lot of interest in extraterrestrial impacts. Seeing that fantastic exposure in Popigai will help me present this to them in the classroom and get them excited about impacts and the effects they've had on Earth throughout its history."

Before I realized it, our party had grown to twenty-one, and I felt that I was getting in over my head. In addition to a lawyer, we even had a stockbroker. A family of three were to drop out, which caused a financial burden by significantly increasing the per-person expedition cost for the rest of us. At the last minute, however, the problem was solved by generous financial support from Jean Dickey, of Sykesville, Maryland, who had long taken an interest in my expeditions to Siberia and wasn't about to see this one aborted. My son, teaching English in Taiwan for three years, said he wanted to come along. One day while describing the proposed trip to my financial adviser, Walter "Rusty" Johnson, there was a long pause, and then he said he'd call back the next day. He did, and said "Count *us* in. Travis wants to come, too." Travis is Rusty's son, then fourteen years old. When I asked Rusty, trained as a nuclear physicist turned financial manager, why he wanted to join us, he said, "Who could pass up a once-in-a-lifetime opportunity like this one? Also, it will give me an opportunity to do a little father-son bonding."

The expedition had gained momentum. We even signed up a limnologist, Dr. Kenton Stewart, from the State University of New York at Buffalo. Ken said he wanted to join us because, "I'm interested in looking at some of the lakes and comparing them to certain lakes I know in North America. Because the Popigai region is so isolated, I think it's a fine opportunity to investigate some of the zooplankton, which are so very important in the food web within lakes."

And finally, a notice in the magazine *Meteorite* about our expedition caught the eye of Geoffrey Notkin, a world traveler and writer about meteorites. He is an amateur paleontologist and meteoricist and has done fieldwork in the United States, England, Iceland, and Chile. Reasons he gave for wanting to come along were, "wanting to participate in one of Roy Gallant's expeditions; also, I've heard that Siberian mosquitoes are among the finest in the world." Between intensive bouts of murdering mosquitoes with his flyswatter, Geoffrey provided a comradery that contributed to making our group a highly congenial one.

We're Off!

Excitement was beginning to run high a month or so before our July 1, 1999, departure for Moscow. After one flight delay out of Dulles in Washington (Rusty and Travis) and one missing duffel bag in Moscow (Ken), the American contingent of seven trickled through customs in Moscow's Sheremetyevo Airport and eventually assembled in the apartment of Valentin Tsvetkov. Katya, who had flown in from Krasnoyarsk, managed to meet all of us at the airport, despite our different arrival times. She had arranged for Dr. Victor Masaitis, distinguished scientist of the Russian Federation, to travel by train from St. Petersburg and meet with us for the several hours before our 11:50 P.M. flight to Krasnoyarsk. Long thought to have been volcanic in origin, the Popigai structure was shown to be an impact crater by Masaitis in 1970. Shattercones and other shock metamorphism features occurring in the jumble of rock within the crater were among the clues that helped convince Masaitis that the depression was due to impacting. Shattercones are large or small rock fragments with characteristic "horsetail" fracture lines formed by compression by the high-energy shockwave generated by an impacting object. The lines occur in a cone shape with the apex of the cone pointing toward the center of the impact explosion. Shattercones are still pretty much of a mystery waiting for some geological sleuth to explain them in detail.

Masaitis's briefing in Moscow included this overview:

"The origin of the Popigai circular-shaped depression for a long time was ascribed to erosion, or tectonic subsidence, or a combination of these processes with volcanic eruptions that occurred in East Siberia about 250 million years ago. But the so-called volcanics at the Popigai site differ from true basaltic to andesitic rocks by an extremely high abundance of inclusions of ancient crystalline rocks and by certain other features. Similar crystalline rocks were found in the form of large blocks around the depression among the fields of the Cambrian and Permian flat-lying sediments. All these enigmatic features attracted our attention and required an explanation.

"Numerous similar impact craters diagnosed for shock metamorphism have long been established for lunar craters. With those studies as background, we began our geological and petrographical study of Popigaian rocks and very soon found shattercones and other features indicating shock metamorphism. It was considered on the basis of geological observations and microscopic study that chaotic breccias together with lavalike and tufflike rocks inside the depression should be regarded as a result of the impact of a giant asteroid some 30 to 40 million years ago.

"On the basis of the enrichment and ratios of siderophiles contained in the crater's impact melt rocks, called tagamites, we concluded that the projectile was an ordinary chondrite with a diameter of 7 to 8 kilometers. It seems to have followed a trajectory from northeast to southwest, according to the distribution of melted material, which occurs mostly in the southwest sector, thus making it an oblique impact. The object had an estimated entry velocity between 15 and 20 kilometers per second.

"Within a short time, we found specific high-pressure phases coesite and diamond caused by compression of previous quartz and graphite. That was clearly additional proof for an impact origin of the crater. Subsequently, geological and geophysical investigation, including drilling programs, confirmed these conclusions.

"Interestingly, with the discovery of the Popigai crater, geological examinations of other Russian territories led to the discovery of other ancient impact craters, or astroblemes."

Within two decades after 1970, the All Russian Science Research Geological Institute, named after A. P. Karpinsky, diagnosed about thirty impact structures, including several with diameters measuring scores of kilometers. According to Masaitis, more than 180 impact structures with diameters between 300 kilometers to several meters have been identified on Earth's land surface.

Lee told me that "It was Masaitis who was largely responsible for those discoveries. Masaitis did more than any other geologist in Russia to validate the impact origins of many structures, and he did this at a time when geologists, usually a conservative lot, were very reluctant to accept meteorite impacts as a significant geologic process."

Impact structures as large as Popigai are especially important to the work of paleoclimatologists who try to reconstruct Earth's ancient climate changes due to catastrophic geological upheavals. Radiometric dating of Popigaian rocks melted by the impact indicate an age of 35.7 ± 0.2 million years. That age sounded a coincidence alarm when it was found to match almost exactly the age of another giant impact crater in Chesapeake Bay halfway around the globe off the Virginia coast. At that time the world's oceans were higher than they are today, lapping the foothills of the Appalachian Mountains. What are now New York, Philadelphia, Baltimore, Washington, Richmond, and Norfolk were all under water. The climate was warm and humid, supporting tropical rain forests on the Appalachian slopes. When the cosmic visitor struck, it blasted out a hole 85 kilometers in diameter and 1.6 kilometers deep in what is today Chesapeake Bay between Norfolk and Richmond. According to U.S. Geological Survey scientist C. Wylie Poag, "It took only a few fiery seconds to brush aside the veneer of atmosphere and ocean and blast deep into the seabed, vaporizing it in a thunderous explosion. A stupendous, supersonic shock wave radiated for thousands of miles in all directions and shook the very foundations of the Appalachians. . . . It would have wiped out all the major cities of the eastern United States, had they existed. Life on Earth would have been shocked, vaporized, pulverized, barbecued, blinded, irradiated, acidified, drowned, starved, and frozen."

Actually, there was a third impact event that has been dated by isotopic ratios of argon for the same time as the Popigai and Chesapeake Bay impacts. It is the Toms Canyon crater located in what is now New Jersey. It seems to have been a gigantic meteorite shower that would put Sikhote-Alin to shame. It generated a monstrous wave measuring hundreds to thousands of meters high that crashed down onto the New Jersey shore.

The Popigai, Chesapeake Bay, and Toms Canyon events occurred toward the end of that geologic epoch known as the Eocene, which saw the greatest mass extinction of life since the demise of the dinosaurs some 30 million years earlier. However, there seems to be no evidence that can link mass extinctions specifically with the three impact craters. Some geologists feel that a crater must be greater than 85 kilometers in diameter to trigger mass extinctions. Later, the close of the Eocene saw a marked cooling of the oceans with the first appearance of ice sheets in Antarctica. Now comes the task of an interdisciplinary group of scientists to try and figure out the extent of the effect of three major asteroidal impacts in geologically quick succession on the biological and climatological evolution of the planet at the close of the Eocene.

A Thorn in Our Petrological Garden

When our group of nine arrives in Krasnoyarsk at about seven the next morning local time, Katya informs us of a series of very unpleasant telephone calls she and her assistant expedition administrator, Sergei Parshikov, have had with Nickolai Andreyevich Fokin, a powerful government bureaucrat in Khatanga. He heads the regional administration there and reports directly to Gennady P. Nedelin, Governor of the Taimyr Autonomous Okrug, or "district." Fokin, it turns out, wants to "tax" our expedition 15 percent of our total expedition costs to enter his territory and be given his blessings—which include an official permit and his authorization to rent a helicopter, "blessings" we much need. He says that our total costs must include the price of our domestic flights in the United States as well!

When Sergei and Katya object and offer Fokin the much lesser amount of $1600 based on expedition costs incurred while in Russia, Fokin shouts accusations and insults into the telephone. He says that what we offer is nothing more than a *podachka,* a Russian expression meaning a mere pittance offered to a beggar just to get rid of him, a humiliating gesture. That *podachka,* Fokin well realizes, amounts to a three-year salary for a typical university professor. His volatility seems well matched with his greed.

We later learn that such outbursts apparently are characteristic of Fokin and have earned him the nickname of "Barking Dog." He accuses us of being media types with elaborate camera equipment and says that our sole interest is to make films of the Popigai crater and then sell them for huge profits back in the United States. The matter is at a stalemate. As a group, we agree that we will fly to Khatanga and see if we can resolve the difficulty there with the possible intervention of other officials who might recognize the legitimacy of our expedition, a group interested only in scientific aspects of the Popigai region. Our "elaborate" camera equipment consists of two hand-held camcorders—mine and one belonging to a Russian member of the crew—and a half dozen or so point-and-shoot cameras. Before Fokin rings off, he boasts that only a week or so earlier he turned back a group of Austrian investigators who refused to pay up.

When we step off the plane in Khatanga, we are attacked not by Fokin but by squadrons of mosquitoes which make us don our mosquito netting hats. Like a musketeer, Geoffrey quickly begins hacking the air with his flyswatter while my son Jon produces a small battery-operated tennis racket affair that electrocutes any and all mosquitoes unlucky enough to be swept into the grid. "Look, they're dropping like flies!" he says triumphantly with a grin. Jon wanted to join the expedition to visit Russia again after an absence of 15 years. A former student in a Russian studies program at the University of Washington, he speaks Russian well and assists Katya as a translator.

Khatanga is the last outpost if you're bound for Popigai or the North Pole. Derelict wooden and concrete buildings line muddy streets, and a general gloom hangs over all. A small bus jostles us to our hotel where we are to spend the Arctic "night" before boarding our helicopter to the crater site, if Mr. Fokin permits. He is still determined to relieve us of as much money as he can. Katya and Sergei immediately begin to work the telephone, calling whichever officials they can to plead our case. Tensions are high. The rest of us amble out onto the puddled streets in two groups in search of shops. We find two in small and tightly closed house-trailer-like structures. Each of our groups in turn is approached by the same three friendly drunks who want to share their vodka with us to help celebrate whatever event brought us here and "to amend past misunderstandings between our two great countries." "If we have vodka," goes a Russian saying, "we can always find a reason to drink it."

A Showdown with "Barking Dog"

By bedtime we still have no word about our future as either potential outcasts or welcome guests. The news is that the next morning we are to appear before Michael Martyshkin, head of the Polar Expedition Group and chief manager responsible for organizing all Russian geological expeditions to the region. We all have lumps in our throats. Will he be another "Barking Dog"? The meeting is to be kept small, so Katya, Sergei, John Warme, Valery Kirichenko, our expedition's chief scientist, and I march up to the entrance of Martyshkin's building and wait in the courtyard. In about five minutes someone approaches and instructs us to follow. This is to be a preliminary meeting before our big meeting with Fokin, or so we have been led to believe.

Martyshkin's office is comfortably large with a big portrait of Lenin glaring down at us from behind his desk. The desk is adorned with four telephones, one of which is red. Maybe I should put in a quick call to Washington, I think. Martyshkin is dressed meticulously in a dark suit, crisp white shirt, and dark tie. He couldn't be more pleasant or gracious, which immediately makes me suspicious. He welcomes us in fluent English, serves us coffee, and offers us brandy and a large box of chocolates to select from, not an uncommon Russian way of greeting foreign dignitaries.

As we sip our coffee, two of his staff pass around for our examination small containers of gold, platinum, and diamonds recovered from his area. He then invites questions we may have. We oblige with a few routine inquiries about the geology of the region and then wait. He then comes straight to the point with a winning smile that reveals two gold teeth.

"You have green lights all the way," he announces. "Immediately I will authorize and schedule your helicopter. I will arrange for two-way radio communications equipment to accompany you, and I will see to it that our meteorologists keep in constant communication with you about weather changes here and where you will be." Whereupon, he strides behind his desk and begins working the telephones, sometimes two at a time. Fifteen minutes later our expedition has been planned and approved down to the finest detail, including our not even having to show our passports to security agents at the airport. Now that's VIP treatment in Russia.

We sit unbelieving. What about Fokin and his threats to dispatch us to the nearest gulag unless we come through with his outrageous "tax"? Katya's and Sergei's frantic telephoning on our arrival has paid off. They got through to Governor Nedelin's office and scored a point in making a high-ranking official see the merits of establishing friendly relations with the West instead of antagonizing it with hardline Soviet authority insensitive to the changes in conditions since the fall of communism. Nedelin's office apparently has ordered Fokin to heel. Barking Dog has been muzzled!

Our "tax," it turns out, was settled at 38,310 rubles ($1583), an amount finally accepted by Fokin's office. When Katya and Sergei take the money to the bank for deposit into an account whose number was given them over the telephone, the bank administrator doesn't know how to handle the transaction. He has to telephone Fokin's office for further instructions. Finally, Katya is given a receipt in my name, and the money is assigned to an account titled "other taxes."

Martyshkin generously comes to our rescue for that unplanned expense and, accordingly, takes it on his own to reduce our helicopter costs by arranging for us to share the helicopter with Russian geologists visiting nearby sites. Then, to our further surprise, he tells us there will not be a charge for our hotel. His final gesture of goodwill is a late afternoon meal at the local Carat Restaurant—delicious reindeer burgers, mashed potatoes, pickled fish, salads, and vodka to wash it all down. Life above the Arctic Circle is improving by the hour.

An Arctic Landscape: Tundra and Hillocks

The helicopter takes our advance party to the crater at 1:30 P.M. to set up the mess/lecture tent, our "Popipooper" toilet tent, and arrange our equipment and supplies. The rest of us take off at 5:30 P.M. on a flight that is spectacular throughout its nearly two-hour duration. We don't have to worry about flying in the dark because there isn't any. We open the small porthole windows, and everyone is poking cameras out of them to catch the hummocky tundra landscape gliding by below. It is desolate and beautiful. Grasses and sedges sometimes gray, other times brown, and then green extend to the horizon, occasionally interrupted by streams and large patches of snow. We roll along with the hills, often dipping or climbing to keep pace with the gentle changes in elevation.

Then the magnificent northwest crater wall comes into view as suddenly as a turned page. We do a lazy circle around our campsite below, already set up by the advance party, and buzz the crater wall before gently setting down on the broad cobblestone shore of the Rassokha River. The crater wall is majestic in its varicolored display of pink sandstones, pale green and yellow carbonate rocks, and darker tagamites—a now silent testament to that catastrophic impact that shook the planet to its mantle some 36 million years earlier.

As soon as we climb out of the helicopter, we are covered with mosquitoes. Within ten seconds every duffel bag, hat, and back is thoroughly covered with only millimeter separations between critters. While Geoffrey swats furiously, Jon electrocutes gleefully. By nine that evening all of our tents are set up along a 100-meter stretch of the sand, shrubs, and dwarf evergreens just above the gently sloping cobblestone embankment. As the helicopter takes off and disappears over the crater wall, it is reassuring to see the long pole that supports the antenna wires of our radio. Our family physician, Dr. Boris Andriyashev, makes tent calls by coming around to each of us with handouts of vitamins. With my GPS I take a reading that locates our Camp Number 1 at 71° 45′ N and 110° 15′ E. The elevation is 17 meters.

Valery Tells All

The next day is July 8 and gets under way with a breakfast of an oatmeal-type porridge with milk, bananas, bread, jam, preserves, tea, cheese, and mosquitoes. Over coffee we listen to a lecture on the history and structure of the Popigai crater by Valery. He worked closely with Masaitis beginning in the early 1970s and subsequently spent fifteen years hammering rocks and drilling into Popigai's floor to a depth of 1.5 kilometers to learn more about its structure, but chiefly to help satisfy the Russian government's hunger for more knowledge about Popigai's impact diamonds. For some ten years he has been chief of the Polar Exploration Expedition. With charts, a pointer, and rock samples, he explains the importance of the northwest crater wall, which rises to a height of some 100 or more meters and is representative of the structure of the entire crater:

"The crater face contains large blocks of allogenic breccias of various rock types that normally would be found in deposits at depths of 2 kilometers or so apart, but here we find them all at the same level," he begins. "Some of the blocks are crystalline rocks from the northeastern edge of the Anabar Shield. And there are Proterozoic sandstones of characteristic pink color, and there are light green and yellow carbonate rocks. Close study reveals Permian Age rocks and Triassic trapps, for example. This all is convincing evidence of a cataclysmic event that resulted in the positioning of these various rocks at one level. All of the features we find here in the northwest wall are typical of the structure of the entire crater.

"In the upper part of the exposure you can see a horizontally oriented layer of tagamites some 50 to 60 meters thick, but drilling has shown they penetrate to a depth of some 500 to 600 meters. They are molten rocks resulting from extremely high temperature (up to 1800°C) during the impact explosion.

"To appreciate the grand scale of the impact event, one should see the entire crater structure, but even the restricted exposure of the northwest rim gives a very good feel for the scale of the cataclysm.

"Our study of the Popigai structure has revealed practically all features characteristic of other structures of this type, including those found in Ukraine, Canada, Africa, and a number of other locations. Popigai has been remarkably well preserved, which allows us to study it in detail. It is not overlain by thick sediments as many structures of this type are in other locations, and thus can be revealed only through geophysical data and core drilling. Here we can see all such structures naturally. At the same time, they are not seriously eroded, thus preserving all the structural elements of structures of this type."

A geologic profile of the area has a hummocky tundra on top, beneath which are Jurassic and Cretaceous sandstones, the deeper down Triassic trapp rock with sills and dykes, then Permocarboniferous rocks of sandstones, shales, and coal. Still deeper down are Cambrian limestones, and then Precambrian sandstone and garnet gneiss.

During the impact, all of this geologic history was blasted asunder and fell back to Earth in a chaotic array, with the lower-density material of suevite tumbling back last and overlaying the somewhat denser and diamond-rich tagamite. Initially, the blast is thought to have dug out a transitional crater with a depth of about 10 kilometers, but almost instantly it was transformed into a multiple angular ring depression with depths of from 2 to 2.5 kilometers. It was then filled in with the products of fragmentation and melting of crystalline and partially sedimentary rocks— allogenic breccias and the tagamite and suevite impactites.

The crater's diameter range of from 80 to 100 kilometers has been estimated in two ways. Gravity surveys indicate a diameter of 82 kilometers. The low-mass anomaly within the crater resulted partly from some material being ejected and other materials being loosened into a less compact mass during the impact. The other method of estimating the crater's diameter is to study the distribution of impactites, which gives a somewhat larger diameter.

In the afternoon, groups of us climb into our two rubber boats, paddle across the river, and listen to Valery as he cracks open rocks and shows us what to look for. Most of us then wander about, hammering away on our own and selecting choice specimens to take home. In Russia you simply do not pocket any old rock and take it home. You need special authorization to remove minerals from the country. Our patron in this case is Oleg Simonov, chairman of the Taimyr Geological Committee. As a postscript to the Fokin episode, Simonov tells Katya that Fokin also once blackmailed his group for a "tax" after the group had arrived at the site.

At one stage a cold front rushes through, dropping the temperature at least 15° within minutes and pelting us with wind-driven rain. One by one we line up to jump across a small mud stream that grows in volume by the minute. Just as the last of our party makes the leap and is caught by Sergei and dragged to safety, what had been the small mud stream explodes into a major mud slide that sends us scattering and tumbles boulders the size of two St. Bernards down the crater wall and into the river.

The fishing is good. Young Travis and several others climb the crater wall to do some net fishing in a small lake, Lake Kumzhalak. They come back with a sack of some two dozen Arctic graylings, troutlike fish with unusually large dorsal fins. With his rod and reel, Keenan successfully casts his luck in the river and comes back with four large fish. Life above the Arctic Circle just keeps getting better, especially when the temperature slowly climbs to around 15°C.

"Down a Lazy River"—for Eighteen Hours

On the eleventh we pack up for the long trip downriver to what would be Camp Number 2. For several hours the camp staff builds a pontoon raft of 5 square meters with narrow slats of wood lashed together and tied to four rubber floats that look like torpedoes. While twelve of us shove off against a head wind in the two rubber boats, the remaining six complete loading our heavy equipment and supplies onto the raft and follow along. You can hum "Down a Lazy River" just so many times before you want the tune to change. In all, we spend eighteen hours cramped in the small boats, with only two stops to make sure that the raft crew is still afloat. They are and make remarkable progress, considering that the river is lowering daily and is so shallow in places that we have to climb out and pull the boats along. The raft crew often has to walk along the shore towing the raft by long lines. The river is shallowing about a foot a day. If we were a week later, this part of our expedition would be very difficult. The unrelenting head wind keeps pushing us against the shore and out of the strong midriver current. At the first stop, Katya finds a beautifully preserved mammoth tooth. The rest of us search but find nothing while two Arctic terns repeatedly dive at us whenever we get too close to their nest.

By the time we pull the boats ashore on a peninsula of sand, which we call our desert "island," I find it hard to know whether it is day or "night" and simply sleep whenever I feel tired. The Sun hangs from about 30° to 10° above the horizon and just keeps doing a shallow sine wave around and around. We have our choice of two rivers for bathing and drinking, one on each side of our V-shaped spit of desert property. Our position, according to my GPS, is 71° 54′ N by 110° 51′ E. The major anomaly at Camp Number 2 is the temperature, which shoots up into the high 20s and mid-30s on the Celsius scale and stays there. The only way to cool off is to wade into one of the rivers. If you lean back just far enough against the gentle current, you can comfortably stabilize yourself in a state of microgravity as an aquanaut. Thirsty? Just tilt back your head and gulp in the water. But no matter how much I drink, I am constantly thirsty since the water lacks thirst-quenching minerals. "Oh, for an ice cold bubbly Coke!" I hear Geoffrey moan a few meters away from me. He is up to his neck in the water, hatted with mosquito netting pulled down under his chin, and vigorously slapping the water as he smashes mosquitoes with his flyswatter.

A Visit to the Dolgans

The plan is to spend three days in our small desert outpost before the helicopter comes for us. That gives us time to cross the river and visit the dilapidated village remains of Popigai, now only a collection of weather-beaten planked structures that once housed a group of about 200 Dolgan natives, people of Mongoloid stock resembling North American Eskimos. Their name Dolgan derives from an Evenk tribal name, so they are most likely an offshoot of Siberia's Evenk ethnic group. The buildings are now crumbling and unfit for habitation. Only one family of six with four dogs occupies the village during our visit, although two elder relatives, grandparents of the children, live nearby in a traditional tepee of heavy cedar bark. The woman, aged about sixty, looks seriously ill, appears ancient beyond description, and is reluctant to talk with Katya.

Popigai is some 300 kilometers from Khatanga, and its few inhabitants live without electricity, radio, medical attention, or modern sanitary conditions. Their food consists of reindeer meat and the fish they are able to net in a nearby lake. Their living conditions amid the relentless swarms of mosquitoes are so bad that some of our party don't have the heart, or stomach, to visit them. They spend the summer months in Popigai, the rest of the year in Novorybnoye, a settlement of some 500 Dolgans located at the mouth of the Khatanga River.

Traditionally, the Dolgans were migratory groups who lived off their herds of reindeer, depending on them for food, clothing, and transportation. But in the 1930s the Soviets, in one of their many failed social schemes, attempted to bring "civilization" to the north people by herding them into newly constructed *faktoriya*, literally "trading posts." There were small wooden houses, a post office, a school room, and a civic center called a "house of culture."

Soon the Soviet authorities realized it was too expensive to maintain so many villages and keep them supplied with food. Several of them were relocated closer to large bodies of water that could be more easily reached by boat and airplane. In the end, most of the settlements were abandoned. Sadly and too late, the Soviet authorities came to realize that they could not easily force a change of a people's way of life. Many of the Dolgans simply dismantled their houses and used the planks to construct their traditional tepees beyond the village perimeter. Today the Russian authorities are severely critical of the earlier Soviet attempts to "civilize" the Dolgan and Evenk people. In the case of the Evenks in the Tunguska region to the west, it's too late. There are few of them left. A 1989 census counted 5243 Dolgans, of whom only 4000 continue to speak their native language of the Turkic language family. Today fewer than a tenth are urban dwellers.

During his pilgrimage through many parts of the Soviet Union in the 1930s, Arthur Koestler had this to say about the Sovietization of Russia's proud indigenous peoples:

"The natives were drawn into the towns, educated, Russified and Stalinised by the pressure-cooker method. The children of the nomads were brought to school, processed, indoctrinated, and stripped of their national identity. All national tradition, folklore, arts and crafts, were eradicated by force and by propaganda. Everywhere in Asia primitive tribes and nations were transformed into a nondescript, colourless and amorphous mass of robots in the totalitarian State."

━•━━ ☲◊☲ ━━•━

On the day the helicopter is supposed to pick us up, the weather closes in around Khatanga and cuts off all air traffic. We receive word by radio. The next day, July 14, half packed with only a few essentials and our tents still standing, we sit by the radio for news about the helicopter, which supposedly left Khatanga around 10 A.M. Judging from the number of mosquitoes, their favorite temperature must be around 10°C, a drop of some 25° from the previous day's high.

Alexander's red cap is black beneath a solid carpet of mosquitoes. Travis shovels in his oatmeal by tucking his spoon up under his mosquito netting. "How do I tell the raisins from the mosquitoes?" he asks examining his cereal bowl, which is more alive than dead.

A Visit to Diamond Land

The helicopter picks us up around 1:00 P.M. With cheers we watch the mosquitoes blown asunder by the prop wash, but I feel as though I still have two or three flying around in my lungs. We help Rusty maneuver his way into the helicopter as he clutches his prize of a set of reindeer antlers which he won in trade for his $29.95 watch. Before heading back to Khatanga, we land at Myak, the core sampling site built in 1974 to search for diamonds. Valery spent five years in this wretched outpost beside Lake Balaganakh. Here, workers drilled for most of the year, small planes landing and taking off from the iced-over lake and carrying core samples to various laboratories for analysis. Today there are several shacks and smashed sheds and crates containing thousands of broken cores of tagamite and suevite which are stacked haphazardly over a hectare or more of the storage site. As Katya remarks, "The little village is lost in the nowhere and taken apart by the Dolgans." Each of us is given a small core section of tagamite as a souvenir. If mine contains diamonds, I'll never know since recovery requires first crushing the rock into fine pieces and then treating the fragments chemically to loosen the diamonds from their matrix. You'll end up with a fragment suitable only for one nostril of a teenage mosquito.

By around 3:00 P.M. we are back in Khatanga. The mosquitoes have followed us, and the other good news is that there is no running water in the hotel. If you ever visit Russia, don't be surprised to find several buckets of water at the ready in the bathroom of your host.

We have our final dinner party that night, with lots of small souvenir gifts for our Russian comrades. The next morning sees us off on our three-leg return trip to Krasnoyarsk, first with a layover in Norilsk, then another in Podkamennaya Tunguska. The temperature has climbed back up to the low 30s on the Celsius scale, and we are all uncomfortable in our heavy clothing, especially in the airplane, where the only air circulation is our hot breathing. After about eight hours, we deplane in Krasnoyarsk. Geoffrey looks around in disbelief, smiles, and sheaths his flyswatter. Jon likewise turns off the batteries in his tennis racket. It is sad to see our group suddenly disperse. The Russians go their separate ways, quickly dissolving in bustling Krasnoyarsk. Jarred Morrow says good-bye to us at the hotel and then leaves to catch a train to Lake Baikal. Those of us left go on to Moscow, where

Ken, Jon, Rusty, Travis, and I catch a flight to Frankfurt. Katya is near tears as she watches her family fragment.

In Moscow at passport control, Rusty courageously suffers verbal abuse by a female passport control officer who rudely lectures him and threatens to fine and detain him because a mosquito got squashed between pages of his passport and hides part of the date on his visa. Stalin would have cheered.

While waiting to board our Lufthansa flight, we watch as grim baggage attendants hurl our souvenir-laden luggage into the cargo hold with a great deal of thumping.

"Sounds as though big rocks are being thrown around," someone says.

CHAPTER 7

Teleutskoye: The Stony Shower of 1904

"Remember John's Rock?" Katya asks during a telephone conversation to plan our next expedition to a Siberian meteorite impact site. I vaguely recall a large rock sitting quite by itself on the forest floor at the Tunguska epicenter when I was there in 1992. I had assumed it was an erratic boulder carried there by glacial ice millennia ago and dropped. The rock has no discernable geological parentage from any rock types native to the Tunguska epicenter region, and it has been ruled out as a glacial erratic, according to John Anfinogenov, the rock's namesake. Over the years John came to develop an elaborate hypothesis accounting for the rock's being where it had no business to be. He speculated that it might have long ago been blasted out of an ancient volcano many kilometers away, hurled asunder, buried into the soft taiga floor on impact, and then later migrated to the surface. He has even considered that the rock may be from Mars, an idea he would like to have investigated.

"Well," Katya continues, "John has asked if we would like to visit a meteorite shower site way down in the Altai district near Mongolia. I don't think much has been published about the place in English, maybe nothing, and not all that much in Russian. He's been there once and says there's an interesting story about the shower, and we might even find a little meteorite."

"Sounds possible," I mumble, trying to be noncommittal. I know from experience that Katya's seeds of an idea have the potential of germinating into de facto expeditions before I realize what is happening. Sensing a spark of interest, Katya's excitement begins to flame. I suspect she has it all planned by now and a crew selected but isn't about to admit it. "Sergei even said he can borrow his brother's trailer for all our gear. And while we're down there near Mongolia we can do a second expedition up in the Altai Mountains!"

"Is that Haydn's Drum Roll Symphony I hear playing in the background?" I interrupt.

"There are great big glaciers to climb and beautiful green rushing streams of glacial melt water," she continues, turning up the volume of her CD player. "They are very swift and all the mountain slopes are carpeted with wild flowers, and Alexei [Rudoy] says there's a little café that serves fermented mare's milk, and . . ."

"No," I break in. "One expedition at a time is enough, and I haven't climbed on ice since my foolhardy climb of Mount Fuji in February many years ago; furthermore, my ice axe is packed away in the attic and it's all rusty. Totally out of the question," I proclaim, letting her know who's in charge. "Besides, there aren't any meteorite craters up in those *very dangerous* mountains," I emphasize. "And what if you fall into one of those *viciously cascading* streams? That will be the end of you because I won't jump in after you. No, it's too treacherous and unsafe. *Pa-ka* (good-bye), I'll talk with you again next week after you regain your senses and after you find out more from John about the Teleutskoye Lake meteorite fall site."

In the moment of silence that follows before she rings off, I can hear that it *is* the Drum Roll Symphony.

＋＋ ━◆━ ＋＋

Although Katya knows the meaning of both *niet* and no, she has never quite accepted their significance. Clear evidence of that foible is that our year 2000 expedition, which was to continue my documentation of the history and current status of Siberian meteorite impact sites, turned into a double-barreled expedition—one to the Teleutskoye (Tele-*oot*-skoi-yeh) fall site and the other one up into the Altai Mountains to risk our necks scampering like mountain goats among glaciers at an altitude of about 3000 meters on the edge of Mongolia. I could think of other ways of visiting Mongolia than by falling down into it from an ice ledge.

Comrade Lenin Gets a Bath

John, a radiation physicist from Tomsk and an authority on the Tunguska site, has done research at the Teleutskoye site and feels that further investigation by our crew of nine might rekindle interest in the lakeside site, if not from the currently research poor Russian government then maybe from foreigners.

To get to the site, I fly from Boston to Moscow where Katya meets me. Around midnight—again one of those impossibly late night Russian flights—we catch a flight to Barnaul, capital of the Altai Republic situated on the Ob, one of Russia's major rivers. The Republic shares its western border with Kazakhstan and its southeastern border with Mongolia. We check into the Hotel Centralnaya, the city's best hotel located adjacent to a large five-story building flying the Russian tricolor flag. Seat of the present government, the building formerly served as headquarters for the Central Committee for the Communist Party. Standing proudly and defiantly in front of the building is an enormous statue of Lenin, not yet toppled as hundreds of other disgraced Lenin statues throughout Russia have been, because the Altai Republic is still strongly communist. When we arrive, I am amused to see a crew of four women on ladders and with long-handled scrub brushes reverently washing down Comrade Lenin.

We check into the hotel and are given a spacious suite of rooms, including a large living room with two wall cabinets filled with crystal glassware and china, although there are no cooking facilities. There is a large foldout couch, two overstuffed armchairs plus three straight-back chairs, and a large refrigerator. Off an entry hall are two bedrooms and a large bathroom with tub, shower, and a seatless toilet. The suite is $36 a night. Small double rooms for the crew come to $6 each. A perfectly adequate dinner for the five of us at a nearby café comes to a total of $11. A bottle of excellent Russian champagne is $2.70. Before settling for that café, our guard and crew chief, Alexey Kovalyov, veteran of our Pallas and Popigai expeditions, had trotted off across the square to examine another restaurant. He came back shaking his head no. "The cockroaches are as big as dogs," he said. Wherever we go, Alexey is my bodyguard and is as inseparable from me as my shadow.

To reach the meteorite site requires first a drive of about 80 kilometers from Barnaul along a two-lane paved road southeast to Troitskoye. Passing seemingly endless fields of buckwheat, we drive in two cars, one hauling a trailer with

192

our gear. Katya keeps in touch with the car behind us with a two-way radio whose battery keeps needing to be charged. At one stage she calls back to Alexey and tells him to stop by a field of beets we have just passed and to pick several for our dinner of borscht that night. Ten minutes later, Alexey radios back and tells Katya that her beet field is a turnip field. The borscht that night is not red.

At Troitskoye we are supposed to meet with a local merchant to get fresh supplies and directions through a labyrinth of another 80 or so kilometers of tractor paths and sandy logging truck roads to the meteorite fall site. Despite our search of the town, our merchant is nowhere to be found. However, we do find his shop and café where he has left us two boxes of supplies: four large chickens, 10 kilograms of potatoes, 2 kilograms of carrots, parsley and other herbs, and three dozen eggs.

On leaving town, we turn southwest onto a series of dirt roads that link remote villages, each with a few to a dozen or so buildings. Drinking water comes from whatever wells and springs we happen to find along the way, and we buy gasoline from local logging trucks. Driver Sergei Kovlov, another expedition veteran, always keeps a hand pump ready for such convenient, although questionable, transactions.

Every now and then we stop at a house for directions to the lake. The only signs along the road read *Ostorozhno Klesch*, meaning "Be careful of ticks." In Russia if the mosquitoes aren't biting, the ticks are. At the site, we have both. Late in the afternoon of July 24, we arrive at the lake and set up camp, where we will be for four days, listening to John lecture, searching the area for meteorites, photographing, and otherwise enjoying our own version of Walden Pond. According to my GPS reading, our coordinates are 52° 39' 27" N by 83° 57' 13" E. John and his wife, Larissa I.

Budayeva, an environmental economist from Tomsk University, camped here on his first expedition to the site in May 1999. The next morning, after a night of heavy rain, while we are listening to one of John's lectures, Sergei Parshikov, our expedition administrator and veteran of the Popigai expedition the previous year, excitedly comes into the lecture tent holding up a small black stone about the size of a pencil eraser. We are all eager for a close look, especially mineralogist Alexander Andreev, who has been on two earlier expeditions with me. John is first to get to the stone. Squinting, he examines it through a 30× hand lens and soon begins to nod his head yes. "I'm almost certain it's a meteorite," he says, looking at Sergei with obvious admiration. The reason why will soon become clear.

How to Find the Meteorites?

If one thing can be singled out to characterize the Teleutskoye site as unique, it is the scant information about an event so highly publicized over much of Russia when it occurred. What information that has become available, however, suggests that the ending to the Teleutskoye story has yet to be written, and possibly will have a surprise ending.

One reason for the site's relative obscurity is its remoteness and the labor-intensive methods required on the part of investigators. You do not search for nice fist-size or larger pieces of rock with a high iron-nickel content that will conveniently set a metal detector into paroxysms of beeps. Instead, you are down on your hands and knees scratching through an impossibly tangled dense forest floor in the company of disease-carrying ticks and searching for tiny nodules of dark stones mostly about the size of the head of a match. Some investigators have preferred scooping up buckets of soil or sand along the edge of the tractor roadway and then sifting the debris through fine mesh screens. It is little wonder that only thirty or so of the tiny rounded fragments have been recovered by these direct-search methods over the decades.

Some astute readers may be wondering how, after about 100 years, little meteorites are still part of the surface rubble at the edges of the logging road. Why haven't they become hopelessly buried? Alexander, who has studied the action of sedimentary materials explained it this way: When you have a mix of gravel and sand and shake it up, the coarser and larger objects tend to migrate to the top while the finer and smaller particles tend to sink to the bottom. That was why we can expect the relatively dense and large meteorites over time to migrate to the top of the fine sand characteristic of the area and that makes up the roadway where the meteorites showered down. The agents of separation are wind, rain, and the horses and tractors continually acting upon the road surface.

What was this shower of a hail of cosmic particles ranging in size from that of a match head to a dove's egg? Like accounts of most meteorite fall sites, the first reports were those of eyewitnesses spread by word of mouth and then reported in the local newspapers.

According to an observer at the Talmensky Meteorological Station, an object was seen to streak down the sky from northwest to southeast near midnight of May 9, 1904. He reported it as a ball of fire "somewhat smaller than the moon at its full phase" and described the light as "blinding bright, bluish white at the beginning and then turning gradually reddish toward the end." When close to the horizon, the object began to shed "sparkles" that formed a trail.

Reports from other eyewitnesses estimate the duration of the fall from one minute to four seconds, but those figures cannot be considered absolute times since one observer might have seen only one part of the fall. An average from many observations places a reasonable estimated time at nineteen seconds from first appearance to the instant of explosion, which reportedly occurred about 15° above the horizon.

Depending on the area of sky visible to this or that eyewitness, some observers reported seeing only a bluish-white light, others only a reddish light. These are not necessarily discrepancies but reflect what segment of the fall was observed—blue while the object was seen near the zenith and red when seen near the horizon where the refractive property of the atmosphere was greater and frictional heating less because of a decrease in velocity.

The fireball was observed over a large region, which helps account for the widespread publicity of the event—over an area of some 455,000 square kilometers. Interviews with numerous eyewitnesses over such a large area, together with professional observers' reports of where they saw the trail of fire, pointed to a general location of the Verkhne-Obsky Pine Forest massif near Teleutskoye Lake, our campsite.

Acoustical phenomena accompanying the visual display were also well documented by eyewitnesses and were reported from a maximum area of some 91,000 square kilometers. Some reported that the object's flight was accompanied by "a loud noise like that of rushing wind then growing into deafening sounds similar to cannons firing, or bouts of thunder." Other eyewitnesses reported not one, but two or more thunderous "shots," all centered on Lake Teleutskoye. The nearly circular area defined by acoustic reports had a radius of some 170 kilometers.

Many eyewitnesses reported that the explosive sounds were immediately followed by a strong ground shock like that from an earthquake. One eyewitness reported a wind strong enough to rustle the leaves of plants and rattle dishes.

An estimate of the meteorite swarm's flight through the atmosphere is about 7.4 kilometers per second, based on the time of the object's flight from the village of Talmenskoye to the time of the explosion over the Teleutskoye Lake area, a distance of nearly 130 kilometers traversed in about nineteen seconds. But this method of estimating the object's velocity seems crude at best due to the uncertainty of both the distance involved and a precise duration of the object's flight.

That the meteorites showered down near the Teleutskoye Lake shore seems probable since the dozen or more samples recovered so far all come from there. The densely wooded nature of the fall site around the lake has made even an approximately accurate mapping of the strewn field impossible; so it is highly unlikely that we will ever determine any of the preatmospheric orbital elements of the original meteoroid since a mass distribution study of the strewn field at present seems impossible. For example, sampling lake-bottom sediments is prohibitive due to the labor-intensive nature of the work. The lake is about 320 meters long, 107 meters wide, by some 2 meters deep, and has a muddy sediment bed about 6 meters thick. Since the present Russian government is not likely to underwrite such an investigation, the only way one could begin would be through private funding.

Reports from Loggers

At the time of the Teleutskoye shower, loggers were working in the area and had set up a half dozen or so huts for shelter and enclosed pits for the collection of melted resin from the area's pine trees. They were awakened around midnight by a thunder clap and the loud clatter of the chondritic stones pelting the roofs of their shelters and striking nearby trees and the lake water surface. The next morning the loggers are said to have collected some thirty fragments, all but four of which have since disappeared without a trace. Those four are now in museums. One of the first on the scene was a police official named Tikhmenev, who interviewed the loggers but failed to get any of their names or where they lived. In his report he included the opinion of some of the loggers that the main mass of fragments probably fell into the lake. By the time officials from the statistical department of the Altai Okrug (district) visited the lake, the loggers had left.

Two major questions remained unresolved: (1) Were there larger meteorite fragments, say in the 1 meter plus range in diameter? (2) Is it likely that the main mass of the meteorite sits in a bog or in lake-bottom sediments still awaiting discovery?

The first official expedition to the fall site wasn't made until the spring of 1909 by V. N. Mamontov at the request of the czar's Academy of Sciences. Although the Russian Academy of Sciences considered the fall an important one, involvement in the Russo-Japanese War of 1905 prevented an investigation earlier than Mamontov's, which had been urged by Academician F. N. Chernyshev, director of the Geological and Mineralogical Museum of the Academy of Sciences, and by the respected investigator V. I. Vernadsky.

Mamontov was able "to inspect Teleutskoye Lake and its surroundings in detail," he later reported. Mamontov had two objectives: to recover as many small meteorites as possible; and to try to discover if the main mass of the fall existed as a single large piece. After several weeks of intense work, he failed on both accounts. The thick and entangled ground cover made it extremely difficult to search the soil beneath, and he found no evidence whatever of large meteoric chunks having struck any trees and left scars. He even scraped down the outside walls of the shelters in an attempt to find small meteorites possibly overlooked by the loggers. He found nothing. The seemingly bottomless soft sediments of the lake made finding an embedded meteorite possible only by "blind chance or with colossal expenditures," Mamontov wrote.

During his expedition, Mamontov managed to visit about twenty villages surrounding Teleutskoye Lake and interviewed fifty-two eyewitnesses of the shower. Not one reported seeing evidence of a large fragment ever reaching the ground, and all said that "the meteorite exploded in the air without reaching the ground." Mamontov did eventually manage to locate some of the logger eyewitnesses. One, Pavel Kachesov from the village of Kamyshenka, said he personally collected twenty-nine fragments. He gave eight to Mamontov, one each to the policeman Tikhmenev and his logging camp supervisor, and the rest to friends. No logger reported hearing any big splash or impact with the ground, only clicking sounds of small stones striking their sheds, trees, and the lake water. By morning, the stones were cold.

In addition to Mamontov's interviews with eyewitnesses, for the first time the government did a questionnaire survey. It was the undertaking of V. I. Galanin, board chairman of the Altai Okrug branch of the Russian Geographical Society, with the support of the statistical department; 262 questionnaires were sent mostly to meteorological stations, of which 233 were completed and returned, and of that number, 154 contained useful information. Mamontov processed the data, which are the basis for the time of the shower (11:34 P.M.), its duration (nineteen seconds), and certain other data cited in this chapter. As the questionnaires were being sent out, two reports of the Altai shower reached the Geographical Society and were accompanied by eight more meteorites. Those, plus the four collected by Mamontov, brought the then total to twelve stones first sent to the Geographical Society in Barnaul, and then later sent to the universities in St. Petersburg and Tomsk. The largest was an elongated piece that measured 3 by 2 by 0.7 centimeters and had a thin dark crust. It had been chipped off another piece. The chipped-off surface was light gray with orange spots resulting from the formation of iron oxides. Slightly smaller, a second specimen showed little grains of iron and a thin network of tiny fractures. Microscopic examination revealed the meteorites as crystalline chondrites rich in iron and to a lesser extent in troilite (FeS). It consists of densely packed relict chondrules with deformed contours.

According to mineralogist T. E. Martynova, in an article currently being prepared for publication, one meteorite specimen was sectioned at Tomsk State University and then analyzed by her at the Mineralogical Museum of the Tomsk State Polytechnical University. She writes:

"The composition is mainly nonmetalliferous (about 60 percent) with the remaining 40 percent being metalliferous. The nonmetalliferous components consist of isometric grains of olivine replaced largely by hydrous ferric oxides. Internal reflections of dark brown color are noticeable.

"The metalliferous component is represented by natural meteorite iron (30 percent) and troilite (10 percent). Natural iron is represented by a nickel/iron alloy exhibiting typical Widmanstätten pattern. The polished section is white and has pronounced anisotropy and high reflecting ability. There are no internal reflections. Meteoritic iron is represented in the form of xenomorphic grains that fill the spaces between grains of the nonmetalliferous component. The prevailing grain size is typically 0.2 to 0.5 millimeters."

Is that the end of the Teleutskoye Lake Meteorite Shower story? Possibly not. As E. L. Krinov and other meteorite investigators were very well aware, one or more large-mass fragments from a fall may travel 15 kilometers or more farther than the shower's low-mass fragments before impacting the ground. The little fragments recovered along the shore of Teleutskoye Lake, then, may mark only the very edge of the trailing edge of a much elongated dispersion ellipse with 1-meter- (or more) diameter fragments waiting to be dug out of the boggy region.

A Surprise Ending

One afternoon as I walk back into our campsite after searching fruitlessly for meteorites along the edges of the logging trail and before the others have returned from their equally fruitless searching, I am startled to see two visitors quietly sitting by the coals of our campfire. One is a young man in his early twenties, slim and neatly dressed in a clean shirt and slacks. Sitting beside him is an older man, heavyset but not fat, dressed in a starched white shirt, a gray suit jacket, and black trousers. His hair is black and neatly combed, his hands and nails are as clean as if he had just come from a wedding. His shoes are also black, polished to a gleam, and have large silver buckles. His eyes, set below large, hairy brow ridges, are very dark, intense, and focused on me. He wears a half smile that barely exposes his teeth set in a jaw as firmly set as a boxer's.

"Who do I have here?" I ask myself. "Bandits, murderers, the KGB?" I decide on none of the above and approach them with a smile and an extended hand of greeting. In Russian I give my name and recite a tongue twister greeting taught to me by Katya and that immediately brings friendly laughter that exposes flashing gold teeth of the older man. It is a traditional Tungus greeting welcoming a guest into one's tepee. The visitor is Andranik Mgdesyan, an Armenian and the absentee rich merchant who had earlier augmented our provisions. He has finally caught up with us at our campsite. The young man beside him is his driver and assistant. If ever I return to that part of the world, or if ever a friend of mine ventures there, a visit to Troitskoe and Andranik's home will be imperative. I will never forget the friendliness expressed by those deep dark eyes, that broad mouth full of noble teeth, and a booming voice that must have carried halfway back to Moscow. One of his bear hugs is a greeting and gesture of comradeship never to be forgotten.

Andranik has driven the four hours from his village to prepare a special feast for us and to invite us to visit him on our way back so that I can interview a woman who, he says, can augment the account of the Teleutskoye meteorite shower. While he is talking, his young assistant lays a fire of dried birch sticks contained within an enclosure of bricks, all of which they brought with them in their van. Pushing up his sleeves, Andranik then begins spearing cubes of pork alternating with chunks of onion, peppers, and tomatoes onto skewers supported above a bed of glowing coals. Dinner that night is shish kebab in the traditional Armenian style. After dinner, we group around the campfire and sing Russian songs, the words to which almost everyone seems to know. Between songs John reads one of his poems. Several years ago he determined to write one poem a day for 120 consecutive days, a Thousand-and-One-Nights endeavor that helps make our last night in camp one unlikely to be soon forgotten. The air is clear and cool, the stars bright, the company sweet, and the forest perfumed with a fragrance so strong that you can almost chew it.

So moved am I by the camaraderie of the evening that during the intervals between John's readings, I start to compose a poem of my own. It is a rambling thing that goes on for several pages of my notebook, praising my Russian companions for their kindness and friendship, their land for its beauty, and the openness and honesty that has so characterized our campfire universe—all stimulated by a full reservoir of emotion and not a little vodka.

At an appropriate break in John's readings, I muster the courage to ask Katya to translate my poem aloud. As she does, I try to read its impression on my audience. Katya reads fluently, smoothly, and with feeling. At one stage, I notice her eyes swelling with tears; then she ends, sits down beside me, and secretly squeezes my hand. For what seems an eternity no one says a word. My companions merely look into the campfire, whose crackling fills the void left by Katya's silence. John is the first to respond. He comes over to me and, in deliberately broken Russian for my benefit, says, "*Bolshoi krasiva,* Roy" ("Greatly beautiful, Roy") and embraces me strongly. Then all the others come with more hugs or playful punches. All want a copy of my poem, and Katya promises them one.

It's late, and we are all tired. How sweet the night. How peaceful the world. How beautiful is this friendship beneath the stars.

By noon the next day we are seated around tables at Andranik's outdoor café listening to an account of the Teleutskoye meteorite shower as related to a woman named Valentina Markitan by her grandmother, one Anastasia N. Merinova, born in 1882 and age twenty-two when the meteorite fell in 1904. According to Markitan, as I interview her, her grandmother related the following:

"It was time to go and mow hay in the meadows, but when we arrived in the valley where we were to mow, we found everything covered with clear water, a new lake where none had been before. We were so surprised that our whole group hurried back to the village to tell the Pop [local priest]. The lake was round and was given the name Schuchye [Pike Lake]."

Markitan further relates her grandmother telling her that the night before the ground shook so much that dishes in the cabinets rattled. No one had an explanation of how the new lake formed.

Could it have been caused by a large fragment from the 1904 shower? At this stage it's impossible to say, but John offered two possible explanations: One, that the blast from the meteorite fall might have triggered an earthquake (a highly unlikely event), but confirmation would have to come from inquiries made of seismological stations to learn if any tectonic disturbances were recorded in the area at the time of the Teleutskoye shower. Another possibility is that the main body of the meteorite broke through the ground and into an aquifer that subsequently released water to the surface. Regardless, Lake Schuchye exists and is located about 25 kilometers east-northeast of our campsite.

So the end to the story of the Teleutskoye Lake meteorite shower has yet to be written.

On our way back to Barnaul to prepare for our expedition up in the Altai Mountains, we were reminded of the brutality and ugliness that was Soviet Russia during the reign of terror under Stalin. This particular reminder was a stretch of dirt road called the "Cheveteh" by the locals, but better known as the Chuisky Voenny ("military road"). The winding valley route it follows is some 2000 years old and for centuries was used for camel and horse caravans from Mongolia and China up into south central Siberia. Archival records recently made public have revealed an awful truth about that winding road through that beautiful valley whose depth and narrowness in places reduce the sky to a mere sliver of blue.

At the turn of the previous century it was surveyed by one Vyacheslav Schishkov, a famous Russian writer, and then laboriously improved in the late 1930s. Further improvement was done from 1941 through 1945 by Stalin's gulag gangs of forced labor—rapists, scientists, murderers, poets, thieves, dissidents, and countless bewildered innocents arrested and imprisoned on trumped-up charges, all mixed indiscriminately into work gangs that were to perish by the millions for the glory of the motherland and Stalin. The tragedy that is the Chuisky Voenny is a 50-kilometer stretch literally built on the bones of 30,000 gulag prisoners, including some German prisoners of war. They were worked to death building the road. As they collapsed from exhaustion, malnutrition, and despair and died where they fell, their bodies were simply covered over and became part of the roadbed. For each mile we drove along that ignoble highway, we traveled atop the bones of 1000 souls who were never privileged to assume their rightful place in history or the dignity of a proper burial.

What of our Altai adventure among glaciers and Katya's beautiful green rushing streams and mountain slopes cloaked in wild flowers? Well, that's another story for telling another time. Our task now is to address the question of where the cache of cosmic bombs that help make Earth such an interesting place is stored in space, how they were made, and the threat they may pose as Near Earth Objects (NEOs), asteroids, and comet nuclei capable of crashing into us and destroying civilization in the blink of an eye.

CHAPTER 8

Target Earth!

"They came from the moon; they came from the earth's volcanoes; they came from the sun; they came from Jupiter and the other planets; they came from some destroyed planet; they came from comets; they came from the nebulous mass from which the solar system has grown; they came from the fixed stars; they came from the depths of space."

This is how, around 1800, Professor H. L. Newton of Yale University summarized the source of the ceaseless influx of cosmic debris that rains down on us from our Chicken Little sky. Each year the sky falls down with more—about 160,000 tons—of that cosmic debris than any subway rider could possibly imagine or even likely be interested in.

But we should be interested, although the astronomical community is pretty much divided on just how worrisome the danger of our being targeted by a monster rock from space actually is. Tom Gehrels, founder of the Spacewatch program of the University of Arizona at the Kitt Peak

Observatory, says that the danger is real although a major impact is unlikely in our lifetime. Nevertheless, he adds, "the energies released [by a major impact] could be so horrendous that our fragile society would be obliterated." Others are not so sanguine.

Of all cosmic assaults on our planet, the Tunguska "marvel" of 1908 commands more world attention today than it did a half century ago. For over nearly 100 years the superblast has been publicized in hundreds of scientific papers, more than 1000 popular articles, more than 60 novels and nonfiction books, and numerous poems, motion pictures, and television documentaries. The bewitching aspect of each is the implied double question hinted at by Gehrels, and by Academician Nickolai Vasiliev in the Foreword to this book: When and where will the next assault be? And how much damage will it cause?

Chicxulub

The time was 65 million years ago in what is now the Gulf of Mexico off the Yucatán Peninsula. A cosmic missile was on a collision course with Earth. It was either a comet nucleus fragment or an asteroid, but we'll probably never know which. Hundreds of millions of years orchestrated its Keplerian dance until on that fateful day, at first with a faint whisper and then a deafening roar to those terror-stricken animals that focused their attention skyward, it came hurtling down out of space, driven by gravity according to Newton's second law of motion, and redesigned the planet in minutes that extended into days, then weeks, months, and who knows how many years? Since we have never witnessed such a devastating event, except for comet Shoemaker-Levy-9's impact with Jupiter in 1994, we can only imagine the terrible calamity as it occurred, one that would defy even the most extravagant among Hollywood's special-effects designers.

In only a few flaming seconds the 10-kilometer-wide object plowed through Earth's atmospheric shield, which protects us against most cosmic intruders. Traveling at between 20 and 60 kilometers per second, it continued to roar earthward, frictional heating with the air turning it reddish-white and hot enough to melt the George Washington Bridge in a blink. The ocean waters off what today is the village of Yucatán's Puerto Chicxulub instantly vaporized as the titan in its final roar excavated a crater up to 300 kilometers in diameter and some 50 kilometers deep, a hole large enough to swallow up forty-five Rhode Islands or almost all of the state of Montana.

The colossal impact instantly vaporized, melted, or ejected more than 200,000 cubic kilometers of Earth's crustal rock and sent a supersonic shock wave racing thousands of miles in all directions, and in the process shook the planet to its mantle roots. Winds and steam unimaginable in their heat and ferocity hurled molten rock fragments and tiny spherules of impact glass thousands of kilometers and raised a towering wall of water that traveled at 700 kilometers per hour and turned the Gulf of Mexico into a sea of chaos, pushing devastating volumes of water scores of kilometers inland all along the Gulf Coast. Planetwide acid rains as corrosive as battery acid soaked the land and poisoned much of the water. Tsunamis and earthquakes were triggered around the globe. Death and destruction came in an instant to all living things unfortunate enough to be within range of that awful event. Hot dust ejected aloft fell back to Earth and ignited possibly 25 percent or more of the planet's forests and grasslands. Smoke and dust then caught up in the global circulation of the atmosphere blanketed the planet to a depth of some 20 kilometers and, augmented by a dense fog of nitrogen oxides, totally darkened the land so that photosynthesis ebbed to a stop possibly for six months to a year.

With the green plant food producers inactive, the links higher up in the food chain were affected. The reduction of heat and light brought on a period of intense cold that snuffed out the lives of untold thousands of species. When eventually the blanket of gloom and doom lifted and the Sun's rays once again flooded the land, the surviving plant and animal species found a vastly altered environment, one that offered an abundance of new ecological nooks and crannies in which to explore evolutionary opportunities. As the lizards found new evolutionary energy and evolved into the dinosaurs after the period of massive extinctions 250 million years ago, the mammals similarly exploited new evolutionary opportunities following the mass extinctions of 65 million years ago that spelled doom to the dinosaurs.

Today the geological thumb print of the Chicxulub event can be reliably read by geologists measuring gravity and magnetic anomalies within the crater. Beneath the veneer of soft sediments of the Gulf floor are some 1000 meters of limestone, laid down in the intervening years, beneath which is a 300-meter-thick jumble of impact breccia rich in quartz, feldspar, and zircon, all of which show shock metamorphism, as does the rock rubble of the Popigai crater. And beneath the breccia is melt rock of a telltale type known as plagioclase feldspar. Chicxulub is undeniably real and a monstrous reminder of Earth's battered past.

Recently new findings have revealed what may be the granddaddy of all mass extinctions, one that occurred 250 million years ago and wiped out 90 percent of life forms on Earth. Although the explosive impact itself did much of the damage, most resulted over longer periods of scores of thousands of years due to associated massive flooding by out-pourings of lava and by changes in ocean oxygen levels, sea level, and global climate conditions. Enough lava oozed out of what today is Siberia to cover the entire planet to a depth of 3 meters if it had spread evenly.

"To knock out ninety percent of organisms, you've got to attack them on more than one front," according to Dr. Luann Becker of the University of Washington, Seattle, who has been studying the event. It is not known whether it was an asteroid or comet fragment or where it struck. At the time of the colossal impact Earth's land masses were clumped as a single supercontinent called Pangaea. The calling card evidence of the strike is exotic molecular structures called bucky-balls discovered in sedimentary rock layers located in what today are China and Japan at the boundary of the Permian and Triassic geological periods. Buckyballs are a complex of sixty or more carbon atoms arranged like a soccer ball with noble gases helium and argon trapped inside a caged structure.

Hits and Misses

Renaissance scholar Lisa Jardine tells us that in 1697 the British astronomer Edmond Halley, of Halley's Comet fame, read a paper to London's Royal Society in which he described the effects "of a Collision of a great Body such as a Comet against the Globe of the Earth, whereby Earth might be reduced again to a Chaos." And when Isaac Newton was in his eighties, he told his nephew John Conduitt that he believed that Earth had narrowly escaped destruction by the 1680 Sun-grazing comet. Over a period of only five years the ESA-NASA *SOHO* spacecraft discovered some 300 "Sun-grazing" comets, one of which plunged into the Sun on February 7, 2001.

According to NASA, a 10-meter-diameter cosmic missile passes closer to us than the Moon's distance each day; and an object 100 meters in diameter crosses Earth's orbit at about the Moon's distance on the average of once a month. In January 1991 a 10-meter-diameter object missed Earth by only half the Moon's distance just twelve hours after astronomers spotted it. On December 9, 1994, Asteroid 1994XM$_1$ missed us by 100 kilometers. It was 13 meters in diameter. The size of a house, the small asteroid would have completely wiped out the greater New York area had it made a direct hit on Manhattan. We can expect to get hit by such house-size objects about once every 100 years. Every 1000 to 3000 years we can expect to be hit by Near Earth Objects (NEOs) ranging in size from 100 to several hundred meters. Fortunately we don't have to worry about those stony objects smaller than about 50 meters in diameter because most burn up in the atmosphere. But if the object is made of iron, then some worrying is justified. For instance, a metal asteroid about 30 meters in diameter carved out a crater 1.2 kilometers across in the Arizona desert 50,000 years ago.

Asteroids about 100 meters and larger in diameter deserve our greatest respect, and we know of some 100,000 of them that inhabit the Solar System this side of Mars. A direct hit by one of these would wipe out a continent. They visit Earth once every 50,000 to 500,000 years. More troublesome are the 1000 or 2000 NEOs roughly 1 kilometer and larger in diameter that collide with Earth once every 300,000 years or so. These are the real Earth crunchers that cause mass extinctions. Chicxulub was one, but that was 65 *million* years ago. If our numbers game is a reliable one, then where are all the more recent impact sites? In any case, as one writer has put it, "We live in a cosmic shooting gallery."

The estimates cited above are only statistical averages. A strike by an object of any of the sizes mentioned does not occur once every 100, 1000, or 10,000 years. Such events occur randomly in time, in a Poissonian process, named after the French mathematician Siméon Poisson. A millennium may pass without Earth being hit by a 50-meter-diameter object, and then we may be hit twice in the next month or the next century. Because we get hit at random and not on any particular schedule, to ask how long we have to wait for the next major strike is meaningless. In Poisson's world of temporal randomness, the bus we are waiting for may be just around the corner or broken down several miles away.

One thing that alerted astronomers to just how often Earth is targeted by bombs from space was a U.S. military report made public early in 1994. According to the report, from 1975 to 1992 military satellites detected 136 high-altitude explosions with a force of 500 to 15,000 tons of high explosives—in effect, small atomic bombs. The report went on to reveal, to the astonishment of the scientific community, that the objects entered the atmosphere at 16 to 48 kilometers per second, that they exploded 27 to 32 kilometers above the ground, and that there probably were 10 times more events than were detected. If that were so, then there are about eighty such explosive events a year.

Currently, the University of Arizona's Spacewatch program detects around twenty new NEOs a month. According to Spacewatch director Robert S. McMillan, as many as nine hundred 1-kilometer-diameter asteroids capable of wreaking global havoc may pose a collision threat to Earth. Of that number, Spacewatch astronomers have so far identified fewer than half. They further point out that new asteroid hazards are being created continually as large asteroids collide and smash up into smaller ones that are then scattered off in all directions. So the numbers game is a dynamic one that changes from year to year. NASA puts the number of NEOs with diameters of 1 kilometer or more at between 750 and 1200.

Just how much energy does a moderate-sized asteroid— say, a 1-kilometer-wide object—pack? Tom Gehrels says we can use the mathematical expression $\frac{1}{2}mv^2$ to calculate the kinetic energy. Let m represent the object's mass and v its velocity of entry into the atmosphere. If the object has a density of 3 grams per cubic centimeter, which we get from meteorites, and the entry velocity is 20 kilometers per second, then an asteroid 1 kilometer in diameter packs a striking force millions of times the explosive forces of the atomic bomb dropped on Hiroshima. Gehrels is reassuring when he tells us that the Spacewatch team knows of only about ten Chicxulub-size objects with Earth-crossing orbits.

At present we suspect that some of the NEOs—possibly 50 percent—are dead comet nuclei. These objects tend to be the most destructive because of their relatively high impact speeds and so are the ones that tend to cause mass extinctions. For instance, a comet with a parabolic orbit—that is, an orbit that is open-ended and does not have a closed configuration—has a velocity of some 55 kilometers per second compared with slightly less than 17 kilometers per second for an Apollo-type asteroid. Unfortunately, we are trying to pin the tail on the donkey rather than on the comet when we pretend to know what comets are and just how they behave. Recall Gene Shoemaker's comment that anyone who claims to know what a comet is doesn't know what he's talking about. Without at least some knowledge of a comet's mass, we are pretty helpless to estimate meaningfully its impact hazard.

That doesn't mean that we don't know at least something about comets. Two spacecraft have flown past two different comets and photographed their cores. The first was the European Space Agency's *Giotto* that passed through Comet Halley's coma in 1984. More recently, in September 2001, NASA's *Deep Space 1* probe flew through the coma of Comet Borrelly, giving us the clearest pictures yet of a comet nucleus. *Giotto* reported a black peanut-shaped nucleus of ices ejecting jets of dust and gases. It also detected a cloud of hydrogen around the comet. The speed of the dust and gas jets was 2800 kilometers per hour, more than twenty times hurricane wind forces. Such jets are presumed to randomly cast off small and large meteoroids that shoot out into surrounding space. The larger ones have velocities of some 100 meters per second while the less-massive ones travel faster, at around 500 meters per second. This cast-off material seems to be the source of the coma, since once free of the nucleus the icy chunks tend to sublime and so add to the gaseous coma and help it expand to a diameter of tens of thousands of kilometers compared with the much smaller size of a few to several kilometers for the nucleus itself. *Giotto* also found that Halley's porous nucleus has a density somewhat less than that of water ice. A spongy coating of sooty carbon material seems to cover some 90 percent of the comet's nucleus. As the nucleus is heated on approaching the Sun, the volatile ices trapped beneath the carbon crust explode and break through the crust, effectively becoming the comet's jets that act like rocket thrusters fired at random. Although *Giotto* somewhat improved our fuzzy image of what a comet is, we still have much more to learn about these "hairy stars" so dreaded in past centuries. Like Comet Halley, Comet Borrelly's 10-kilometer-long nucleus of rock and ice shot jets of gas and dust into the coma. The nucleus was seen to have rugged terrain, smooth rolling plains, deep fractures, and very dark material.

Project Spaceguard

In 1992 NASA invited more than 100 scientists and military experts to take part in two workshops. The first, called "The Spaceguard Survey," dealt with scanning the skies for Earth-threatening asteroids and comets. The second was called the "Near-Earth-Object Interception Workshop." Its purpose was to propose ways of either destroying NEOs that pose a threat before they can destroy us or of nudging them into an orbit that would take them safely away from Earth.

Our ability to protect the planet from an NEO on a collision course with us depends on four things: the object's mass, its velocity, the amount of warning time, and our technological ability to deal with the object, either to destroy it or to interfere with its flight path to alter its course.

It now seems that nuclear weapons technology is the only technology that may be able to ward off disaster for errant asteroids and comets. The idea would be to mount a nuclear warhead atop a rocket and send the rocket on a course that would intercept the NEO and blow it to bits safely away from Earth. Such a nuclear explosive might be implanted within the nucleus of a large comet or beneath the surface of a "soft" rocky asteroid and then detonated to pulverize the object. To do this, workshop members foresaw a vehicle with an engine for maneuvering and landing on the object, as *NEAR-Shoemaker* landed on asteroid Eros in February 2001. It would also need a device to bore beneath the surface. Although this scheme could destroy the asteroid or comet nucleus, there is also the possibility of shattering the object into a shotgunlike blast that might end up hitting

Earth as a destructive swarm of cosmic missiles instead of an equally destructive single bullet.

A less ambitious plan would be simply to crash a rocket into the threatening asteroid or comet. This, according to Newton's first law of motion—that a body in motion tends to remain in motion at a constant speed in a straight line unless acted on by an outside force—would nudge the object into a new and nonthreatening orbit. Success would depend on the force of the impacting rocket and might be limited to objects smaller than 100 meters in diameter.

For objects with a diameter near 1 kilometer, a much more ambitious plan has been suggested. Mine the object by drilling and blasting away chunks of its mass. Each time a bucket of rock were jettisoned off the object, Newton's third law—stating that for every action there is an equal and opposite reaction—would result in a slight change in the object's orbit. According to one estimate, the equivalent of about 1000 tons of asteroid or comet nucleus a year would have to be blasted away at a velocity of 100 kilometers per hour for a period of 10 years to effectively alter the object's course.

Nuclear devices exploded near or at the surface of a metallic or especially massive stony asteroid could nudge the object into an orbit that would detour around Earth. Another possibility considered by workshop members was flying a crewed mission to the intruder, landing on it, and then fitting it with thrusters that would propel the object away from Earth—in other words converting the threatening object into a remotely controlled spaceship. To avoid flying a rocket out to meet an NEO, powerful lasers operated from Earth, or from the Moon, might be used to nudge the intruder off course. One advantage of the laser approach would be that we could observe the effects of each burst on the object's orbit and adjust successive bursts accordingly, as with tracer bullets. The approach most favored by work-shop members was the explosion of a nuclear warhead at an appropriate distance from an NEO in order to alter its course so that it would miss impacting Earth.

Brilliant Mountains

The more we look into schemes now being considered to protect our battered, although resilient, planet from cosmic hazards, the more they sound like tales of science fiction. But we should recall that many of yesterday's science fiction stories are today's science facts. Before the Apollo flights to the Moon who would have dreamed of soft landing a space probe on tiny Eros some 195 million miles away, let alone designing probes that could reach the outer giant gas planets and then carry on into interstellar space bearing greetings from Planet Earth?

One of the most imaginative proposals made at the workshop was given the name "Brilliant Mountains." In this proposal, nuclear rockets would be sent out to capture small nearby asteroids and then return with them, shepherding them into orbit around Earth where the flock would be kept in storage. Asteroids with masses of 1000 to 10,000 tons could be parked in Earth orbit. Then in the event an incoming NEO were found to be on a collision course with Earth, a Brilliant Mountain of just the right mass could be nudged out of Earth orbit and into a new orbit that would intercept the NEO and destroy it at a safe distance from Earth. It has even been suggested that such cosmic missiles—whether comet nuclei or asteroids—could be directed down to Earth by some unscrupulous superpower to selectively target a con-sortium of enemy nations.

An early warning system to detect cosmic invaders, and a means to destroy them before they destroy us, is the concern of every nation. It is, therefore, an effort that requires global cooperation. The U.S. House of Representatives recognized that fact when in its NASA Multiyear Authorization Act of 1990 it said:

"The Committee believes that it is imperative that the detection rate of Earth-orbit-crossing asteroids must be increased substantially, and that the means to destroy or alter the orbits of asteroids when they threaten collision should be defined and agreed upon internationally."

A number of astronomers, prominent among them Duncan Steel, a research astronomer at the Anglo-Australian Observatory, have given much thought to an NEO detection program. According to Steel, $300 million a year, divided among participating nations, would build and staff six observatories strategically situated around the globe. While optical telescopes would spot potential intruders, radar would be used to pinpoint their orbits precisely and so provide warning of any on a collision course with us. Unfortunately, such a full-scale international detection program has not been initiated, and probably won't be until a major impact catastrophe jolts politicians' concern, but then, of course, it would be too late. It had been proposed that the Spaceguard Survey span some twenty-five years during which time virtually all major Earth-crunching asteroids capable of unleashing global havoc could be spotted and their orbits precisely calculated. That means an estimated 2000 to 3000 Earth-crossing asteroids with a minimum diameter of 1 kilometer. According to Steel, in the process of identifying 99 percent of such major killers, we would probably discover about half of, say, potential problem asteroids with diameters of about 0.5 kilometer.

We would find an even smaller percentage of, say, 100-meter-diameter objects capable of wiping out the state of Connecticut or Switzerland. And even if we did detect one, it would not be until the object were closer to us than the Moon, too close to take any action without an interceptor device parked and ready in Earth orbit.

The detection task, although approached on a limited basis so far, is not easy because it calls for international political, as well as financial, cooperation. Aside from a Spaceguard detection program, one requirement would be the development of a very powerful (100-megaton) nuclear explosive, one about five times the force of the asteroid impact that blasted out Arizona's Meteor Crater. Its development would further require several test explosions. But under existing and projected nuclear test ban treaties, such a program could not be started. It will be interesting to see what may develop over the next decade or so on an international level. A glimmering of hope has come out of the European Space Agency (ESA) with its two projected missions called *GAIA* and *BepiColombo*. *GAIA*, scheduled for launch sometime around 2010, will be able to detect NEOs as small as 500 meters in diameter and will enable astronomers to make very precise, long-term orbit determinations. *BepiColombo* will be designed to sniff out NEOs orbiting between Mercury and Earth. These objects are especially dangerous since they can approach Earth unseen against the glare of the Sun. My own view is that little more will be done because of what I call the Dry Faucet Syndrome; that is, it will take a catastrophe, such as turning on the faucet only to discover that there is no more fresh water, to precipitate action, and by then it will be too late.

Some astronomers view Project Spaceguard with a jaundiced eye. Among them is astrophysicist Dr. Jerry LaSala of the University of Southern Maine, who admits that he is more than a little skeptical. "While blowing up small asteroids from within, and redirecting asteroids with rocket thrusters built into them are theoretically possible, the chances of being able to apply these methods to a really threatening object are nil," he says.

He feels that most likely we would have too little lead time to intercept an intruder, "and how would we respond?" he asks. "How would we know which way to deflect it? The intruder's motion would be almost entirely radial to the line of sight, with only a small tangential component, but it's that tangential component that would govern whether it hits or misses Earth. Unless the uncertainties in that small quantity are practically zero—an inconceivable requirement—there's a considerable danger that small course corrections could *increase* the probability of collision! In 1912, a deflection of the course of the *Titanic* by perhaps 0.01 degree a few days before the fateful night of April 14 would have been enough to cause it to miss the iceberg. But if you had been steering the ship, would you have known in which direction to deflect it?"

"Furthermore, course deflection by exploding nuclear bombs near the incoming object can't work because conservation of momentum is inexorable. While the exploding bomb releases lots of energy, the momentum transfer to a nearby object in space is small. The Brilliant Mountains idea is perhaps the most technically feasible, if we overlook the enormous engineering obstacles, but it still suffers from the orbital uncertainty problem," LaSala concludes.

Each chapter of this book has, in a way, been a prelude to this final chapter, since an understanding of the various impacts reported is essential to our ability to assess the potential danger from impacting objects. These objects pose a threat to small local levels the size of a village to metropolises the size of New York, Paris, or Tokyo and could bring devastation on a global scale that would snuff out civilization as we know it and spell doom to species numbering in the hundreds of thousands. It is tantamount to an evolutionary restructuring of life. Clearly we must continue to study the Tunguska Event and other impact sites in order to identify those objects capable of "splitting the sky apart." In some small but significant way a knowledge of what the Tunguska object was, and how it behaved once in the atmosphere, just might help prepare us for future impacts. We should be mentally prepared, at least, for the next Tunguska Event may occur not on a local scale but on a continental or global scale and blast humanity back into the Stone Age. Whether the next catastrophe will be on a local or global scale, we do not know. It is not though a matter of *if* one or the other will happen, but *when*. The ultimate questions are, "Will we be ready?" and "What, if anything, could we do?" Right now the answers are "No" and "Nothing."

In a commencement address delivered at his university in Sri Lanka, Sir Arthur C. Clark concluded with the following:

"In one of his last books, Carl Sagan pointed out that no really long-lived civilization could survive unless it develops space travel, because major asteroid impacts will be inevitable in any solar system over the course of millennia. Larry Niven summed up the situation with the memorable phrase: 'The dinosaurs became extinct because they didn't have a space programme.' And we will deserve to become extinct, if we don't have one."

It is comforting, if not reassuring, to know that those of us in the astronomical community—from professional astronomers, to planetarians, to the cadre of amateur astronomers the world over whose telescopes nightly survey the sky for misbehaving stars, undiscovered asteroids, and comets and who add immensely to the data bank of NEOs—are keeping watchful eyes on what's going on out there. A combination of studying the effects of past impacts, which this book has had as its focus, and current efforts to understand and evaluate what's out there now to threaten our towers and our gardens, seems a logical and desirable thing to be doing. Finally, however, the politicians, not the scientists of the world, are the ones who will decide what is best for us. The scientists can do little more than point the way.

References

Alvarez, Walter. *T. rex and the Crater of Doom.* Princeton, NJ: Princeton University Press, 1997.

Barnes-Svarney, Patricia. *Asteroid: Earth Destroyer or New Frontier?* New York: Plenum Press, 1996.

Baxter, John, and Thomas Atkins. *The Fire Came By: The Riddle of the Great Siberian Explosion.* Garden City, NJ: Doubleday, 1976.

Beatty, J. Kelly. "Impacts Revealed," *Sky & Telescope*, February 1994, pp. 26–27.

Ben-Menahem, Ari. "Source Parameters of the Siberian Explosion of June 30, 1908, from Analysis and Synthesis of Seismic Signals at Four Stations," *Physics of the Earth and Planetary Interiors*, Vol. 11 (1975), pp. 1–35.

Benton, Michael J. "Later Triassic Extinctions and the Origin of the Dinosaurs," *Science*, Vol. 260 (7 May 1993), pp. 769–770.

Bottomley, R., R. Grieve, D. York, and V. Masaitis, *Nature*, Vol. 388 (1997), pp. 365–368. (Popigai crater)

Boyarkina, A. P., V. A. Bronshten, and A. K. Stanyukovich. "Non-stationary Interactions of the Shock Waves in the Gasdynamical Problems of the Meteorites." In *Interactions of the Meteoric Matter with the Earth* (in Russian). Novosibirsk: Nauka (Siberian Branch), pp. 138–156.

Bronshten, V. A. *Physics of Meteor Phenomena*. Dordrecht: Reidel, 1983.

Bronshten, V. A. *Meteors, Meteorites and Meteoroids*. Nauka (Siberian Branch), 1987.

Bronshten, V. A. *Tunguska Meteorite: The History of Research*. Moscow: A. D. Selyanov, 2000.

Brown, John C., and David W. Hughes. "Tunguska's Comet and Non-thermal ^{14}C Production in the Atmosphere," *Nature*, Vol. 268 (11 August 1977), pp. 512–514.

Chapman, Clark R., and David Morrison. *Cosmic Catastrophes*. New York: Plenum Press, 1989.

Chapman, Clark R., Daniel D. Durada, and Robert E. Gold. "The Comet/Asteroid Impact Hazard: A Systems Approach." Boulder, CO: Office of Space Studies, Southwest Research Institute, 2001.

Chernyshev, Alexander. "Tsaritsinsky Meteorite and Its History," *Vecherniy Volgograd* (newspaper), 24 July 1980. (In Russian)

Chladni, E. F. *Ueber Feuer Meteore*. Wein, 1819.

Chyba, Christopher, Paul J. Thomas, and Kevin J. Zahnie. "The 1908 Tunguska Explosion: Atmospheric Disruption of a Stony Asteroid," *Nature*, Vol. 361 (7 January 1993), pp. 40–44.

Clark, Sir Arthur C. "Spaceguard Revisited." Convocation address as Chancellor, University of Moratuwa, Sri Lanka.

Coleman, David L., and Sarah K. Kennedy. *The Pocket Guide to Asteroids*. Dubuque, IA: Jensen Scientifics, 2000.

Cook, J. M. *The Persians*. London: The Folio Society, 1983.

Consolmagno, Brother Guy. *Brother Astronomer*. New York: McGraw-Hill, 2000.

Cox, Donald W., and James H. Chestek. *Doomsday Asteroid: Can We Survive?* New York: Prometheus Books, 1996.

D'Alessio, S. JU. D., and A. A. Harms. "The Nuclear and Aerial Dynamics of the Tunguska Event," *Planetary and Space Science*, Vol. 37 (1989), pp. 329–340.

Desonie, Dana, David Levy, and Eugene Shoemaker. *Cosmic Collisions*. New York: Henry Holt, 1996.

References

Dmitriev, A. N., and V. K. Zhuravlev. "The Tunguska Phenomenon of 1908: A Coronal Microtransient," *Geologiya i Geofizika*, Vol. 27, No. 4 (1986), pp. 10–19.

Emiliani, Cesare, Eric B. Kraus, and Eugene M. Shoemaker. "Sudden Death at the End of the Mesozoic," *Earth and Planetary Science Letters*, Vol. 55 (1981), pp. 317–334.

Farrington, O. C. *Meteorites*. Chicago, 1915.

Gallant, Roy A. "The Sky Has Split Apart," *Sky & Telescope* (June 1994), cover and pp. 38–43.

Gallant, Roy A. *The Day the Sky Split Apart*. New York: Atheneum Books of Simon & Schuster, 1995.

Gallant, Roy A. "Tunguska Revisited," *Meteorite!* (February 1995), cover and pp. 8–11.

Gehrels, Tom, ed. *Hazards Due to Comets and Asteroids*. Tucson: University of Arizona Press, 1994.

Glass, Billy P. "Silicate Spherules from Tunguska Impact Area: An Electron Microprobe Analysis," *Science*, Vol. 164 (2 May 1969), pp. 547–549.

Halpern, Paul. *Countdown to Apocalypse*. New York: Plenum Press, 1998.

Hodge, Paul. *Meteorite Craters and Impact Structures of the Earth*. Cambridge: Cambridge University Press, 1994.

Hou, Q. L., E. M. Kolesnikov, L. W. Xie, M. F. Zhou, M. Sun, and N. V. Kolesnikova. "Discovery of Probable Tunguska Cosmic Body Material: Anomalies of Platinum Group Elements and REE in Peat Near Explosion Site of 1908," *Planetary and Space Science*, Vol. 48, No. 15 (2000), pp. 1447–1455.

International Workshop Tunguska—'96, Program Abstracts, Department of Physics and Commission for International Relations, University of Bologna, Italy.

Jackson, A. A., and Michael P. Ryan. "Was the Tungus Event Due to a Black Hole?" *Nature*, Vol. 245 (14 September 1973), pp. 88–89.

Khotinok, R. "Observations of Bright Bolides and the Search for Meteorites," *Science and Life*, No. 1 (1998). (Tsarev fall)

Khotinok, R. "New Meteorites of the USSR: The Stony Meteorite Shower at Tsarev."

Kirova, O. A. "Scattered Matter from the Area of Fall of the Tunguska Cometary Meteorite," *Annals of the New York Academy of Sciences* (1964), pp. 235–242.

Kolesnikov, E. M. "Search for Traces of Tunguska Cosmic Body Dispersed Matter," *Meteoritics*, Vol. 24, No. 4 (1989), p. 288.

Kolesnikov, E. M., T. Boettger, and N. V. Kolesnikova. "Finding of Probable Tunguska Cosmic Body Material: Isotopic Anomalies of Carbon and Hydrogen in Peat," *Planetary and Space Science*, Vol. 47 (1999), pp. 905–916.

Kolesnikov, E. M., A. L. Stepanov, E. A. Gorid'ko, and N. V. Kolesnikova. "Element and Isotopic Anomalies in Peat from the Tunguska Explosion of 1908 Area Are Probably Traces of Cometary Matter," *Meteoritics and Planetary Science,* Vol. 34, No. 4, Suppl. A85 (1998).

Komarov, Viktor. "Stones in the Field," *Zvezdochet* ("Star Counter"), No. 5 (1998). (Tsarev fall)

Korobeinikov, V. P., S. B. Gusev, P. I. Chuskin, and L. V. Shurshalov. "Mathematical Model and Computation of the Tunguska Meteorite Explosion," *Acta Astronautica*, Vol. 3 (1976), pp. 615–622.

Krinov, E. L. "Publication of the USSR Academy of Sciences," pp. 238–240. (Teleutskoye)

Krinov, E. L. *Principles of Meteoritics*. New York: Pergamon Press, 1960.

Krinov, E. L. *Giant Meteorites*. New York: Pergamon Press, 1966.

Kronk, Gary. *Meteor Showers: A Descriptive Catalog*. Hillside, NJ: Enslow Publishers, 1988.

Kulik, L. A. "The Problem of the Impact Area of the Tunguska Meteorite of 1908," *Doklady Akad*. Nauk SSSR (A), No. 23 (1927), pp. 399–402.

Levin, B. Yu., and V. A. Bronshten. "The Tunguska Event and the Meteors with Terminal Flares," *Meteoritics*, Vol. 21, No. 2 (30 June 1986) pp. 199–215.

Lewis, John S. *Rain of Iron and Ice: The Very Real Threat of Comet and Asteroid Bombardment*. Reading, PA: Addison-Wesley, Helix Books, 1996.

References

Lockyer, Norman. *The Meteoritic Hypothesis*, 1890.

Mamontov, V. N., "In Search of the Altai Meteorite." Report prepared in the village of Kemerovo of the Kuznetky Uezd, July 24, 1909.

Masaytis, V. L., A. N. Danilin, M. S. Mashchak, A. I. Raykhlin, T. V. Selivanovskaya, and Ye. M. Shadenkov. *The Geology of Astroblemes*. St. Petersburg: Nedra, 1960. (Popigai)

Masaytis, V. L., and O. N. Simonov. "Popigai International Expedition—'98."

Mason, Brian. *Meteorites*. New York: John Wiley, 1962.

Mastny, Lisa. "Coming to Terms with the Arctic." *Worldwatch*, January–February 2000, pp. 24–36.

Merrill, George P. *Minerals from Earth and Sky, Part 1: The Story of Meteorites*. Washington, DC: Smithsonian Institution Series (1934).

Monikov, S. "The Stony Visitor," *Znamya*, 1997. (Only date evident; Tsarev fall)

Montanari, A. In V. L. Sharpton and P. D. Ward (eds.). *Global Catastrophes in Earth History: An Interdisciplinary Conference on Impacts, Volcanism, and Mass Mortality*. Boulder, CO: Geological Society of America (1990), pp. 607–616.

Mowat, Farley. *The Siberians*. Boston: Little, Brown, 1970.

Nininger, H. H. *Out of the Sky*. New York: Dover Publications, 1959.

Norton, O. Richard. *Rocks from Space*. Missoula, MT: Mountain Press, 1998.

Oliver, C. P. *Meteors*. Baltimore, 1925.

Pilipenko, P. P. Report dated February 12, 1909, published by the Tomsk State University Mineralogical Laboratory, Russia. (Teleutskoye)

Poag, C. Wylie. *Chesapeake Invader: Discovering America's Giant Meteorite Crater*. Princeton, NJ: Princeton University Press, 1999.

Rasmussen, K. L., H. J. F. Olsen, R. Gwozdz, and E. M. Kolesnikov. "Cosmic Iridium and Carbon from the Tunguska Impactor," *Meteoritics and Planetary Science*, Vol. 34 (1999), pp. 891–895.

References

Rasputin, Valentin. *Siberia, Siberia.* Evanston, IL: Northwestern University Press, 1991.

Rogan, Mary. "Please Take Our Children Away," *The New York Times Magazine* (4 March 2001), pp. 40–45.

Steel, Duncan. *Rogue Asteroids and Doomsday Comets.* New York: John Wiley, 1995.

Stern, S. Alan, and Paul R. Weissman. "Rapid Collisional Evolution of Comets During the Formation of the Oort Cloud," *Nature,* Vol. 409, No. 1 (February 2001), pp. 589–591.

Stöffler, Dieter, and Phillippe Claeys. "Earth Rocked by Combination Punch," *Nature,* Vol. 388, No. 24 (July 1997), pp. 331–332.

Summers, Carolyn, and Carlton Allen. *Cosmic Pinball.* New York: McGraw-Hill, 2000.

Taplin, Mark. *Open Lands.* South Royalton, VT: Steerforth Press, 1997.

"An Unusual Meteor," *Bor 'ba* (newspaper). December 24, 1922. (Tsarev fall)

Vogt, Gregory L. *The Search for the Killer Asteroid.* New York: Millbrook Press, 1994.

Zavarnitsky, A. N., and L. G. Kvasha. "Meteorites of the USSR." Moscow: USSR Academy of Sciences, 1952. (Teleutskoye)

Zotkin, I. T., R. V. Medvedev, and S. S. Gorbatskevich. "Durability Characteristics of the Tsarev Meteorite," *Meteoritics,* USSR Academy of Sciences, No. 46 (1987).

Note: Readers wishing to learn more about the Spaceguard and Spacewatch programs discussed in Chapter 8 are encouraged to search the Web using those two search words. Up-to-date information about which nations are currently funding NEO and NEA detection programs will be found on the sites. Readers may also wish to search the Web using search words such as "Tunguska," and "Popigai."

Conversion of
Metric to Standard Units

1 centimeter = 0.39 inch

1 meter = 39.37 inches

1 kilometer = 0.62 mile

1 hectare = 2.47 acres

1 gram = 0.035 ounce

1 kilogram = 2.2046 pounds

$°Fahrenheit = (°Celsius \times 1.8) + 32°$

About the Author

Professor (emeritus) ROY A. GALLANT has been digging around in Siberian meteorite impact sites since 1992. Over the years he has organized eight Russian expeditions that have earned him the alias "the Indiana Jones of Astronomy" and have taken him from the top to the bottom of Siberia—from above the Arctic Circle and southward to Mongolia—and from Kamchatka in the Russian Far East westward across the Urals. Gallant's quest has not been for meteoric "gold" but to document the impact sites and bring to the English-speaking world scientific accounts of what fell where with what consequences. Much of what Gallant reports has either been buried in obscure Russian scientific journals or is freshly researched material never before published. Many of his articles about his Siberian expeditions have appeared in *Sky & Telescope* and in the journal *Meteorite*.

A teacher of astronomy for many years (from the university level down to the elementary grades) until the year 2000, Gallant was also director of the Southworth Planetarium of the University of Southern Maine for twenty years. He has taught astronomy at the Maine College of Art, was a guest lecturer for the University of Illinois's National Science Foundation funded Astronomy Program, and was a member of the faculty of New York City's Hayden Planetarium.

His best-selling National Geographic book, *Our Universe*, which has sold more than two million copies, won him a Geographic Society of Chicago award. He has also received the John Burroughs award for nature writing, the Thomas

Alva Edison Foundation Award for science writing, and several other awards. His most recent recognition is the Maine Library Association's Lifetime Achievement Award.

Among the nearly 100 books he has written are many for young people. The *School Library Journal* has called him "one of the deans of American science writers for children." Professor Gallant is a Fellow of the Royal Astronomical Society of London and a member of the New York Academy of Sciences. He lives in Rangeley, Maine.

★ Expedition sites
Map locations are only approximate.

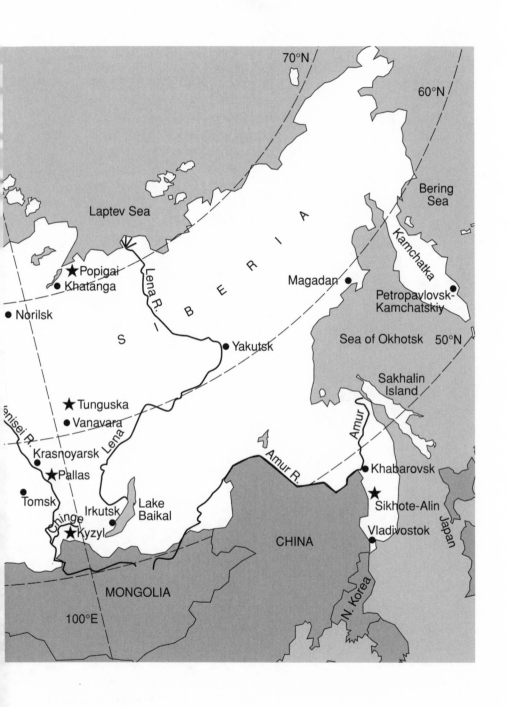

70°N

60°N

Laptev Sea

Bering
Sea

Kamchatka

★ Popigai
● Khatanga

Magadan ●

Petropavlovsk-
Kamchatskiy

● Norilsk

Lena R.

S
I
B
E
R
I
A

● Yakutsk

Sea of Okhotsk   50°N

Sakhalin
Island

★ Tunguska
● Vanavara

Lena

Amur

Amur R.

● Khabarovsk

★

enisei R.

● Krasnoyarsk
★ Pallas

● Tomsk

★ Kyzyl

Irkutsk

Lake
Baikal

Sikhote-Alin

Vladivostok ●

Japan

hinge

CHINA

N. Korea

MONGOLIA

100°E